Organizational alternatives in Soviet-type economies

T0312027

Also by Nicolas Spulber

Quantitative Economic Policy and Planning (co-author)
Socialist Management and Planning
The Soviet Economy: Structure, Principles, Problems
The State and Economic Development in Eastern Europe
Soviet Strategy for Economic Growth
The Economics of Communist Eastern Europe
Foundations of Soviet Strategy for Economic Growth (ed.)
Study of the Soviet Economy (ed.)

Organizational alternatives in Soviet-type economies

NICOLAS SPULBER
Distinguished Professor of Economics
Indiana University

CAMBRIDGE UNIVERSITY PRESS
CAMBRIDGE
LONDON · NEW YORK · MELBOURNE

CAMBRIDGE UNIVERSITY PRESS
Cambridge, New York, Melbourne, Madrid, Cape Town, Singapore,
São Paulo, Delhi, Dubai, Tokyo, Mexico City

Cambridge University Press
The Edinburgh Building, Cambridge CB2 8RU, UK

Published in the United States of America by Cambridge University Press, New York

www.cambridge.org
Information on this title: www.cambridge.org/9780521179966

First published 1979
First paperback edition 2010

A catalogue record for this publication is available from the British Library

Library of Congress Cataloguing in Publication data
Spulber, Nicolas.
Organizational alternatives in Soviet-type economies.
1. Europe, Eastern – Economic policy.
2. Europe, Eastern – Economic policy – Addresses,
essays, lectures. 1. Title.
HC244.S62   338.947   78-68378

ISBN 978-0-521-22393-5 Hardback
ISBN 978-0-521-17996-6 Paperback

FOR BERNIE

Contents

Acknowledgments

I wish to express my special gratitude to the *International Development Research Center* of Indiana University, sponsor of the research involved in the preparation of the volume, and to Professor George J. Stolnitz, former Director of the Center, for his unstinting support. I am also greatly indebted to a number of colleagues who have guided my steps through the difficult phase of preliminary research and documents selection. I am grateful to those who took the time and trouble to write to me about the most significant positions involved, notably the Professors: Branko Horvat, of the Institute of Economic Studies, Belgrade – for his advice concerning Yugoslavia; Ivan Berend, of the University of Budapest; Alan Brown of the University of Windsor, Ontario, Canada; Zoltan Kennessey of the UN Statistical Office, New York; Janos Kornai, of the University of Budapest; and Paul Marer, of Indiana University, Bloomington – for their remarks concerning Hungary; Włodzimierz Brus, of the University of Oxford, England (formerly of the University of Warsaw, Poland); Andrzej Brzeski of the University of California, Davis; Andrzej Korbonski, of the University of California, Los Angeles; Janusz G. Zielinski, of the University of Glasgow, Scotland; and Claus Wittich of the University of Southern California, Los Angeles – for their suggestions concerning Poland; and Vaclav Holesovsky, of the University of Massachusetts, Amherst – for his advice concerning Czechoslovakia. Special thanks are further due to the publishers of the copyrighted materials included in the selected essays who have graciously granted me the permission to use them. (Each source is clearly indicated at the appropriate place in the text).

A number of my colleagues and students have read parts or the entire draft of my introductory essay. Among them, Professors George M. von Furstenberg and H. Scott Gordon of Indiana University, Professor Arthur W. Wright of Purdue University, as well as Mrs Judith McKinney (who has also edited a number of the selected essays) deserve particular thanks for helpful criticisms and suggestions. Finally, the members of the Secretariat of the Department of Economics of Indiana University, particularly Mrs

Barbara Hume and Linda Parker have done outstanding work in transcribing an almost illegible manuscript into the final draft.

Neither the sponsor nor any of the aforementioned persons who so kindly helped me, bear any responsibility for the use I made of their advice in my introductory essay or in my comments, nor for the selections made and their translation, arrangement, and presentation.

Introduction

The Soviet-type organization and management of the socialist economy – usually referred to in the West as the Soviet *model* and in the East as the Soviet *mechanism* – emerged in the USSR, with its present characteristics, in the late 1920s and early 1930s. The characteristics are: (i) interlocking political–economic leadership of the state and the economy under a hierarchically structured Communist party; (ii) integration of large sectors of the economy into a single state-owned complex; (iii) centralized directive planning as a means of management and of performance control (with reluctant reliance on market mechanisms); and (iv) centralized determination of the economy's short-run or long-run goals under the assumption of complete identity of the interests of all members of the society.

It is this model – based in some essential respects on Marx and Engels' conception of socialism as interpreted by Lenin – that has been implanted in, or emulated by, all the other socialist countries since World War II. Alleging that it embodies the revolutionary essence of Marxism-Leninism, Soviet leaders continue to present the model as having universal validity and application. Yet its premises, its component parts, and their arrangement have all been targets of wide-ranging, deep-probing and often devastating critique in certain of the socialist countries. As one outgrowth of the crises and upheavals that have shaken Eastern Europe since the 1950s, clearly defined alternatives to the Soviet-type organization and management have been proposed and, in some cases, actually implemented.

While the Soviet Union's leadership – and for that matter, Communist China's leadership as well – never departed from the fundamental conception of the interlocking of the state and the economy into a centrally-directed servo-mechanism – though the latter has had to undergo at times deep adjustments and rearrangements in both countries – in Eastern Europe a number of alternatives were evolved by bringing into question the Soviet premises concerning the organization of the decision-making processes, the scope of socialist ownership, the nature and role of planning, the interaction of goals and of incentives in the socialist society. The full content of this significant critique, or the rationale of all these alternatives have, however, thus far not been systematically examined. This book presents and analyzes both the main thrust of this critique and the fundamental features of the suggested alternatives.

As we shall point out in detail in this study, in Marx and Engels' vision of socialism, the following changes necessarily occur if capitalism is overturned: (i) a communes-state, administered from below, replaces the military-state bureaucracies and any permanent managerial strata; (ii) collective ownership replaces private ownership of the means of production and new economic regularities supersede the law of value characteristic of capitalism; (iii) planning in kind, in an increasingly naturalized (non-monetary) economy, replaces markets and exchange as production and distribution of free goods supersede the traditional operations of buying and selling of commodities; and (iv) private interests merge in a single, clearly perceived and freely accepted, collective interest. In the Marxian conception of socialism, the structuring of the decision makers and of the decision process; the interactions between constraints and new economic laws; the interplay between controls and the complex procession apparatus of a fully unified economy; and finally, the selection of the objectives of control, do not raise any particular difficulties. The appropriate solutions combine harmoniously in the new crises-free socioeconomic order and allow the new society to rapidly surpass the highest productivity levels attained under capitalism.

Actually, each of the four key issues mentioned – organization, ownership, economic instruments, and goal-determination – involved in Soviet practice a number of painful choices. Consider the question of the decision makers and of the decision process. Which specific organs – say the Communist party, the Soviets (Councils of toilers), the trade unions, separately or in some combination – should exercise the main executive functions in managing the economy? To whom should lower-level executive and operational functions be delegated? Should the state executive power act through an *ad hoc* commission which would appoint and control the operational managers? Should the state administration be entirely separated from the day-to-day operational management of the economy? Can the working class by itself administer both the state and large-scale production without generating a vast bureaucracy?

Consider next the possible variations in the scope of socialization and their impact. To start with, should the leaders of the *workers' states* arising in less developed countries proceed immediately to the mass collectivization of peasant landholders? Or should they rather attempt to work out compromises with, and make concessions to, private agents in agriculture, small-scale industry, and trade? Further, which normative rules and which economic laws would be called into play if socialization were to be limited only to the commanding heights of the economy, while most of agriculture, small-scale industry and retail trade were to be left in private hands? Directly dependent on these choices are the scope assigned to certain markets, the role of monetary relations, and the uses of costs and prices in the sphere of centralized decisions and in planning itself – questions which Marxians subsume under the heading of the law of value and its possible interrelations with other specific economic laws of socialism.

The third primary issue, that of the possible combinations between planning and markets, raises a host of questions concerning the nature of the plan itself, the strategy of development, the organization of the economy's branches and firms, and the specific methods of managerial coordination. A vast range of choices is possible concerning the scope of the plan, and its instruments of implementation. Further crucial choices may involve the determination of the structure, growth, and uses of investable resources; the relations and transactions between different sectors, branches, and firms; dispositions concerning inputs, output assortments, and performance control; and the methods of management coordination.

Finally, how should the workers' interests (as producers and as consumers) interact with the planners' preferences? How should the social welfare function be decided and the scope of pricing and other stimuli be defined in everyday practice, so that the system operates efficiently? How should one avoid increasing discrepancies between goals pursued and results achieved?

The Soviet economic model was ultimately molded not only by Marx and Engels' conceptions of socialism as interpreted by Lenin, but also by Russia's underlying cultural–historical matrix, the constraints under which the Soviet regime has had to function, and the adjustments which the leaders of the system have had to make in order to make their normative conceptions operational.

At the beginning of the Soviet regime, the newly emerging economic system seemed to conform closely to Marx and Engels' fundamental outline. During the period of *War Communism* (June 1918–April 1920), a growing structure of Councils (Soviets) was indeed resolutely displacing the old state machine. The private ownership of the means of production was being suppressed throughout all sectors. Planned centralized allocation in kind of critical inputs and outputs was becoming typical as markets and monetary relations were disintegrating. The needs of the workers and of their fighting *avant garde* took precedence over everything else as the policy makers were waiting for the revolution to spread toward the industrial heart of Europe. True, at the same time, out of these same

Soviets, and out of the Communist party itself, a military–state–economic bureaucracy was irresistibly beginning to emerge, and the locus of decision making was shifting away from the Councils. But on the surface, at least, the new system conformed closely to the 'model of the centralized directive system of planned economy in its purest historical form ever implemented'[1] – as the Bolshevik leaders had indeed promised they would install.

Yet just as the new system reached its 'purest historical form', a retreat had to be sounded: economic chaos and famine following the Civil War were becoming widespread and menacing while the hope of the spread of the revolution toward the West was rapidly waning. The immediate, compelling necessity of recovery in agricultural production dissipated the illusion that simply waiting for massive help from the West could eventually allow socialist Russia to reach the highest levels of capitalist output. The pursuit of the compelling goal of recovery forced the introduction of structural changes in the economy's mechanism: the scope of socialization was drastically curtailed; the naturalization of the economy was halted and the centralized coercive regulation of production and distribution were thoroughly modified; a new balance was struck between what the policy makers perceived as being the public interest and what diverse strata of the peasantry perceived as being their own interests. Thus, a new Soviet economic system emerged under the label of the *New Economic Policy* (NEP) inaugurated in April 1920. In this new system, the scope of socialization was limited to the economy's commanding heights, i.e. to the complex of large-scale industry, banking, transport and wholesale trade. Within this complex, strict financial bookkeeping, accounting and cost control – at centrally determined prices – replaced the earlier simplistic naturalization of inter-firm relations. The array of coercive measures covering the collection and allocation of output outside the state sector was dispensed with, particularly in agriculture, where outright requisitions were replaced by a tax in kind. Markets and monetary relations were reestablished for labor, consumer goods, and services.

The NEP worked: private-based agricultural output recovered to its pre-war levels and pulled with it the state-based industrial sector. But the NEP barely provided an answer to the disquieting question: how could a country resolutely engaged in the transformation period from capitalism to socialism ultimately reach and surpass the highest output indices of capitalism, when its basis was constituted of technologically-backward, privately-owned, peasant agriculture? Instead of the expected automatic upsurge in productivity following the revolution, the country was barely

1 See the well documented book of Laszlo Szamuely, *First Models of the Socialist Economic System, Principles and Theories*, Budapest, Akademiai Kiado, 1974, p. 22.

catching up with its pre-war levels. The necessity of defining policies and priorities and of adjusting accordingly the entire economic mechanism came thus again to the fore. As I pointed out elsewhere,[2] the Communist leadership split wide open on these issues. The *right*-wing of the Communist party, led by Bukharin, advocated that the NEP be continued since in the given circumstances this system alone could guarantee a continuous growth in total output and balanced economic development including an appropriately developed industrial sector. In contrast, the *left*-wing opposition, led by Trotsky, advocated substantial changes in both priorities and the economic system, in order to step up the growth of industry in general and a military–industrial base in particular. According to the left, this required changes in the NEP system to make agriculture provide the tribute necessary if industry was to grow. Stalin eventually defeated both of these factions, while implementing the basic goals and methods suggested by the left. In so doing, he transformed the country's economic system and created the Soviet model as it is known today.

Under Stalin, the state's direct controls over production and distribution were again expanded with the aim of encompassing the entire economy. The private sectors were curtailed through collectivization of agriculture and socialization of trade, small-scale industry, and handicrafts. Short-term, indicative policy and planning were replaced by directives and comprehensive plans, and a vast centralized economic administration extended its direct controls over the activities of each firm. Standards of living were driven down, a tribute was extracted from agriculture, a high investment rate was secured, and inflexible priorities were enforced with respect to certain inputs, outputs, and the growth of various branches and industries. Stalin thus created in peacetime what Oskar Lange correctly defined as a *sui generis* war economy – a sort of hybrid between the two preceding Soviet economic models.

From the 1930s on, Stalin's economic mechanism was proclaimed by the Russians to be the socialist model *par excellence*. It was held to be universally valid for, and applicable in, any country undergoing a transformation from capitalism to communism. This model was the one copied by each Communist leadership after its accession to power in Eastern Europe and in Asia.

The Soviet model proved suitable for mobilizing investable resources and for concentrating them on a limited number of projects and priorities selected by the leadership. At the same time, the centralized, coercive, Soviet-type organization and management also gave rise to deep crises: Yugoslavia in 1948–51, Hungary in 1954–57, Poland in 1956–57, and

2 See N. Spulber, *Soviet Strategy for Economic Growth*, Bloomington, Indiana, Indiana University Press, 1964.

Czechoslovakia in 1963–68. During these crises, the dysfunctional consequences of the system became clearly visible. Those consequences were the continuous growth of a vast and cumbersome bureaucracy, marked deterioration in the quality of inputs and outputs, persistent lags in technology, distortion of incentives, and increasing discrepancies between goals and performance. The trade-offs between advantages and disadvantages appear to have been acceptable in countries at a relatively low level of development (China, Albania, Bulgaria, and Romania) but increasingly unacceptable in countries at a higher level of development (Hungary, Poland and Czechoslovakia) which had important ties with international markets. It was in these three more advanced countries and in Yugoslavia (which made the earliest break) that the rationale of the Soviet economic model and its underlying premises were seriously probed and challenged, and that operational alternatives to it were devised and, up to a point, implemented.

Particular interest attaches to each of the four crises mentioned above for several reasons: First, each of them imparted new directions to the search for change. Second, each of them stressed different solutions. Third, each of them led to a reconceptualization of the underlying assumptions of a socialist system. Finally the degree of departure from the Soviet model varied from case to case. The Yugoslavs started the process of system change by tackling the issue of the decision makers and of management structure. The Hungarians pursued it by attempting to modify the balance between the public and the private sectors and the rules of the economic order. The Poles continued it by examining the range of possible combinations of planning and the market, but under the overall priority of the plan. The Czechoslovaks concluded it by exploring the interrelations between interests, incentives, and the planners' preferences.

Tito's Yugoslavia began its overt process of change after a series of policy rifts with the USSR and the expulsion of Yugoslavia in 1948 from the international organization of the Communist parties. To cope with the external pressures, coupled with the alienation and disenchantment of its own workers and the dismal results of its efforts at autarkic industrialization, the Yugoslav leadership dramatically turned the country's attention to the dangers of bureaucratization *à la Russe*. It proclaimed its decision to 'transfer the management of national enterprises to the workers engaged in them', and to proceed henceforth in the building up of socialism 'without the use of any ready-made forms . . . following our own road, taking account of the specific conditions which exist in our country'.[3]

---

3 J. B. Tito, 'O radničkom upravljanju u privrednim preduzecima' (On Workers' Management in Economic Enterprises). Speech of June 26, 1950, in J. B. Tito, *Govori i članci* (Speeches and Articles), Zagreb, Naprijed, Vol. v, 1959, p. 205.

While the Yugoslav leadership changed a number of other significant elements of the country's economic mechanism, the Yugoslav economic reforms focused mainly on so-called *workers' self-management*. As one of the Yugoslav leaders, Edward Kardelj, put it for the Yugoslav Communists, 'the main dilemma of socialism' consists in whether 'self-management or state-management persists and grows stronger'.[4]

Hungary's search for ways of modifying the Soviet-type economic mechanism took a somewhat different direction from that of Yugoslavia. The dislocations brought about in the early 1950s by the faithful application of the Soviet strategy of development brought to the fore the question of investment priorities in a small, agrarian country, poorly endowed with raw materials and traditionally heavily dependent on foreign trade. The ensuing debate among policy makers, planners, and economists centered on possible changes in the scope of socialization and in the nature of the methods to be applied, particularly to peasant agriculture. The measures set forth in 1953 by the Communist Premier Imre Nagy were reminiscent of the policies propounded by Bukharin in the mid 1920s. These measures aimed at the mutually reinforcing growth of state industry and private agriculture: eventually, the latter would be transformed under the leadership of the former, through voluntary formation of cooperatives and flourishing domestic and foreign trade. Although the NEP-like Nagy solution was finally rejected and the country engulfed in an open revolt (1956), the Hungarian debates brought into dramatic focus the second group of primary issues to which we have referred above, namely, the interrelations between the public and the private sector in the transition to communism, and the specific operational rules of the socialist economic order.

The Polish economic crisis and open revolt of 1956–57, which erupted shortly after the Hungarian upheaval, was also precipitated by dislocations from attempting to implement a Soviet-type strategy of development. The Polish debates and attempts at reform focused, however, on a different set of problems from those in Yugoslavia or Hungary: the scope of the plan, and the possible utilization of various planning instruments. The country's Economic Council did propose reforms which reflected the Yugoslav and Hungarian experiences. But, moreover, the Poles explored the numerous theoretical implications of linkages between plan and market, and of the uses of governmental instruments under socialism – our third group of primary issues.

The fourth major attempt at reform in the socialist camp took place in the 1960s in Czechoslovakia. In 1948, Czechoslovakia was the most

4 E. Kardelj, 'The Principal Dilemma: Self Management or Statism', *Socialist Thought and Practice*, October 24, 1966, p. 16.

developed country of Eastern Europe, enjoying the highest per capita income in the area. After the Communist takeover in February 1948, the country underwent deep structural changes in order to transform itself into the military–industrial workshop of the socialist bloc. The structural readjustments and the heavy-handed application of the Soviet strategy of development, however, brought about a marked deterioration in economic performance, which became particularly severe in the early 1960s. A thorough-going debate on the country's economic mechanism gathered momentum throughout the 1960s, and in 1968 a bold attempt was made to put an end to the country's deteriorating performance. The Czechoslovak Communist leadership tried to discard its directive planning system, to end the stream of incessant injunctions (called in Czech *jet-rebismus* or *we must* -ism), to modify priorities and incentives, and to give the country socialism *with a human face*. The main thrust of the reform was the search for a new balance between collective and private interests, with due consideration of what the private preferences really are and what their satisfaction entails. But the Czechoslovak upheaval, like the Hungarian, ended with the intervention of Soviet troops, cutting off any possibility of direct experimentation. The Czechoslovak debates illuminate, however, many of the critical issues of a socialist economy, and prove very important for an understanding of the questions connected with our fourth group of basic issues and choices, which concern the interrelations between public goals and private wants under socialism.

This book examines in detail the range of subjects touched upon in this introduction. The book falls into two parts. Part I, *Analysis of Issues* examines the conceptions involved in the structuring of management, the scope of socialization and rules of the economic order, plan–market combinations, and goals determination. A concluding chapter contrasts the Soviet objections to market-oriented variants with the critique of the limits to improving the Soviet model's *modus operandi*.

Part II, *Selected Essays*, presents four groups of essays and documents from the economic literature produced in Eastern Europe, particularly during the four crises indicated (Yugoslavia, 1948–51; Hungary, 1954–57; Poland 1956–57; Czechoslovakia, 1963–68). Each of the four sections opens with an article by a Soviet writer presenting the historical or the current Soviet position on the given topic. The other essays of each section illustrate the wide range and the tenor of the specific criticisms directed in periods of crisis against the fundamental elements of the Soviet-type model of organization and management of the socialist society. Selected for their pertinence as well as for their originality, the essays document and support the main analytical propositions advanced in Part I. Eleven of the essays have appeared only in their author's native language; the others have been previously translated into English, but have been published (with two exceptions) in journals or books printed in Eastern Europe which have a rather limited circulation. The new translations were made by the Israel Program for Scientific Translations located in Jerusalem. All the translations used, whatever the source, have been edited and carefully rechecked against the originals. I have tried to avoid repetition, although at times this was impossible if the integrity of the documents was to be preserved. I have indicated in the short introductory notes to the four sections of essays the weight to be attached to this or that document according to its source and the special limitations of this literature because of self-censorship by the authors, official taboos, peculiarities of the Marxian vocabulary, and a propensity under socialism to use Aesopean language that conveys meanings different from the literal ones.

We now have sufficient historical distance to enable us to look back at the *main* crises of Soviet-type socialist organization. Most of the critical alternatives have been clearly sketched. All have illustrated the incessant struggle for more functional systems with more efficient performance. All can now be analyzed jointly in a single conceptual framework, rather than in isolation within their respective national contexts. The single framework is the approach I have chosen. The book will, I hope, prove of interest to students of comparative economics, economic planning, economic development, and economics in general. All are areas in which the study of alternative models of organization plays a significant part.

1 The decision makers and the decision process

The frame of reference

In Marxian theory, the socialist economy evolves from a commodity-producing, market-directed system dominated by private interests into a non-monetary, planned, collectivist system. As the economy is thus transformed, new kinds of management structures must necessarily emerge. While these general ideas of Marx, Engels, and other socialist revolutionaries are quite clear, they sorely lack in detailed elaboration. Indeed, the founders of 'scientific socialism' deliberately avoided details in order to ward off the epithet utopians.

Consider the question of an economic system's decision makers. According to Marx and Engels, the state – no matter the form of government – is both the result of the division of society into classes and an instrument of the dominant class. In the capitalist system, the state is simply a 'capitalist machine, the ideal personification of the total national capital'. The management of both the state and the economy is accordingly in the hands of a bourgeois class 'freed from directly productive labour', which arises 'side by side with the great majority, exclusively bond slaves to labour'.[1] It is for the benefit of the bourgeois class that the prevailing relationships in production and the forms of ownership on which they rest are maintained by the parasitic civil–military bureaucracy staffing the state apparatus.

When the proletariat seizes political power and socializes the means of production, thus changing both production relations and ownership forms, it simultaneously unleashes a series of processes which in time will change not only the role of the state, but also the nature of social management and the scope of economic coordination and control. The state as an administrative and coercive apparatus will eventually become unnecessary, because there will be no classes to be kept in subjection; state

1 Frederick Engels, *Anti-Dühring. Herr Eugen Dühring's Revolution in Science*, Trans. from the 3rd German edition (1894), Moscow, Progress Publishers, 1975, sixth printing, pp. 330 and 334.

interferences will become superfluous in one domain after another: thus 'the state will wither away of itself'. The unlimited expansion of the forces of production which has in the meantime become possible will sweep away the division of labor that underlies class divisions. No bureaucratic–military parasitic apparatus will henceforth be needed to enforce supervision or controls: man will ultimately be freed of the extraneous objective forces – political, social or economic – which have hitherto governed his history and social organization.[2]

In regard to the management of firms or enterprises which are the *component* elements of the economy, Marx makes a crucial distinction between a coordinating function and a supervisory function. He considers coordination indispensable in all cases where individuals must cooperate, since cooperation requires a 'commanding will to coordinate and unify the process'. Supervision, however, is typical only for the 'modes of production based on the antithesis between the laborer, as the direct producer, and the owner of the means of production'; that is, supervision is bound to disappear when the means of production pass into the hands of the direct producers.[3]

If the general thrust of the Marxian conception is clear, important specific questions nevertheless remain. What forms will the new processes take? At what pace will they unfold? How are transitions from one phase to the next to be prepared and effected?[4]

By the time of World War I, three main tendencies had emerged in this respect among the European Marxians – the German Reformists, the Russian Bolsheviks, and the intermediate Austrian socialists, called Austromarxists. The most articulate spokesmen of these three groups were Karl Kautsky, Lenin, and Otto Bauer, respectively. The ideas they propounded played an important role in clarifying the socialist positions concerning the pathway to socialism. Many of these ideas are still important, I believe, for understanding both the debates and the reforms actually proposed in the contemporary socialist countries.

In his later writings on the proletarian revolution, the Social Democratic leader, Karl Kautsky, visualized his party taking power after a struggle which did not necessarily include violence and bloodshed. For him, the revolution was to be a careful, methodical process of transforming the state machine and the organizational structures of the economy, as well as

2 K. Marx, *Capital, A Critical Analysis of Capitalist Production*, reproduction of the 1887 edition, Moscow, Foreign Languages Publishing House, in three volumes, 1954–62, Vol. I, pp. 487–8 and Engels, *Anti-Dühring* . . . , pp. 405–8.
3 *Capital, ibid.*, Vol. III, p. 376.
4 The question of transitions from one socialist type of organization to another has elicited an important debate also among non-Marxist economists. See my paper 'On Some Issues in the Theory of the Socialist Economy', in *Kyklos*, Vol. xxv, 1972, Fasc. 4, pp. 715–35.

implementing various changes in the forms and principles of income distribution.[5] The existing state apparatus could serve the workers' interests, provided it was cleansed of the 'vestiges of the monarchy as well as [of] bureaucratic and military privileges'. The economy, however, required systematic and wide-ranging structural transformations. Socialization of the large firms had to be carried out, albeit gradually, keeping in mind that the management of such firms requires not dilettantism but comprehensive technical and economic training as well as constant study of the development of science and of the market. Kautsky rejected as inefficient the management of such enterprises by state bureaucrats, the introduction of bureaucratic directive planning, and the vesting of regulatory powers in mandatory industrial associations carrying out administrative mandates. He found devoid of imagination the idea of transforming capitalist enterprises into cooperatives, collectively owned by their workers.[6] Such a solution, he noted, would transform the workers into entrepreneurs submitting to the same vagaries of the market as the previous capitalist owners – viz., competition, instability, and bankruptcy. The better-suited establishments would crowd out the weaker ones and eventually hire the latter's displaced workers, while isolated enterprises of the same branch would organize themselves into trusts. The formation of entirely self-sufficient collectives he also considered incompatible with more developed forms of production. Kautsky advocated instead a flexible choice of management forms, with proper adjustments for scale, type, and significance of the given enterprise, and with maintenance of private ownership, entrepreneurship, and initiative in small establishments.[7]

The use of a wide variety of management forms was also stressed by other socialist leaders, including Otto Bauer, who suggested the formation of so-called joint control managerial organizations, allowing for various forms of cooperation among employees, consumers, the scientific community, and the state.[8] Each socialized branch of industry would be managed by a board of directors, whose members would be elected by the branch trade unions, by representatives of the consumers, and by the state. As the revolution unfolded, land would be nationalized step by step, with the idea of eventually developing technically advanced socialist farming. Farm workers would be organized just as the workers in industry, and

5 See Karl Kautsky's classic work, *The Class Struggle* (Erfurt Programme) [1892] trans. by William E. Bohn, Chicago, Kerr & Co., 1921, pp. 90–1 and *The Labour Revolution* [1925], trans. by H. J. Stenning, New York, The Dial Press, 1926.
6 See Karl Kautsky, *Le Programme Socialiste*, Trans. by L. Remy, Paris, Librairie des Sciences Politiques et Sociales, 1910, pp. 109ff.
7 *The Labour Revolution*, pp. 128ff., 169ff., 209 and 223ff.
8 *Ibid.*, pp. 180ff. See also Otto Bauer, *La Marche au Socialisme*, trans. by F. Caussy, Paris, Librairie du Parti Socialiste et de l'Humanité, 1919, pp. 23ff.

would be encouraged to engage in productive cooperation of associations of various forms.

The Bolshevik vision of the transition period to communism is substantially different from those of the reformists and Austromarxists. On the eve of the Russian revolution of October 1917, Lenin thought how the workers could *immediately* eradicate both the old state machine and the market economy, and replace them with a new, non-hierarchical, non-bureaucratic system, integrating both the state's administration and the management of the economy. In Lenin's interpretation of Marx, the workers in arms had to destroy the existing civil and military administrations and rapidly concentrate in their own hands all the executive, legislative, judicial, and economic powers as well. Following the example of the Paris Commune of 1871 (which emerged after France's defeat by Germany in the war of 1870), the proletariat should erect a non-hierarchical state by organizing itself as the ruling class. In Lenin's words, 'the principal lesson of Marxism regarding the tasks of the proletariat during a revolution in relation to the state' is that it must 'smash the bureaucratic–military machine' and replace it with institutions in which first 'the majority, and then *the whole population without exception,* proceed to discharge state functions'.[9] The proletariat cannot dispense at once with all administration and subordination, but it can and should submit all administration to the decision of the workers in arms.

The crux of the Leninist conception of a non-hierarchical system was the assumption that capitalism had reached a level of development in which everyone could discharge both administrative and managerial functions. According to Lenin's pre-October 1917 writings, the creation by capitalism of large-scale production, transportation, and communication had made it possible to simplify administrative functions to the point where they could be reduced to 'simple operations of registration, filing and checking'. Because of this, a 'reversal to primitive democracy' had become possible – a reversal which for Lenin explicitly implied 'control and supervision by *all,* so that *all* may become "bureaucrats" for a time and that, therefore, nobody may be able to become a "bureaucrat" '.[10]

The idea that state administration and management (both coordinating and supervising) are essentially nothing more than registration, filing and

9 V. I. Lenin, 'The State and Revolution', in *Collected Works,* Vol. 25 (June–September 1917), Moscow, Progress Publishers, 1964, pp. 415 and 420. In an earlier writing, Lenin speaks of the replacement of 'the old state machine, the army, the police force and bureaucracy [officialdom]' not only by 'a mass organization, but a universal organization of the entire armed people'. 'Letters from Afar: Fifth Letter, The Tasks Involved in the Building of the Revolutionary Proletarian State', *Collected Works,* Vol. 23, (August 1916 through March 1917), Moscow, Progress Publishers, 1964, p. 340.
10 *Ibid.,* pp. 420–1 and 481.

checking which everyone could perform in rotation – computers had not yet appeared on the horizon – came to be enshrined in communist revolutionary theory. Nikolai Bukharin, whom Lenin considered an outstanding Communist theoretician but whom Stalin later had shot, proposed an interesting hypothesis on the eventual disappearance from history of *specialized* organizers, administrators and officials. Organizational functions are obviously necessary, Bukharin stated, and hence will be necessary in the future. But the continued existence of specialized staffs of leaders and organizers (even under the Soviets) was due to lack of uniformity within the working class and within its party. Eventually, the growth of productive forces and education would homogenize the entire population and, at the same time, result in 'a colossal overproduction of organizers'; such overproduction would nullify the stability of specialized groups. In the transition to communism, however, 'a *tendency* to "degeneration", i.e., the excretion [sic] of a leading stratum' may be unavoidable. This tendency will nevertheless eventually be offset by the growth of production and education and by the fact that neither one would henceforth offer a shield for the exploitation of others.[11]

Thus, in the Leninist frame of reference, the bureaucratic administrative form – i.e. administration by specialized personnel working in offices – was viewed as parasitical under capitalism, and as a transitional form of administration under socialism. (It would be totally unnecessary under communism.) A certain degree of reversion to primitive democracy was considered to be immediately feasible under socialism, given the advanced level of organization inherited from capitalism. A complete reversion was of course imperative and unavoidable in the future, as the overproduction of organizers would necessarily reach 'colossal' proportions.

Primitive democracy in theory, and partyarchy in practice

As soon as the Bolsheviks seized power, it became plain that the question of managing both the state machine and the nationalized enterprises was far more complex, more difficult, and more demanding than Bolshevik theory had assumed they would be.

Consider first the state administration. In accordance with his prerevolutionary postulates, Lenin and his followers perceived the Soviets (Councils) of Workers, Peasants, and Soldiers as the new state machine ready to replace the old state apparatus. Accordingly, the Bolsheviks encouraged the Soviets to displace the old institutions and to concentrate executive, legislative and judicial powers in their own hands. The Bol-

11 Nikolai Bukharin, *Historical Materialism, A System of Sociology* [1921], Trans. from the third Russian edition, New York, Russell & Russell, 1965, pp. 310–11.

shevik revolution was supposed to have given all power to the Soviets, i.e. to the organs of the exploited and the oppressed organizing themselves as the ruling class. In backward Russia, however, the 'exploited' were not the industrial workers alone. They shared the Soviets with the peasants, to whom certain concessions had to be made. Furthermore, from the very instant of victory, the revolution moved away from its intended ideal of a reversion to primitive democracy. The Soviets, supposedly elected directly by the masses, quickly spawned executive committees and secretariats at the district and regional levels, and, at the national level, a central government comprised of numerous *commissariats* (ministries) with rapidly growing bureaucracies.[12] Finally, within the executive committees, secretariats, and commissariats, the real power was concentrated in the hands of the Communist party. The simple Marxian principle that the new state would consist of 'the proletariat organized as the ruling class'[13] in practice became more complicated: the proletariat, in alliance with the peasantry, was presumed to rule through its Soviets; in fact, the Soviets ruled through inner appointed bodies, which were actually run by the Communist party, which was, in turn, ruled by a narrow group of leaders.

From their dominant supervisory position, the party staff were able to mobilize the former bureaucrats and technicians as coordinators. By 'hemming them in' the party was able to use their talents to bring order out of chaos in industry, agriculture, and transport; above all they were able to win the civil war. As Lenin himself told us, the Red Army could not have solved the problem of administration if it had not trusted the former 'General Staff and the big specialists in organization'.[14] Nevertheless, while a bureaucracy thus irresistibly proliferated, the official exhortations for government by all continued unabated. Thus Lenin proclaimed:

First, every member of a Soviet must, without fail, do a certain job of state administration; secondly, these jobs must be consistently changed so that they embrace all aspects of government, all its branches; and thirdly, literally all the working population must be drawn into independent participation in state admini-

12 See *Le testament de Varga,* edited by Roger Garaudy, Paris, Grasset 1970, pp. 51ff. Eugene Varga, one time people's commissar for Finances of the brief Hungarian Soviet Republic of 1919, lived in the USSR from 1920 until his death in 1964. His 'testament' first circulated in the illegal publications of the Soviet underground, but its authenticity has never been seriously questioned. The process of creating 'inner bodies often at two or three removed from directly elected bodies' actually remains typical of today's Soviets also. See Derek J. Scott, *Russian Political Institutions,* New York, Praeger, 1961, p. 111.

13 See Lenin's comments on this key quotation from Marx and Engels' *Communist Manifesto,* in 'Proletarian Revolution and Renegade Kautsky', *Collected Works,* Vol. 28 (July 1918–March 1919), Moscow, Progress Publishers, 1964, pp. 260ff.

14 'Report of the Central Committee', Eighth Congress of the RCP (B) [Russian Communist Party (Bolshevik)], March 8, 1919, in V. I. Lenin, *Collected Works,* Vol. 29 (March–August 1919), Moscow, Progress Publishers, 1965, p. 156.

stration by means of a series of gradual measures that are carefully selected and implemented.[15]

Even though such exhortations were increasingly unrealistic, Lenin refused to concede that systematic day-to-day work in any field could only be done (in Max Weber's phrase) by 'officials working in offices'. This was especially true of highly complex organizations involving hundreds and even thousands of people. As the reversion to primitive democracy became more and more elusive, Lenin attributed the phenomenon of bureaucratization to *temporary* factors – the wretched cultural level inherited from capitalism, the exhaustion of the masses through war and revolution, or the perfidy of former bureaucrats who, 'thrown out through the door . . . creep back through the window'[16] to poison and corrupt with their old habits and mentalities.

Lenin certainly knew that a new bureaucracy, more complex and more independent of the masses than ever before, had been evolving directly from the Soviets: yet he continued to treat bureaucratism as a transitional phenomenon which would disappear once the temporary factors had passed. Whether out of deceit or wishful thinking, Lenin established an important precedent: his successors too treated bureaucracy not as an unavoidable division of labor or an evil preferable to dilettantism, but as an accidental phenomenon. They too were to point to the low cultural level, to the insufficient mobilization of mass initiative, and to the past rather than to the present bureaucratic needs and propensities.

Meanwhile widespread changes were taking place in bureaucratic structures and in the economy as well. Private enterprise and market relations were being systematically repressed and replaced with central supervision. Initially, enterprise directors and managers were placed under workers' *control*. When this arrangement proved unsatisfactory, *corporate management* – with the workers appointing the administrators and specialists was attempted. As this second arrangement soon failed as well, Lenin finally had to acknowledge the need for the party or the state to appoint managers who would be *independent* of direct supervision by the workers. Henceforth *one-man management* at every important level was proclaimed indispensable.

Thus Lenin discarded without apparent qualms the simplistic theory he had formulated on the eve of the revolution, namely, that 'the workers shall organize large-scale production on the basis of what capitalism has already created, relying on our own experience as workers, establishing strict, iron discipline backed up by the state power of the armed work-

15 'Draft Programme of the RCP (B)', V. I. Lenin, *Collected Works*, Vol. 29, p. 109.
16 'Report on the Party Programme', March 19, 1919, in Lenin, *Collected Works*, Vol. 29, p. 183.

ers'.[17] He rationalized that both the coordinating and supervisory functions created immense difficulties because every factory, industry, and railway built on the basis of large-scale engineering embodied 'the concentrated experience of capitalism'.[18] Implicitly, this argument conceded that, to run such enterprises, one could not rely on his earlier theory that a mechanism of social management was at hand, and that the economy could be organized as a *postal system,* with the workers hiring workers, foremen and accountants on behalf of the whole society.[19] His new theory stressed the following:

Large-scale machine industry – which is precisely the material source, the productive source, the foundation of socialism – calls for absolute and strict *unity of will* which directs the joint labours of hundreds, thousands, and tens of thousands of people. The technical, economic and historical necessity of this is obvious, and all those who have thought about socialism have always regarded it as one of the conditions of socialism.[20]

It was 'sheer muddle', Lenin continued, to think that in a developed socialist society, with no social division of labour or fixed professions, the replacement of people performing administrative functions each one in his turn will be simple and automatic. Management was necessarily the job of the individual administrator – and who this administrator would be was a special question that depended on what workers or experts were available and what kinds of administrators were needed.[21]

Accordingly, Lenin began now to attack the tendency to restrict the powers of managers. He stressed repeatedly that it was *absolutely essential* to concentrate all authority in the factories in the hands of the management and insisted that the latter 'must have authority independently to fix and pay out wages, and also distribute rations, working clothes, etc.'[22] In Lenin's new one-man management system, the party would not, of course, relinquish its own authority. The party reserved to itself the right to *choose* all the managers. Moreover, the 'freedom to maneuver' granted to managers was sharply reduced by the creation of numerous central planning and supervisory agencies.

17 Lenin, 'The State and Revolution', p. 426.
18 'Report of the Central Committee', Eighth Congress, Vol. 29, p. 154.
19 'The State and Revolution', pp. 426–7.
20 'The Immediate Tasks of the Soviet Government', published April 28, 1918, endorsed by the All-Russia Central Executive Committee, and reaffirmed by Lenin against the partisans of corporate management in his 'Speech on Economic Development', March 31, 1920, Ninth Congress of the RCP (B), *Collected Works,* Vol. 30 (September 1919–April 1920), Moscow, Progress Publishers, 1965, p. 475.
21 'Reply to the Discussion on the Report of the Central Committee', March 30, 1920, Ninth Congress of the RCP (B), Lenin, *Collected Works,* Vol. 30, p. 465.
22 'The Role and Functions of the Trade Unions under the New Economic Policy', Decisions of the RCP (B), January 12, 1922, in Lenin, *Collected Works,* Vol. 33 (August 1921–March 1923), Moscow, Progress Publishers, 1966, p. 189.

Thus the Communist party not only shadowed but also penetrated the supervisory apparatus emerging from the Soviets and the managerial structure of the state sectors of the economy. The party, in principle only the theoretical inspiritor of the new system, thus became both its co-ordinator and its supervisor. Indeed, following the revolution, it began to be extolled as the only force capable of 'uniting, training and organizing a vanguard of the proletariat and the whole mass of the working people', without whom the 'dictatorship of the proletariat is impossible'.[23]

Thus the idea of the reversion to primitive democracy was soon abandoned, and the idea of a coordinating and controlling vanguard was substituted for it. As the party took control over the state machinery and the management hierarchy, it of course generated a ponderous bureaucracy of its own. Thus the leadership of the new socialist society almost from the beginning was vested in three bureaucracies – party, state and managerial – each autonomous yet intertwined with the others. Eventually, Lenin himself came to speak openly of a 'bureaucratic ulcer', of a 'serious malaise'.[24] He even suggested that *ad hoc* inspection groups of workers and peasants, whose honesty has been tested, be formed to verify and appraise the work of the Communist bureaucrats. 'We must have non-Party people controlling the Communists',[25] declared Lenin. But the injunction was hollow, because all power rested with the latter, not with the former.

At Lenin's death, the Soviet bureaucracy of party, state and management was more complex, more stratified, and more vast than Russia had ever seen. Already before Lenin's death, Trotsky became the most vocal opponent of the bureaucracy. His opposition might seem, at a distance, to hark back to the earlier tendencies toward utopian democracy; in fact, it took place on an entirely new plane. Trotsky focused on the party's own 'bureaucratic degeneration' and on the ways to cure it and avoid it in the future. In the *New Course*, written in 1923, Trotsky attacked not the bureaucracy *per se* – after all, he had participated with Lenin in its creation – but rather 'the excessive authority of committees and secretaries' *within the party*. He attributed the bureaucratic degeneration of the party to inertia – 'the methods and administrative manners accumulated during these long years' – to concentration 'solely upon questions of administration, appointments and transfers', and finally, to the 'changing social

23 'Preliminary Draft Resolution of the Tenth Congress of the RCP (B)', March 1921, Lenin, *Collected Works*, Vol. 32 (December 1920–August 1921), Moscow, Progress Publishers, 1965, p. 246.
24 'Report on the Political Work of the [Central Committee of the] RCP (B)', March 8, 1921, Lenin, Vol. 32, pp. 190 and 191.
25 'Instructions of the Council of Labour and Defense to Local Soviet Bodies', Draft, May 21, 1921, Vol. 32, pp. 388 and 389.

composition' of the party.[26] To cope with the forces of degeneration which flowed from the party's 'new tasks . . . new functions . . . new difficulties, and . . . new mistakes', Trotsky offered a diagnosis and proposed a cure:

> The proletariat realizes its dictatorship through the Soviet state. The Communist party is the leading party of the proletariat, and consequently of its state. The whole question is to realize this leadership without merging into the bureaucratic apparatus of the state, in order not to expose itself to a bureaucratic degeneration.[27]

Trotsky's struggle for the New Course thus represented an earnest attempt to separate two deeply intertwined and inseparable elements: the party's own internal regime, and its total involvement in both the state administration and the economic management. He suggested that the party could insure 'a vibrant and active democracy' internally: to do so, however, it had to remember that Communists are only in the state apparatus and in the economy '*hierarchically* dependent upon each other', but 'all *equal* in the determination of the tasks' in the party.[28]

In actuality, the party could not isolate itself from the power relations it constantly manipulated. Moreover, the party had always been hierarchically organized, and had tended to become monocratic under Lenin. Stalin, Lenin's successor, eventually transformed the party into a pure monocracy: through successive, bloody purges, he made the party into a pliable and subservient instrument. But Stalin's own *personality cult* added little beside byzantine ritual to the basic mechanism inherited from Lenin.

Thus by the late 1920s the Communist party had established itself at the top of a complex bureaucratic system. It was the overseer, organizer, coordinator, developer and manipulator of the state and the economy. It operated through the Soviets and their committees, bureaus, and presidia, through the state's civil and military institutions, through the state's regulatory boards and ministries, through the trade unions and professional or non-professional groups – reaching down into every plant, office, or association. To this day, all key administrative, managerial, cultural posts are staffed by the party's hierarchs. Lists of key jobs and lists of privileged party individuals – called the *nomenklatura* – are highly correlated, reflecting the party's goals and policies.[29]

While no system could be managed without at least *one* hierarchical level, systems may of course become burdened with complex, overlapping,

---

26 Leon Trotsky, *The New Course* and Max Shachtman, *The Struggle for the New Course*, New York, New International Publishing Co., 1943, pp. 14, 15, 18.
27 *Ibid.*, p. 24.
28 *Ibid.*, p. 25.
29 *Le testament de Varga*, pp. 64ff.

and often offsetting layers of control. Lenin's system is clearly uniquely complex. The widely ramified party and economic bureaucracies have no analogues in the modern world, except perhaps – and only up to a point – in war economies and in the fascist regimes. In this system, allegiance is due not to the workers' state, but to the party and, as became true under Stalin, directly to the supreme party leader himself. The party's key officials – indeed the entire partyarchy – are permanent probationers of the party leader, entrusted with a revocable commission and subject (like the French *commissaires royaux* of the late Middle Ages) 'to specific instructions regulating . . . functions and duties, to disciplinary controls, to sudden transfer or dismissal'.[30] As a result, any crisis or power shift within the top party hierarchy deeply affects the stability of the administrative–managerial bureaucratic pyramid. This is so to this day in spite of attempts to convert this *partyarchic* system into a more stable, self-regulating system with its own internal rules of operation (e.g. like the British civil service).

It is otiose to debate whether the Soviet-type bureaucracy as a whole – party leaders, state administrators, and managers – constitutes a social class or merely a caste. To be sure, in a fully nationalized economy of the Soviet type, there are no private capitalists and entrepreneurs: these Marxian classes have disappeared under socialism. But distinct strata are still there: industrial workers, collectivized peasants – half-peasants, half-workers – bureaucrats, intellectuals. With Ludwig von Mises, I believe that under socialism differences in social functions do exist which lead to classes directly analogous to Marx's classes under capitalism. 'There will be those who issue orders and those who are bound to obey these orders unconditionally; there will be those who make plans and those whose job it is to execute these plans.'[31] The directors of the Soviet system issue the orders and make the plans; they are the coordinators, the decision makers, the supervisors; it is of little importance whether they do it in the name of the workers, the party, or its vanguard – themselves.

Workers' self-management and the partyarchy

The first systematic attempts to disentangle the management of the economy from the administration of the state were undertaken in Yugoslavia. Those attempts began soon after its break in 1948 with the Soviet Union and the other Communist East European countries. The theoretical

30 See Hans Rosenberg, *Bureaucracy, Aristocracy and Autocracy, The Prussian Experience 1660–1815*, Cambridge, Massachusetts, Harvard University Press [1958], 1968, p. 17.
31 Ludwig von Mises, *Bureaucracy* [1944], New Rochelle, Arlington House, 1969, pp 99–100.

justifications for the Yugoslav departures from Stalin's methods and procedures have undergone many changes. One main contention has, however, remained constant: Tito's Yugoslavia intends to create, and has indeed created, a new system of economic management that is a unique alternative to centralized bureaucratic management *à la Russe*. The new Yugoslav system is called 'workers' self-management'.

In launching the new system in 1950, Tito explained that it was merely another step toward communism. The transition to workers' self-management meant that the functions of the state in administering the economy were no longer exclusive, and that the workers were 'beginning to take up their right as producers to manage production'. This would 'prevent the infectious disease known as bureaucracy [from] becoming endemic in our economy'. The bureaucratic disease, Tito added, 'is carried with incredible ease and rapidity from bourgeois society, and it is dangerous in the transitional period because, like a squid with a thousand tentacles, it holds back and hampers the correct process and speed of development'.[32]

Under workers' – or, more accurately, *employees'* – self-management, the employees of an economic enterprise form an 'organization of associated labor' that is supposed to manage the enterprise through a 'workers' [employees'] council'. The state owns the physical assets of the enterprise, but the collective of employees becomes the manager. In enterprises with fewer than 30 workers, the workers' council consists of the entire work force; in larger enterprises, the council consists of from 15 to 200 elected members. (Most of the enterprises in question are industrial ones: crop raising and animal husbandry remain mostly in private hands.)

The basic unit of the Yugoslav social organization is the commune, a unit of municipal government. A commune supervises all the self-managed enterprises within its jurisdiction, except for those of more than local significance, which fall within the purview of the republic. In order to reduce the direct involvement of the state in the economy, central planning directives were eventually replaced by indicative planning. Market relations between enterprises were permitted to expand, and indirect regulatory instruments of control over the activities of enterprises – a vast array of taxes, subsidies and regulations – were put into effect.

The establishment of workers' management was originally presented as a form of reversion to primitive democracy, a new framework within which 'the entire economy [was] in the hands of the people', who, by their 'ceaseless process of work and management would surmount and van-

---

32 J. B. Tito, 'On Workers' Management in Economic Enterprises [1950], in *Selected Speeches and Articles*, Belgrade, Naprijed, 1963, pp. 108 and 111.

quish the economy's backwardness'.[33] Inevitably, though, just as in the Soviet Union of 1918, the simplistic assumptions underlying 'primitive democracy' rapidly proved erroneous. The division of labor within the enterprise could not be easily swept away. Management was not merely a kind of mechanical registration, filing and checking. And the employees (the 'direct producers') could not henceforth participate in the most important decisions. In practice, the Yugoslav self-managed firm quickly came to resemble closely the capitalist corporation with its board of directors exercising only broad control over the executive management. Moreover, in Yugoslavia as elsewhere, executive management became concentrated in the hands of a highly educated, technically skilled elite.[34]

Numerous studies of the Yugoslav experience with workers' self-management have underlined the decisive influence of the professional managers in every phase of business policy and operations – investment decisions, new technology, product lines, marketing, public relations, and so on.[35] As a Yugoslav writer puts it, the professionals, i.e. those occupying key technological and administrative positions, 'have incomparably greater opportunities to shape business policies than those who are more or less responsible for the actual execution of individual operations'. The workers' councils often do little more than discuss the possible implications of the managers' expert reports 'from the aspect of what personal earnings and what income for their enterprise the proposed programmes or projects will insure'.[36] The notion that *every* person employed in an enterprise could participate equally in the management is a naive idea that continues to be taken more seriously outside, rather than inside, Yugoslavia.

Thus a systematic and sustained effort was made in Yugoslavia to dismantle centralized planning *à la Russe* and replace it with a unique form of socialist market relations.(From the peak of decentralization in 1966, some gradual recentralization has occurred particularly from 1971 on – but never significantly above the level of the national republics.) The official term 'workers' self-management' overstates, however, the case of decentralization: within it, the directors of enterprises play the decisive role in regard to such formerly centrally-determined decisions as output mix, pricing, plant sites, and investment outlays. Moreover, whatever the changes in the operation of enterprise management, the League of Communists (as the party is called in Yugoslavia) strongly influences the

33 *Ibid.*, p. 113.
34 See *Yugoslav Workers' Self-Management.* Proceedings of a Symposium held in Amsterdam, January 7–9, 1970, edited by M. J. Broekmeyer, Dordrecht, Holland, Reidel Publishing Co., 1970, p. 198.
35 *Ibid.*, pp., 98ff.
36 D. Bilandžić, 'Workers' Management of Factories', *Socialist Thought and Practice*, No. 28, October–December 1967, pp. 39 and 45.

workers' councils, the trade unions, and the municipalities, whose representatives are supposed to appoint the managers. The latter's careers depend on the party's good will. The party (at the federal or republican levels), never relinquished the role of selecting, controlling, and manipulating the managerial elite.[37]

Thus the non-Stalinist way of running the economy coexisted with the *Stalinist* way of appointing and shifting the leading 'cadres' of the economy and of insuring that party men were in command wherever it counted. Moreover, for fifteen years (1951–66), 'there hovered over the workers' councils the continuing presence of the all-powerful secret police'.[38] In 1966, the police chiefs were dismissed, but the party did not abandon its extensive overt or covert presence in the self-management structures.[39] Although the party came to be torn between the fear of losing its supremacy and the fear of losing credibility on its democratization drives, it did not renounce its power. As Milovan Djilas put it, those who look 'to the workers' councils and to self-management for an escape from the bugbears of Stalinism . . . ignore the reality that the party bureaucrats and oligarchs, too, have their vested interests in these organizations'.[40]

Much has been written since 1966 about the party's 'struggle within its own ranks against bureaucratic usurpation of self-management rights and of self-management practice',[41] and about the party's efforts 'to gather sufficient strength to remove radically, within its own organization, all the legacies and excrescences of the etatistic stage'.[42] Much has also been said about the necessity of shifting the center of gravity of the League's action from the exercise of power to ideological–political activity.[43] There are even references to transforming the party into a 'self-management organ, that is, a more or less democratic organization, which, so to speak, is subordinated to society and which carries out what society decides'.[44] But

---

37 *Radnička klasa u socijalizmu* (The Working Class in Socialism), a collection of articles by nine authors, Zagreb: Naše Teme, 1969, pp. 143ff.
38 See M. Djilas, *The Unperfect Society*, London, Methuen, 1969, p. 159.
39 'The pressure of economic and political practicability has – contrary to the principles of our programme – led to the further merging of Party and State leadership and leadership of economic management.' See Edvard Kardelj, 'The Principal Dilemma: Self-Management or Statism', *Socialist Thought and Practice*, No. 24, October–December 1966, p. 18.
40 *The Unperfect Society*, p. 160.
41 J. B. Tito, 'Current Problems of the Struggle of the League of Communists of Yugoslavia for the Implementation of the Reform', *Yugoslav Survey*, Vol. VII, No. 25, April– June 1966, p. 3590.
42 'The Fifth Meeting of the League of Communists of Yugoslavia', *Yugoslav Survey*, Vol. VIII, No. 1, February 1967, p. 36.
43 'Theses on the Further Development and Reorganization of the League of Communists of Yugoslavia (LCY)', *Yugoslav Survey*, Vol. VIII, No. 3, August 1967, p. 44.
44 Interview with Vladimir Bakarić, member of the Central Executive Committee of the League, *Borba*, August 14, 1966.

in practice the Yugoslav League of Communists has continued to reinforce and extend its controlling and guiding powers for a variety of reasons – for example, to prevent hostile forces, 'bureaucratic, technocratic or elitist', from driving a wedge between the economic aspects of the management reforms and their political and social aspects.[45]

We see, then, that in Yugoslav enterprises power tends to concentrate in the hands of the managers and of technicians, not in the workers' collectives. Moreover, just as in other socialist countries, the Yugoslav party and state continue to exercise pervasive control over enterprise managers. Even though state administration and economic management have been disentangled up to a point, the economic bureaucracies of both party and state continue to grow. These facts discredit any claim that the workers themselves are actually in charge of production, or that the Yugoslav state is in the process of withering away.

Diversity of participatory forms in decision making

It is evident that the degree of worker participation in decision making and management can vary widely, whether the enterprise is publicly, collectively, or privately owned. Further, no management form is necessarily wedded to a given system, and no single form is capable of avoiding the consequences of social and professional differentiation, bureaucratization, or alienation. Worker participation may involve any of a wide range of issues – e.g. hiring and firing, wages, work conditions, job rotation, welfare and safety, input mix, administrative tasks, commercial policy, and profit sharing. The participation may take the form of advice or of actual control. The locus of participatory decision making may be limited to a plant – or, within a plant, only to certain departments – or it may extend to a complete enterprise, a whole industry, or even an entire economy.[46]

Under public ownership (as in the state sectors of the socialist countries) or collective ownership (as in collective or union-owned firms), the workers may actually have fewer recognized rights than in capitalist firms. In both the USSR and Yugoslavia, with decision making in the hands of the party-controlled management, and with the unions reduced to organizing fringe benefits or prodding for higher productivity, the workers are deprived of any legal possibility of exercising countervailing power against the management. Strikes, for example, are banned on the theory that the

45 Edvard Kardelj, 'The Class Position of the LC Today', *Socialist Thought and Practice*, No. 37, December 1969, pp. 6ff.
46 For a detailed up-to-date discussion, see Michael Poole, *Workers' Participation in Industry*, London, Routledge & Kegan Paul, 1975.

workers could only strike against themselves. Like their Soviet counterparts, Yugoslav leaders in the late 1960s dismissed the existence of 'so-called strikes in our country'. Demands for the right to strike were entirely devoid of sense and superfluous since the 'working man in Yugoslavia is invested with far broader rights than the mere right to strike'.[47]

However broad the workers' rights are alleged to be in Yugoslavia, the evidence supports the view that, under workers' self-management, management has 'power without responsibility' while the workers' councils have 'responsibility without power'.[48] Managers are selected for their party loyalty rather than for their managerial expertise, and they need not assume responsibility for business failures. The enterprise director – as in the USSR – may even avoid certain risks: when the party considers it expedient, it helps the enterprise in need; when not, it lets the employees bear the burden of failure.

For a while, to be sure, two tendencies opposed each other in this self-management system. One pushed for the suppression of party–state intervention in the selection of cadres, and for entrusting the 'direct producers [the workers] themselves' with the hiring and firing of managerial personnel. The other tendency, which finally got the upper hand, pushed for the affirmation of the role of the party: in the words of a spokesman, Josip Vrhoveć, a leader of the Croatian party and member of the Presidium of the League, 'self-management without a party' would mean the denial 'of the leading role of the working class as the chief standard bearer of progress' – a denial which no Communist party could tolerate.[49]

The first tendency above, emphasizing the role of the enterprise council 'as an agency independent of the state and having the right to elect the manager', has appeared not only in Yugoslavia but also in other East European countries. Supporters of this tendency have stressed that only *real independence* from party–state influence can permit an enterprise to make decisions primarily on the basis of entrepreneurial criteria – primarily profit:[50] without such independence a proper business spirit cannot exist. As von Mises has rightly noted, the business spirit is not generated by the mere trappings of business techniques – acquisition of office furniture, prompt reply to inquiries, and the like – nor by granting the manager a

47 'Introductory Address by Krste Crvenkovski at the Sixth Session of the Presidency of LCY', *Socialist Thought and Practice*, A Yugoslav Quarterly, No. 36, October–December 1969, pp. 112–13.
48 V. Rus, 'Influence Structure in Yugoslav Enterprises', *Industrial Relations*, Vol. 9, 1970, p. 151.
49 *Vjesnek*, March 23/24, 1975.
50 See for instance, 'Everything about the Law on Enterprise', *Hospodarski Noviny*, Vol. 11, 1969.

share in profits. Rather, a manager acquires such a spirit through the penalty of 'his share in the losses which arise through his conduct of business'.[51]

The current Yugoslav system, no less than the Soviet, shelters the manager from this constructive discipline. Under the centralized planning of the Soviet economy, the requisite quality of the good manager is the ability to bargain with his superiors for low targets for his enterprise, and adroitly to pad his results in fulfilling and overfulfilling those same targets. In the less centralized Yugoslav system, *party* conformity and docility are sufficient. In either case, nothing akin to the 'business spirit' generated by the capitalist market can be created.

The dismantling of central planning machinery and the expansion of market relations are certainly capable of stunting the development of a centralized economic bureaucracy. But even at decentralized levels of the Yugoslav system, orders can be given, managers can be appointed or dismissed, organizational structures can be penetrated, and diversification, mergers or liquidations can be ordered. Thus the ostensibly independent enterprise may in fact remain chained to a bureaucratic apparatus, better camouflaged but no less inclined to growth and proliferation than the Soviet kind which it has superseded. As the Yugoslav economist Ivan Maksimović points out, 'none of the essential competencies of the state administration with regard to its influence upon the economy' has been altered in Yugoslavia by various decentralization schemes. The state authority (and behind it the party) exerts 'great influence at various points of the vertical axis [municipalities, republics] of the system, and is also strong at the level of working organizations'.[52] Administrative manipulations and arbitrariness (behind the screen of market relations) and party selection of managers on the basis of political loyalty indeed encourage the expansion of party–state bureaucracies in patterns not different in essence from those prevailing in the USSR. Ultimately, the Yugoslav leaders, like their Soviet counterparts, justify enormous socialist bureaucratization, not by reference to a party–state system of totalitarian authority, but on grounds of the 'low cultural level of the masses' – masses who, in the far future, will certainly enjoy a long-promised, but always elusive, reversion to primitive democracy.

---

51 L. von Mises, *Socialism* [1936], Trans. by J. Kahane, London, Jonathan Cape, 1969, pp. 216–17.
52 I. Maksimović, 'The Economic System and Workers' Self-Management in Yugoslavia', in *Yugoslav Workers' Self-Management*, ed. by Broekmeyer, *op. cit.*, p. 134.

2 Constraints and normative rules

The frame of reference

For the Western economist, economic principles are empirical generalizations meant to transcend the historical moment and the specific framework with reference to which they happen to have been formulated. As Marshall noted, however, these generalizations are only 'statements of tendencies more or less certain, more or less definite'.[1] For Marx, in contrast, an economic law was rigorously tied to a given socio-economic framework; within its specified realm, each economic law 'works with iron necessity towards inevitable results'. Indeed, for Marx, such laws expressed all of the interlocking forces which govern the entire social movement 'as a process of natural history', independent of the will, consciousness, and intelligence of its participants. Therefore, according to Marx and the Marxians, any scientific investigation into economic history must lay bare the laws which 'regulate the origin, existence, development, death of a given social organism'. Marx's own goal in *Capital* was precisely to uncover *the law of motion* of modern society.[2]

For Marx, the regulatory principle of a system of producing goods for sale – that is, a commodity-producing private-exchange system such as capitalism – was the law of value. The law of value in Marx's writings encompassed the basic forces which determine the production and exchange of commodities under capitalism: the formation of product and factor prices and the choice of input and output mixes. For all his insistence on concrete historical circumstances, however, Marx failed to treat a series of important concrete questions: What happens to commodities (goods bought and sold), to their values, and to the law of value itself, when the workers overturn capitalism, seize the means of production and

1 Alfred Marshall, *Principles of Economics*, ninth (Variorum) edition with annotations by C. W. Guillebaud, London, Macmillan, for the Royal Economics Society, 1961, pp. 33ff.
2 'Preface to the First German Edition' of *Capital* and notes of a reviewer of *Capital* quoted approvingly by Karl Marx in the 'Afterword to the Second German Edition' of this work; see, *Capital, A Critical Analysis of Capitalist Production*, Vol. 1, *op. cit.*, pp. 8–9 and 17ff.

start laying the foundations of a system of cooperative production, not for profit, but for common use? What becomes of market relations, trade, small-scale industry and handicrafts during the transition from capitalism to communism, i.e. during the so-called transformation period of the former into the latter? What kind of economic relations will then develop between the dominant working class – controlling the economy's industrial and banking complexes and the state's economic levers – and the working peasants who are presumed to be its allies and to accept its leadership? Will private, small-scale agricultural and industrial production and trade be encouraged or, rather, discouraged and finally liquidated through the formation of cooperatives (collectivization) throughout the entire economy? How will the cooperatives' controlling parameters be adjusted and what normative rules will the system's controllers have to obey in the evolving conditions of the transformation period?

Engels, who addressed certain of these questions, posited that, after the takeover of the means of production in the advanced capitalist countries, the production of commodities would necessarily give way to production for common use, i.e. to mere products destined for social distribution (free goods) rather than for market exchange. Values, prices and money would then tend to vanish, while anarchy in production and market spontaneity would be supplanted by conscious organization and by physical planning 'without the intervention of much vaunted "values" '.[3] But Engels did not specify how these various processes and the associated categories of value, prices and money, might interact within the framework of planned management in a predominantly backward peasant economy such as that of Russia at the beginning of its transformation period.

In the early 1920s, two Soviet theoreticians, Nikolai Bukharin and Evgenii Preobrazhenskii, formulated the basic outlines of the Bolshevik theories as they were to apply to Russia. These outlines, which often received Lenin's enthusiastic approval, were to play a decisive role in shaping Communist thought and economic policies for decades to come.[4] According to Bukharin, the proletariat and the peasantry, as the 'class bearers of different economic models', would of necessity clash. A struggle

3 See Engels, *Anti-Dühring . . .* , *op. cit.,* pp. 335–6, and 367. See also Paul M. Sweezy, *The Theory of Capitalist Development, Principles of Marxian Political Economy,* New York, Oxford University Press, 1943, pp. 52ff.

4 See N. Bukharin, *Ekonomika perekhodnogo perioda,* Chast' I: *Obshchaia teoriia transformatsionnogo protsessa* (Economics of the Transition Period, Part I, General Theory of the Transformation Process), Moscow, Gosizdat, 1920. (A translation of Bukharin's book is available in English under the title *Economics of the Transformation Period, with Lenin's Critical Remarks,* New York, Bergman Publishers, 1971. Useful because it provides Lenin's remarks along with Bukharin's text, this English translation is unfortunately often inaccurate.) See also N. I. Bukharin and E. A. Preobrazhenskii, *The ABC of Communism,* trans. by Eden and Cedar Paul, London, Unwin Bros., 1922.

between a proletarian *socializing* tendency and a peasant *commodity-anarchical* tendency, or between a state *plan* and market *anarchy*, was inevitable. Even after the revolution, the proletariat would have to combat a persistent and continuously renascent capitalism in the countryside, since the peasants' small commodity production 'is nothing else but the embryo of capitalist production'.[5] To the extent that a conscious social regulator (the plan) would increasingly replace the spontaneous forces of the market (the exchange economy), commodities would, as Engels foresaw, necessarily be converted into mere products and lose their former economic character.[6]

Furthermore, as both socialization (nationalization) and centralized state administration eliminated commodity production – i.e. as the economy increasingly became a system of cooperative output for the production of goods for the common use – the market value itself, 'a category of the capitalist commodity system in its equilibrium', would become 'the least useful [category] for the transition period'.[7] Finally, money, the social link of the developed exchange economy, would increasingly lose the character of universal equivalent and become, as Bukharin puts it, 'a conventional – and thereby an extremely imperfect – symbol of the circulation of products'. Socialism would thus evolve into a full-fledged cooperative system of production, that is, into 'a moneyless system of account-keeping'.[8]

Only a few years later, practice was to show that the Soviet economy could not possibly function other than as a monetary economy, and eventually the theoreticians of the transformation process under the Soviets were ordered shot by Stalin. Nevertheless, their schema, which corresponded to the traditional Marxian vision of the transformation period, remains to this day embedded in the foundations of Soviet economic theory. Put differently, Communist theory continues to be based on a schema according to which the plan necessarily supersedes the market and the law of value, commodities change into free goods, and value loses

5 Bukharin speaks indeed of the workers and peasants as representing two different models – 'kak klassovymi nositeliami razlichnykh khoziaistvennykh tipov', *Ekonomika . . .* , p. 85. See also in *ibid.*, pp. 83, 86 and *The ABC of Communism*, pp. 334–5.

6 *Ekonomika . . .* , p. 134. Lenin adds: 'not "product" . . . but product designed for social use and not through the market'. The Lenin note is in the indicated English translation, p. 219.

7 *Ekonomika . . .* , p. 135. This is in agreement with Marx: cf. K. Marx, *Critique des Programmes de Gotha et d'Erfurt*, Paris, Ed. Sociales, 1950, pp. 23ff.

8 K. Marx, *op cit*. In a judicious analysis of the 'Major Features of the Economy and Ideology of War Communism', published in *Acta Oeconomica* of the Hungarian Academy, Vol. 7 (2), 1971, pp. 143–60, L. Szamuely shows clearly the part which the idea of 'naturalization' of the economic life played in the overall ideology of the Bolsheviks concerning the transition period. See particularly pp. 150ff. See also L. Szamuely's book, *First Models . . .* , *op. cit.*, pp. 31ff.

its significance. Thus modern Soviet pronouncements on socialist transformation and proposals for reforming the socialist economic mechanism cannot be understood without reference to this basic schema and its underlying assumptions.

We noted in the introduction (pp. 1–2) that, in Eastern Europe, both the schema and its underlying assumptions have been openly questioned. The reason was the gradually dawning perception that the *subjective* policy decisions of the leadership could deliberately accelerate or decelerate the allegedly *objective* processes of nationalization, cooperativization or collectivization. Furthermore, the impact of those subjective decisions could vary enormously depending upon the size, factor endowment, level of development and relation to the world market of each country considered.

Stalin's new economic laws and the old law of value

Under the pressure of crises and emergencies, Soviet policy makers themselves revised, if not the basic conception itself, then at least their timetables and immediate policies for the complete liquidation of the commodity-producing private-exchange economy. During War Communism, they had indeed aimed at its outright annihilation. However, after the civil war, the utter collapse of the national economy, and the launching of the NEP, they admitted the necessary coexistence of socialist relations at the economy's commanding heights with commodity production and market exchange in the rest of the economy. Following the economic recovery of the mid 1920s and the beginning of Stalin's comprehensive planning in the late 1920s, they emphasized anew the necessity of overcoming commodity production and exchange through agricultural collectivization and the expansion of the state's centralized administration. Finally, after Stalin's death, when the distortions and dislocations created by the continual emphasis on capital goods, and particularly military goods, became all too evident, the leaders again resigned themselves to the persistence of commodity production and exchange for at least a few more decades. It would be that long before a new, vast, effort to reorganize the countryside, more ambitious even than the earlier collectivization, would finally transform the farmers into workers, concentrate them into agri-towns, and detach them irrevocably from the last vestiges of private ownership, namely their tiny private plots.

Whatever the actual changes or the projected phases might have been under other circumstances, Soviet policy makers have always been preoccupied with the following questions. Will the socialist character of the economic relations prevailing in the state sectors survive in the long run if, on the one hand, markets continue to exist for consumer goods, and if, on the other hand, freedom is granted to the workers to choose their jobs? Will these state-socialist relations expand if the peasants continue to market parts of their collective output and play an important role as producers from their private plots? Are not the socialist links between the workers' state and the peasants weakened by the persistence of such markets? When and how can these contradictions be finally overcome?

As the drives for collectivization, industrialization and pervasive planning gained momentum in the early 1930s, the Soviet economy was officially described as *dualistic* – part socialist, part commodity-exchange, with the former outweighing the latter. The socialist nature of the economy was said to assert itself through the state ownership of the commanding heights, the 'planning principle . . . embodied in the organs of the Soviet State, in their acts and measures',[9] and the production of non-marketed products. (These last were capital goods and raw materials reserved for the use of state-owned firms, or traded, within narrow limits, with the farm sector.) Commodity-exchange was said to assert itself through the existence of collective farms (*kolkhozy*) – with the farmers using state land as if it were their own, owning the seed and their labor, and disposing of their collective and individual output (from their private plots) to a large extent as marketed commodities – and through the state's own sale of consumer goods. Eventually, however, the law of value would be overcome: the collective farms would change into state farms, production as well as distribution would involve products only, and therefore, production for sale, values, and money would cease to exist. Implicitly, the labor market would also eventually disappear.

At the time, the economic categories of capitalism were viewed as transitional rather than inherently *necessary* for socialist production relations:

The commodity form in the Soviet economy is *not an internal necessity of socialist production relations*, it is conditioned by the dual character of the economy in the transition period. . . . The dual character is shown by the fact that an important part of production in agriculture is still accounted for by the individual peasant sector, and by the fact that the collective farms still place on the market part of their production which has not been socialized.[10]

9 See I. Lapidus and K. Ostrovityanov, *An Outline of Political Economy, Political Economy and Soviet Economics,* trans. from the Russian, New York, International Publishers, 1930, p. 470.

10 P. Bulat, ed., *Osnovy teorii sovetskogo khoziaistva* (Foundations of the Theory of the Soviet Economy), Leningrad, Leningrad Department of the Communist Academy, 1931, p. 279 (emphasis supplied). For an interesting Marxian discussion of this particular passage, see M. Samardzija, 'Problems of Commodity Production in Socialism and Economic Theory in the USSR Today', *Socialist Thought and Practice,* No. 4, December 1961, pp. 98–9.

The idea that production and distribution should increasingly be conducted on the basis of *material accounting* and *engineering,* rather than economic categories and criteria, remained unquestioned until the late 1930s. The overthrow of the law of value seemed close at hand. Stalin proclaimed that socialism was *completed* in the USSR in 1937, and Marxists everywhere, including the American economist Paul M. Sweezy, affirmed that in the socialist economy the law of value was receding into oblivion as the planning principle became supreme:

It follows that in so far as the allocation of productive activity is brought under conscious control, the law of value loses its relevance and importance; its place is taken by the principle of planning. In the economics of a socialist society, the theory of planning should hold the same basic position as the theory of value in the economics of a capitalist society. Value and planning are as much opposed, and for the same reasons, as capitalism and socialism.[11]

From the early 1940s on, however, circumstances brought about a significant change in the Soviet view of the role of the law of value in the USSR. As the heavy toll of the war and the disquieting consequences of some fifteen years of high-handed planning became increasingly apparent, Soviet policy makers, planners, and economists began to emphasize not the overcoming of the law of value, but its objective existence, and its possible uses in a socialist system. Economic necessity, objective limitations, orderly process of development henceforth came to be emphasized, in sharp contrast to the over-optimism of the early five-year plans and the expected early demise of the law of value.[12] Following World War II, as pressures for economic rationality mounted in the USSR and socialist Eastern Europe, Stalin himself made official the new status of the law of value under socialism. In his last work, *Economic Problems of Socialism in the USSR* (1952), Stalin distinguished two socialist economic laws which interacted with the law of value, instead of the single all-encompassing planning principle. The two socialist laws were the so-called *basic law,* leading the system to secure 'maximum satisfaction of the requirements of society', and, inherent in the first, the *law of balanced proportionate development of the national economy,* allowing for uninterrupted growth.

11 Paul M. Sweezy, *The Theory of Capitalist Development, op. cit.,* pp. 53–4.
12 See 'Teaching of Economics in the Soviet Union', *American Economic Review,* Vol. xxxiv, No. 3, September 1944, pp. 501–30 (trans. from *Pod Znamenem Marksisma* by Raya Dunayevskaya). The article generated an interesting discussion in the USA: the translator, Raya Dunayevskaya, stressed the revisionist character of this article, while P. A. Baran asserted that the latter did not revise but rather reaffirmed the tenets of Marxian orthodoxy. See *The American Economic Review,* Vol. xxxiv, No. 3, September 1944, pp. 531–7; *The American Economic Review,* Vol. xxiv, No. 4, December 1944, pp. 862–71; and *The American Economic Review,* Vol. xxv, No. 5, September 1945, pp. 660–4.

Diametrically opposed economic laws, both interacting with the law of value, were said to lead capitalism and socialism in opposite directions:

instead of maximum profits, maximum satisfaction of the material and cultural requirements of society; instead of development of production with breaks in continuity from boom to crisis and from crisis to boom – unbroken expansion of production; instead of periodic breaks in technical development, accompanied by the destruction of the productive forces of society – an unbroken process of perfecting production on the basis of higher techniques.[13]

According to Stalin, an undisturbed economic expansion required that socialist planners correctly perceive the *requirements* of the new laws and conform in every way to them. In short, if the laws of capitalism were deemed to act spontaneously and blindly under that system, the laws of socialism would bring benefits only if the planner first recognized them and then conscientiously used them.[14] Moreover, the new laws did not supplant but rather harnessed the law of value. While the latter may reign spontaneously only at the periphery of the state complex, it can be used to nudge *the entire socialist sector* toward rational resource utilization, rigorous accounting discipline, and methodical production efforts. Indeed, as consumer goods are produced and sold by state-owned firms,

such things as cost accounting and profitableness, production costs, prices, etc., are of actual importance in our enterprises. Consequently, our enterprises cannot and must not function without taking the law of value into account. Is this a good thing? It is not a bad thing. Under present conditions, it really is not a bad thing, since it trains our business executives to conduct production on rational lines and disciplines them.[15]

Stalin thus transformed the planning principle from the immanent law of socialism, into two related principles which would operate only if the planners correctly assessed the conditions propitious for their functioning. And the law of value, far from disappearing, would exercise a beneficial influence on socialist planning.

A number of years earlier, at the beginning of the all-out industrialization drive, Stalin (quoting Lenin) had asserted that the USSR faced an

---

13 J. V. Stalin, *Economic Problems of Socialism in the USSR*, New York, International Publishers, 1952, p. 33.
14 Stalin obviously patterns his recognition and use of the alleged law of balanced proportionate development on the Hegelian–Marxian approach to freedom and necessity. 'Freedom does not consist in the dream of independence from natural laws, but in the knowledge of these laws, and in the possibility this gives of systematically making them work towards definite ends.' (See F. Engels, *Anti-Dühring, op. cit.*, p. 136.) By extension, the freedom of the planner consists in knowing the law and conforming to it.
15 Stalin, *Economic Problems* . . . , pp. 19 and 20.

inescapable dilemma: 'perish, or overtake and outstrip the advanced countries'.[16] Stalin's solution then was a strategy of industrialization based on 'the premise that a fast rate of development of industry in general, and of the production of the means of production in particular, is the underlying principle of and the key to the industrialization of the country'.[17] Eventually, Stalin's premises and policy choice were proclaimed to embody a so-called law of priority growth of the production of the means of production, the 'objective economic law of extended reproduction [i.e., growth] in the machine age'.[18] Thus the law of balanced proportionate development, itself proclaimed in 1952 to be inherent in the basic law of socialism, turned out to have embodied in itself still another law, the priority growth of the means of production.

In the early years of socialist rule, the East European Communist countries followed Stalin's interpretations of the planning principle and of the economic laws of socialism unquestioningly. Following the dictator's death, however, both Stalin's ideas and the earlier concepts of Bukharin and Preobrazhenskii came under sharp critical examination there. Accompanying the questioning of basic precepts were attempts to introduce various concrete modifications of the socialist economic mechanism they had borrowed from the USSR.

Laws and resource shifts

In an institutional framework in which the teachings of Marx and Lenin provide the doctrinal foundation of the socio-economic system, no substantive changes in that system's components, interconnections, policy parameters of normative rules can be undertaken without reference to the established doctrine. As is often the case with such doctrine, however, Marxism–Leninism offers vast scope for reinterpretation and restatement.

Thus, as the Yugoslav Communists in the late 1940s prepared to break away from Stalin's economic mechanism, their main spokesman, Boris Kidrić, propounded the then startling idea that the socialist economy was, after all, also a system of production of goods for sale, a system within which the law of value 'operated actively'. This was so, even though the law of value had ceased to play the key role in the allocation of resources:

16 See J. V. Stalin, 'Industrialization of the Country and the Right Deviation', in *Works,* Vol. 11, Moscow, Foreign Languages Publishing House, 1954, p. 255.
17 *Loc. cit.*
18 A.I. Pashkov, *Ekonomicheskii zakon preimushchestvennogo rosta proizvodstva sredstv proizvodstva (Economic Law Concerning the Faster Growth of Output of Producers' Goods),* Moscow, Gosplanizdat, 1958. See also G. N. Khudokormov, ed., *Political Economy of Socialism,* trans. from the Russian by Don Donemanis, Moscow, Progress Publishers, 1967, pp. 246–7.

The law of value exists without the shadow of a doubt in our economic system, and it *operates actively,* but it has ceased to be the fundamental law of the socio-economic development, as it had been in the pre-socialist social formations based on the production of commodities. The fundamental socio-economic law of our development has become socialist planning, which means, among other things, the conscious and logical utilization of the objective law of value, fully recognized and dominated.[19]

What was startling about Kidrić's position was not the reinterpretation of the then-established doctrine, but the changes which this reinterpretation foreshadowed with respect to both economic policy and the institutional arrangements of ostracized Yugoslavia. Indeed, Kidrić was thus proclaiming the readiness of Yugoslavia's leadership to rely henceforth on market forces and on market mechanisms as indispensable adjuncts to planning. Theoretically, Kidrić did not advance any original ideas. Already in the mid 1920s, I. Stepanov-Skvortsov and A. A. Bogdanov had dismissed as nonsense Bukharin's and Preobrazhenskii's contentions that under socialism 'commodities, prices, wages, etc., exist and do not exist', while planning calculations, capital formation, and consumption could be carried out 'without knowledge of the value of the product'.[20] But both Stepanov-Skvortsov and Bogdanov had been crushed (Bogdanov committed suicide), and their position was branded as heretical.

After Stalin's death, the new premier of Hungary, Imre Nagy (1953–55) attempted to achieve a decisive shift in economic policy by proclaiming it as necessary to conform with Stalin's own economic laws. At the time, the first East European long-term development plans and the accompanying collectivizations (1949–53) had had disastrous effects in a number of countries – and particularly so in Hungary. By 1953, the exaggerated growth targets, the massive allocations to heavy industry, the strenuous efforts to achieve industrial autarky (despite the lack of domestic raw materials), and the pressures for rapid collectivization had brought about severe dislocations throughout the area. Under the label of *New Course,* all the Communist governments of the area tried to correct past policies and to shift national priorities. All of these governments expressed the desire to increase investments in agriculture, to raise agricultural production, and to allow the peasants more leeway in forming collectives and in joining *and* quitting them.

19 Boris Kidrić, 'Karakter robnonovčanih odnosa u FNRJ' (Character of the Commodity–Monetary Relations in Yugoslavia), *Kommunist,* No. 1, January 1949, and 'Teze o ekonomici prelaznog perioda u našoj zemlji'(Theses on the Economy of Transition Period in our Country), *Kommunist,* No. 6, November 1950, *passim.* (Emphasis supplied.)
20 I. Stepanov-Skvortsov, 'Chto takoe politicheskaia ekonomiia?' (What is Political Economy?) and 'Preniia po dokladu I. Stepanova-Skvortsova' ('Discussion on the Report of I. Stepanov-Skvortsov') in *Vestnik kommunisticheskoi akademii,* Moscow:

In Hungary, however, Nagy went further: he attempted to transform what was supposed to be a *temporary* retreat into a far-reaching, well-coordinated and *lasting* system change. What Bukharin had suggested for the USSR in the 1920s, Nagy reaffirmed for Hungary in the 1950s. The socialization of the commanding heights was sufficient to limit and shape the development of privately-owned agriculture. The collectivization of agriculture could proceed at a measured pace. The simultaneous growth of both state-owned industry and privately-owned agriculture was compatible with socialism.[21]

To start with, Nagy, like other East European leaders, stressed that the over-ambitious goals of the first long-term plan had exceeded his country's productive capacity and depressed its standard of living. Like the others, he advocated that industrialization be slowed down, agriculture encouraged, unprofitable collective farms dissolved, and regulations against wealthier peasants abandoned. But Nagy made an additional move which the other Communist leaders were careful to avoid (or reluctant even to consider): he proposed that cooperation with the peasantry be henceforth put at the core of the regime's strategy of development. Such cooperation implied for him the limitation of socialization and the encouragement of both collective and independent farm production; expansion of private small-scale industry, handicrafts and trade; and a significant rise in the standard of living. The proposal involved changes not only in policies, but in the very parameters and normative rules of the system. Nagy stressed that the new program amounted to a methodical return to a mixed economy in which central planning guidance was flexibly combined with the broad utilization of market mechanisms – a system akin to the one which had prevailed in the Soviet Union before Stalin inaugurated comprehensive planning in 1929, and in Hungary from 1946 to 1949. According to Nagy, for a country of small peasant holdings heavily dependent on farm output and foreign trade, the NEP system was necessarily 'the basis of building socialism during the transition period', i.e. during the *entire* historical phase meant to lead to communism.

Komakadizdat, No. 11, 1925; and A. A. Bogdanov, *A Short Course of Economic Science*, second ed., London, Dorrit Press, 1927.

21 Two texts, N. Bukharin's *Put' k sotsializmu i raboche krest'ianskii soiuz* (The Path to Socialism and the Worker–Peasant Alliance) [1925] and his *Doklad na XXIII chrez-vychainoi leningradskoi gubernskoi konferentsii VKP (b)* (Report to the Extraordinary XXIII Conference of the Leningrad District RCP (b)) [1926] embody the indicated positions as formulated by Bukharin and as accepted by Stalin until the beginnings of 1928; see *Put' k sotsializmu v Rossii*, Izbrannye proizvedeniia N. I. Bukharina (The Path to Socialism in Russia, Selected Works of N. I. Bukharin), edited by Sidney Heitman and trans. by Eugenia Zhiglevich, New York, Omicron Press, 1967, pp. 247ff. and 317ff. For Hungary, see *Imre Nagy on Communism: In Defense of the New Course*, Praeger, 1957, pp. 194ff.

Nagy and his associates claimed that all of Hungary's economic misfortunes had come from the 'violation of the laws of development of the economy worked out by comrade Stalin'. The reference to Stalin's law of proportionate development of the national economy was interpreted by Nagy to mean, for Hungary, not the need to stress heavy industry (as Stalin had done in the Soviet Union) but rather the necessity to develop light industry and agriculture. In short, Nagy challenged the contentions (1) that the so-called alliance of workers and peasants could be strengthened by forced collectivization rather than by broadened market connections; (2) that socialism could be built without the political cooperation and agreement of the peasantry; and (3) that forced-production on collective farms could yield higher results than the combined productions of cooperatives and independent peasants. In Nagy's words:

Fear of the market, fear of the development of peasant farms, fear of the revival of capitalism as a result of the NEP policy – in other words, underestimation of the power of authority of the People's Democratic government, a disguised lack of faith in the concept of federation between peasants and workers – this is characteristic of the representatives of the extreme 'left wing' agrarian policy, who incline somewhat more toward 'militarist communism' than toward a properly developed and continued NEP policy.[22]

Nagy's was a resolute attempt to revise national priorities, to expand the role of markets, to promote both collective and individual farming, to increase peasant marketings, to reduce planning regulations, and to establish mutually advantageous trade with other countries. Resolute or not, though, the attempt was thwarted in 1955 after less than two years of experimentation. Subsequently, the revolutionary upheaval of October–November 1956, quelled by the intervention of Russian tanks, finally foreclosed the NEP option. A few of Nagy's measures, after being tried in Yugoslavia, were eventually implemented within narrow limits in Hungary itself. But the idea of re-establishing the NEP system, a system predicated on a *lasting coexistence* of the socialized commanding heights and the peasantry moving at its own pace toward the formation of cooperatives, was completely discarded. This specific alternative to Stalin's economic mechanism, devoid of Yugoslavia's peculiar emphasis on new management forms and justified with Stalin's own economic laws – was stamped out in the Soviet bloc.

On the manipulation of parameters and rules

The debate on Stalin's laws did not die down with Nagy's political failure. Actually, a whole theoretical literature developed around them, first in

22 Nagy, *ibid.*, p. 200.

Hungary and then in Poland, particularly during the crises years of 1955–57. Thus in 1956, a Hungarian economist, Tamas Nagy (no relation of the deposed premier Nagy) made the following critique of the then official textbook of political economy, the basic school text in all European socialist countries:

The textbook, following Stalin, justifies the necessity of the survival of commodity production and trade in socialism only by the existence of collective farms. But this thesis is untenable, and also leads to incorrect conclusions. Could a socialist society, with its complicated division of labor, where abundance of products has not been reached yet, where work has not yet become a life necessity of first importance, that is, an economy in which every important branch has to be based on material interest – could such a society exist without commodity production and exchange in case it has no collective farms? It could not exist.[23]

Nagy thus affirmed that a modern, complicated division of labor in an economy constrained by scarcity inescapably generates a system of production for sale *whether or not* the existing enterprises are nationalized. In the same vein, the dean of Polish economists, Edward Lipiński, noted that the product of any enterprise in or outside the state sector

turned out for exchange, necessarily represents 'value' and therefore it represents an outlay of social labor which entitles the enterprise to an equivalent [share] out of the aggregate product of the labor of society. This is irrespective of the fact whether the enterprise produces means of production or consumer goods.[24]

Following these and similar writings, the idea that the socialist economies were or would soon become systems of production of free goods rather than of goods for sale and exchange became to a large extent discredited. By the mid 1960s, some Czech writers felt free to note that since it was 'impossible to effect the division and distribution of labor from one center . . . the market is the only criterion of whether a given quantity of labor has been expended in the best interests of society'. In short,

the commodity–money mechanism provides a natural driving force making for flexible adaptation of production to consumer demand and tending to reduce the cost of production and improve the quality of the use values produced.[25]

23 T. Nagy, 'A politikai gazdaságtan néhány kérdéséröl' (Some Issues of Political Economy), *Közgazdasági szemle*, Vol. III, No. 6, June 1956, pp. 657ff. The textbook refered to by Nagy, entitled *Political Economy*, was issued by the Institute of Economics of the Academy of Sciences of the USSR, in 1954. An English version based on the second Russian edition [1955] and translated by C. P. Dutt and Andrew Rothstein, was published in London, by Lawrence and Wishart, in 1957.

24 E. Lipiński, 'O przedmiocie ekonomii i prawach ekonomicznych' (On the Subject of Economics and Economic Laws) *Ekonomista*, No. 5, 1956.

25 Z. Šulć, 'Creative Development of Marxist Economic Thinking', *World Marxist Review*, June, 1965.

The law of value, instead of being barely tolerated as a subordinate economic factor, was thus thrust to the forefront in four East European countries. The campaign against the premise of the progressive annihilation of the exchange economy under socialism grew into increasingly open assertions of the role of markets, or rational approaches to resource allocation, and of substantive modifications of the Soviet-type system of administrative management.

Now it was precisely such far-reaching implications of the questioning of basic precepts that Soviet policy makers tried to avoid. The official Soviet economic textbooks did eventually accept modification of Bukharin's and Stalin's theories about commodity production; for example, they conceded that producers' goods are also commodities, just like consumers' goods. But they maintained to the end that under socialism commodity production and exchange necessarily spring only from the persistence of a certain *form of ownership*, viz., collective ownership in agriculture. They fully upheld the assumptions that all economic categories such as value, price, wages, profits, and even the market necessarily have a dialectically *emphemeral* character, as a result of socialization and planning.[26]

Oskar Lange was probably the only well-known East European economist who tried to reconcile those increasingly differing – and increasingly irreconcilable – Soviet and East European perceptions of the nature of socialism and of its laws. Lange, who had affirmed in 1953 that Stalin's *Economic Problems of Socialism in the U.S.S.R.* was 'a great event in the history of learning, particularly in . . . Political Economy'[27] felt finally free to suggest in 1957 (after the beginning of Nikita S. Khruschev's 'destalinization' drive) that after all there were more economic laws than Stalin had been able to identify. Lange now asserted that all economic laws could be classified into four groups: (1) laws which operate in *every* system, such as the laws of production and growth: (2) laws *specific* to a given system, such as the law of planning under socialism; (3) laws of an *intermediate nature* operating in several systems, such as the laws of value and of monetary circulation in exchange economies; and finally, (4) *institutional* laws arising from the organizational forms of the managerial superstructure and affecting incentives in particular. Lange then added that the socialist state could, in the early stages of socialism, use 'extra-economic force', i.e. 'voluntaristic' administrative decisions, but that when higher levels of development were reached such methods had to be discarded: in

26 G. N. Khudokormov, ed., *Political Economy of Socialism, op. cit.*, pp. 129ff.
27 See O. Lange, 'The Economic Laws of Socialist Society in the Light of Joseph Stalin's Last Work' (trans. of 'Prawa ekonomiczne socjalizmu w świetle ostatniej pracy Józefa Stalina', from *Nauka Polska*, No 1, Warsaw, 1953), *International Economic Papers*, No. 4, 1954, pp. 145ff.

the latter stages, as 'the economic laws of the socialist society more and more become operative, the role of the extra-economic force of the state recedes'. In short, administrative edicts must in time be necessarily replaced by the interplay of all four types of laws – general, specific, intermediate or institutional – including of course the law of value, all interacting harmoniously under socialism.[28]

But a large number of East European economists dismissed both Stalin's laws and any possible attempt of reconciling the opposite views which emerged from the debate around them. In the already mentioned review of the official Soviet economics textbook, Tamas Nagy chastised the Soviet propensity to 'fetishize' Stalin's laws:

> The [Soviet] textbook creates the impression that the economic laws of socialism determine the development of socialist society in all details, and that procedure in accordance with the laws was ensured because the laws could be discovered and known, and also because of the harmful consequences of not proceeding in accordance with these laws. Actually ... the economic laws, in socialism too, describe only the general tendencies, and although it is very important to discover them, they must not be interpreted as exactly describing reality.[29]

Nagy argued (i) that one can never encompass under some single fundamental law the complex elements of the development of any economic system; (ii) that the formulation of fundamental laws is no substitute for the objective study of the actual growth and development of a system; and (iii) that socialism is obviously beset by 'problematical and unsolved issues' which require strenuous and methodical research and analysis.[30]

Another Hungarian economist, Peter Erdös, noted that as general tendencies Stalin's laws may at best define the main thrust of economic development, but not the concrete details and complications of this development itself. Indeed, the alleged laws are in no way guides to practical planning, since the state, try as it may, cannot prescribe every economic activity of the country's economic organizations. Moreover, the exact realization of the prescribed plans would not at all prove that the chosen plan was the only one possible and that its realization was in any way required by the said laws.[31]

Finally, Lipiński stressed that economic regularities evidently operate everywhere, and everywhere, policy tries to 'use' laws, though not always aptly. Marxism, he remarked, does not contain a specific economic methodology. One may therefore legitimately assume that any method or

28 O. Lange, 'Political Economy of Socialism' (lecture held on November 18, 1957, in Belgrade), *Problems of Political Economy of Socialism*, edited by Oskar Lange, Calcutta: People's Publishing House, 1962.
29 T. Nagy, 'Some Issues . . . ', *op. cit.*   30 *Loc. cit.*
31 See Peter Erdös, 'A tervgazdálkodás néhány elméleti kérdéséröl' (Some Theoretical Issues of Economic Planning) *Közgazdasági szemle*, June 1956.

means of investigation, even if employed by 'bourgeois economists', may be used if it is effective. Economic laws do not change because ownership relationships are reshuffled: what changes is the locus of decision making, not the essence of the decision. In short, Stalin's views on the influence of the law of value on production, on its educational role, and on its subordination to the law of planned proportionate development were dubious, unclear, and had little to do with economic theory.[32]

In fact, these economists, just as the Soviet or the East European policy makers, knew full well that behind Stalin's, Imre Nagy's or even Lange's exercises in doctrinal casuistry, lay serious and complex policy and economic issues. What indeed is a socialist economy? Is it an economy producing free goods, or goods for sale and for the market? What is the role within it of such 'old' economic categories as prices, wages, and profits? Are the socialist policy makers 'subjectively' speaking free to manipulate the economy's parameters (for example to contract or expand socialization, collectivization, and markets) and are they thus able to determine the operation within it of different economic laws?

In the 1950s Peter Erdös dismissed ironically the entire matter:

On reading some recent books, the unsuspecting reader may find himself lost in an enchanted forest of economic laws. Here the laws have their own hierarchy, superiority and subordination, where they mutually determine and modify one another as well as every economic event. Once hurt, the laws immediately retaliate. Our clinging to these laws, turning them to our own use, seems analogous to the dead souls' clinging to the ship of Charon. . . . And even the fact that our destination is not the pit of hell, but rather the marvelous socialist future to which there is a single route, precisely defined, does not change this inevitability of laws. This omnipotence of laws, their power to determine every detail of development, is in strange contrast to the fact that the majority of the actually formulated economic laws are too general and unfit to help solve any practical problem.[33]

But these complex issues cannot be dismissed with sarcasm: neither the manipulation of a system's parameters nor the implications of the alleged operation within it of this or that economic law can be viewed lightly. Stalin's laws are kept on the books precisely because they appear useful to his successors as they were to him. First of all, like the entire Soviet dialectical analysis which distinguishes the economics of socialism from the economics of capitalism, these alleged laws place a screen between the opposing systems. What is condemned in capitalism as the exploitation of labor, surplus-value and production for profit, can be conveniently extolled as social labor, social surplus and production for social needs when talking about socialism. Secondly, the laws enhance the importance of the

32 Lipiński, 'O przedmiocie ekonomii . . . ', *op. cit.*   33 Erdös, *loc. cit.*

economic targets set by the policy makers: socialist plans can be proclaimed as faithfully reflecting these laws, and therefore need to be accepted unquestioningly and implemented in all their details. Pointing to conformance with laws bestows upon an official policy the stamp of scientific truth, and sanctions any necessary attacks against doubters, deviationists, or heretics; as Tamas Nagy once put it, the laws justify everything: 'Whatever there is, and as it is, is in conformity with the laws.'[34] Finally, the entire discussion of laws helps perpetuate belief in the vigor of the Marxian analytical method, a method which alone can bare the laws of motion of any system, including socialism.

Not everybody, of course, is allowed to specify which laws operate when and where under socialism. This is a political privilege appropriated and jealously guarded by the highest policy-making echelons – the party in each country (and in the Soviet zone of influence, the Soviet party). The economists are supposed simply to repeat what the policy makers have already decided; only at certain critical junctures can the economists break free of this tutelage and enjoy intoxicating moments of freedom to criticize.

34 T. Nagy, *loc. cit.*

3 Choice of instruments and requirements on the processor

The frame of reference

According to Marx and Engels, the socialization of the means of production accelerates a series of processes already started under capitalism. Those processes lead to the radical transformation of the economy and of the society. After socialization, the economy can be organized 'rationally'. All interpersonal relations are placed on new bases. Barriers of all kinds, disturbances, and the waste of products and of the means of production are abolished. Market anarchy is replaced by a definite plan. Technology is unceasingly revolutionized. Unbroken prosperity is assured.

Following the concept of the French Utopian Saint-Simon, Marx and Engels saw the socialist economy as organized into a single vast producing company which allocates its means of production and manpower to produce for the needs of all according to plan. The massive integrated company emerges from a long, historic process, starting with the appearance of the modern factory and machine manufacture. Indeed, as Engels noted, with the modern factory *social* production replaces *individual* production, because the planned organization of large groups of workers within each plant becomes indispensable. Eventually, the owners of factories coalesce into holding companies and trusts aimed at regulating production and replacing market competition with monopolistic control. In time, the state steps in and places whole branches of production under its direction – a fact which demonstrates that the owners of production have become superfluous. Production without a plan 'capitulates' to the invading forces of socialism and their principle of production according to a definite plan.[1] Capitalism cannot bring socialized production and individual appropriation into harmony with one another, nor can it cope with both continuous change in production forces and rigidly maintained production relations. Only socialization makes such harmony possible, by suppressing individual appropriations and by changing production relations.

1 See F. Engels, *Anti-Dühring*, op. cit., pp. 320–1, 330ff.

Through socialization, the means of production lose the 'quality of capital' (i.e. of means of exploitation) and the goods produced lose the character of commodities (i.e. of goods which can be bought and sold). All the productive forces of the society are integrated into a *single coun-trywide cooperative workshop,* while society itself is progressively trans-formed into a kind of giant household. As in the American Indian and Slavic communities of old, the entire community thenceforth uses all its means of production in direct association for production, applies its manpower wherever needed, and distributes its product first according to work performed, and later according to individual needs. As commodities change into free goods, and as values and money vanish, production is organized according to a comprehensive plan based on the increasing mastery of socio-economic laws.[2]

A new, more versatile and better endowed labor force emerges in this unified country-wide workshop-cooperative. Under capitalism, modern machinery allows 'variation of labour, fluency of function, universal mobility of the labourer'. But capitalism squanders these possibilities and stunts the development of manpower. After socialization, the innate and acquired powers of the laborers can finally develop to the fullest. No divisions, contradictions, or antagonisms thenceforth impede the growth of the vast communal workshop. The allocation of work tasks among members of the commune does not generate conflicts between general and individual interests. Such conflicts exist only in societies in which the distribution of labor is forced upon individuals, and in which everybody has a specific and exclusive sphere of activity.[3] In such societies, Marx wrote, man is 'a hunter, a fisherman, a shepherd or a critical critic, and must remain so if he does not want to lose his means of livelihood'. But in the communist society, 'nobody has one exclusive sphere of activity . . . [and] each can become accomplished in any branch he wishes'. Society, he concludes, 'regulates the general production and thus makes it possible for me to do one thing today and another tomorrow, to hunt in the morning, fish in the afternoon, rear cattle in the evening, criticize after dinner, just as I have in mind, without ever becoming hunter, fisherman, shepherd, or critic'[4], and presumably be equally efficient in each capacity.[5]

2 *Ibid.,* pp. 335–6, 366–7. See also Karl Kautsky's *The Class Struggle* (Erfurt Program) [1892], *op. cit.,* pp. 95ff.

3 *Ibid.,* pp. 349 and Marx, *Capital,* Vol. I *op. cit.,* pp. 421ff. and 487–8.

4 Marx and Engels, 'Feuerbach: Opposition to the Materialistic and Idealistic Outlook', 'The German Ideology' [1845–1846] in Karl Marx and Frederick Engels, *Selected Works,* Moscow, Progress Publishers, 1969, Vol. I, pp. 35–6. A similar passage can be found in Bukharin's and Preobrazhenskii's *The A.B.C. . . .,* p. 72.

5 In his book, *Les Maîtres Penseurs* (Paris, Grasset, 1977), the French author André Gluck-smann noted ironically in this connection that Raphael and Mozart had also been the 'victims' of the division of labor (p. 202).

In short, it did not occur to the founders of modern socialist theory that within the single, highly-developed, communal, producing company the old problems of *organization, information and coordination* might persist. They implicitly assumed that all decisions and production processes would mesh perfectly in all their phases, and that no differences among branches or technical stages of production, no losses or failures of any kind would interfere with the perfect dovetailing of inputs and outputs. They further assumed that direct calculations in *labor time* (rather than in money-value terms) would simplify rather than complicate the tasks of the planner. Finally, as I said, they thought that specialization was unnecessary and harmful. Moreover, they believed that the *fluency of labor* observable at the very beginning of the industrial revolution (when the simple machines of the time required unskilled operatives) would increase rather than decrease as industrialization progressed.

This was the framework — inspired by Marx and elaborated by Engels and Kautsky in the tradition of ideas and trends at the end of the nineteenth century — that Lenin and the Bolsheviks applied to the economy and society of early twentieth-century Russia. Writing just after the Bolshevik revolution of 1917, the leading Communist propagandists Bukharin and Preobrazhenskii repeatedly stressed that the fundamental goal was the integration of the economy and society into a unified 'single, countrywide "syndicate" ': 'society . . . will be transformed into a huge working organization for cooperative production. . . . No longer will one enterprise compete with another; the factories will all be sub-divisions, as it were, of one people's workshop, which will embrace the entire national economy of production.'[6] As the working class assumed the role of the organizer of production and the old technological hierarchy collapsed, all activities would be carried out on the basis of a 'general directive system . . . careful calculation and bookkeeping'.[7] Machines would be furnished where needed; workers would be assigned by rotation to various jobs; unified accounting would keep all waste in check; goods would be provided not for the market, but for use; and money would be replaced by temporary tickets or tokens.[8]

Whatever changes occurred as the Soviet Union proceeded from War Communism, to the NEP, to the Stalin era, and on into the post-Stalin period, certain basic features of the Soviet economic mechanism have not changed. The Soviet government has always regarded the central complex of the state sectors (the so-called commanding heights of the economy, comprised of large-scale industry, transport, banking, and trade) as a *unified establishment* which must eventually encompass the economy in

6 Bukharin and Preobrazhenskii, *The A.B.C. . . .* , p. 70.
7 *Ibid.,* pp. 75 and 79.   8 *Ibid.,* pp. 70, 74 and 398.

its entirety. The economy must be integrated by a single center of command, a centralized system of accounting and bookkeeping, and a uniform set of operating instructions and injunctions. Put more formally, the purposive socialist society must unify and control its *economic processor* in accordance with the blueprint conceived by Marx and Engels. But the process of integrating the economy raises many complex problems not foreseen by the founders of modern socialism. Moreover, once an integration is achieved, the restructured economy does not, indeed cannot, function as Marx, Engels or Lenin assumed it would.

The purposive economy in operation

Soviet policy makers devised a variety of measures to transform the economy into a unified country-wide organization for cooperative production. As we have seen, to do this they had first to determine who would be the managers and what would be the scope of their decision makeup; second, what normative rules these managers would have to follow. Further, they had to face the thorny issues of establishing priorities and targets and of insuring that the economic processor in its entirety, as well as each of its components, would carry out these targets.

The roles of the basic component of any advanced industrial economy, the *enterprise,* differ widely between a market-directed and a centrally-administered Soviet-type economy. In the former, leadership of an enterprise stands at the center of a web or organizational, financial, and supply and demand relations. The organizational links define the structure of the enterprise: the levels of management; the loci of centralized and decentralized decisions (e.g. hierarchies *versus* 'profit centers'); and the ties with other enterprises or firms. The financial links involve connections (such as contractual obligations) with creditors and debtors, and with various 'financial intermediaries'. The supply and demand relations consist of linkages with suppliers and buyers. Those linkages, which depend on such things as price elasticities, gradations of competition, and shifts in taste, in turn affect input mixes, output assortments, changes in technology, investment allocations, contracting and subcontracting, manpower recruitment and training, marketing patterns, and ultimately, the organizational and financial links themselves.

By contrast, in the centrally administered economy *à la* Stalin, the top directors of the system both determine and supervise the organizational links, and financial connections, and the supply and demand relations of the enterprise. The latter is but a division of a given ministry (or other central directorate), which in turn is an integral part of the centrally-run complex managed by the party–state. The internal levels of supervision and control in the enterprise and its external relations with other enterprises are rigidly controlled by the system's top directors. All financial connections are monitored by the State Bank, within the framework of a unified bookkeeping and accounting system. Both suppliers and buyers are precisely identified. Input and output assortments are centrally determined, as are most prices; and changes in technology, capacity use, investment allocations, and manpower utilization, are centrally prescribed. Access to the specific capital goods and raw materials earmarked for a given enterprise is governed by a centralized Material Technical Supply System.

In fact, the Soviet-type enterprise is not simply a sub-division, as it were, of one massive workshop. Rather, it is the focus of an intertwined set of monitoring activities by diverse agencies: its own ministry; the State Bank; the Material Technical Supply System; central or regional agencies for planning, technology, and manpower, and so on. Most of the liberty appropriated by – rather than granted to – the operating manager of an enterprise results from his adroit maneuvering to play off one monitor against another, to juggle obligations and evade controls in order to fulfill or overfulfill planned assignments which the top directors consider most important.

Definite plans are periodically and regularly established for the Soviet economy, and, as Engels foresaw or at least suggested, the individual enterprise assignments and their aggregates are formulated in physical terms. But the specific practical model of Soviet directive planning is the German war economy of World War I, not Engels' sketchy suggestions. In the Soviet view, as in the Imperial German *Kriegswirtschaft,* planning means centrally administered production by issuing detailed instructions and injunctions to each operating enterprise. Soviet planning is not market-oriented: it relies on fragmented and closely circumscribed markets (for example, for labor and consumers' goods) only because centralized procedures are not expedient there.

The core of each plan consists of a series of interlocking physical balances of scheduled outputs (including net imports) and distributions to specific addressees by key products or aggregates of products. For the first quarter century of the Soviet system, the top directors systematically extended the scope of the physical balances to encompass more and more products. At one point, under Stalin, there were no fewer than 10,000 central balances, which formed the core of an even greater number of ministry-level balances. Eventually, the process of centralization became impossibly cumbersome, and the number of central balances was sharply reduced. Not long after, an increased though still subordinate role was assigned to the so-called synthetic balances, i.e. to the balances in money terms, derived from the physical balances by applying centrally determined prices. Nevertheless, the mechanistic view of clock-like central regulation of all production processes has not been abandoned. Indeed, the hope is now to use computers to achieve truly complete, effective centralized administration.

In the meantime, the frequent discrepancies between goals and results, the failure of plans to mesh, and the enormous waste inherent in the centralized administration of production are viewed as temporary. Publicly, at least, Soviet leaders consider theirs to be the only true form of economic planning. They dismiss Western versions of planning – for instance, indicative plans which attempt to provide a consolidated frame of expectations for private firms that is compatible with government policy aims – as formalistic and ineffective. In fact, there is no logical reason why planning has to mean a centralized system which attempts to control all production and distribution by directives stated in physical terms and identified down to the level of each and every enterprise. The expanding literature on planning and programming in the Western countries, along with their growing practical experience, show that the aims of government policies can vary widely; that numerous kinds of instruments can be used to pursue those aims; and that centralization and decentralization can be mixed in various proportions. Thus the Soviet version of planning is but one extreme variant in a broad spectrum of possibilities.

Soviet policy makers and planners see in the state, as Bukharin put it, 'the concentrated and organized force of society' – that is, the promoter of new production relations and the developer of the material forces of production. In the early Stalinist period, it was held that the state leaders could overcome any and all bottlenecks and thus could shape the future *at will*. Toward the end of Stalin's reign, though, a more moderate view came to prevail. Voluntarism was tempered with realism, and economic constraints began to be recognized. Yet the moderation did not bring with it any major changes in the official approaches to planning or to the overall strategy of development. Even since the end of the Stalin era, Soviet leaders have continued to visualize the state-owned complex as a single, unified enterprise which will eventually transform and absorb the entire economy, including the agricultural sector. They have continued to believe (or at least argue) that, in time, the top directors will be able to master both social and economic laws (and eventually even reshape them at will), and monitor all production and distribution processes. True, current practice may indicate that human will alone cannot purge the future of uncertainties, disturbances or failures and that unification of the economy does not really ease the problems of coordinating a vast variety of inputs and outputs, nor does it allow the center to fully control even the most important production processes. Nonetheless, the vision of a single, harmonious national enterprise producing for use, not for sale, has not been called into question, at least in the USSR.

In certain East European countries, however, the situation has been different. The disappointing results of the Soviet model have been felt more keenly there. Moreover, as we have seen, the underlying Marxian assumptions of socialist economics and, more particularly, the Soviet interpretation of those assumptions, have prompted the search for alternatives. That search has led to an open break with Saint-Simonian, Marxian assumptions concerning the organization and functioning of the economy as a single fully integrated enterprise allocating its resources in accordance with an overall plan.

Enterprise methods in the economy vs. economic methods in the enterprises

This open critique has evolved slowly, even reluctantly. It did gain momentum in the first few years after Stalin's death, but then faltered after attempts at reform in Hungary and Poland in the mid 1950s. Subsequently the critique re-emerged under the protective umbrella of Moscow's own tortured attempts at economic reform.

In the mid 1950s, sharp criticisms of the Saint-Simonian concept of the single enterprise were voiced by several outstanding economists. For instance, Edward Lipiński, suggested that the whole idea was technically unworkable:

One national, wholly centralized enterprise cannot exist or function. Such an 'enterprise' can be imagined only as a single, gigantic, automatically functioning mechanism, one factory comprising many departments. Maybe something like that will be created in the distant future. . . . At the present level of technology, the role of man and his creativity is still decisive. Therefore, the individual enterprise will long continue to be the 'production unit', the center of disposition, decision, dynamics and adaptation.[9]

Soon afterwards, Oskar Lange noted that the concentration of many steps of production in one enterprise could undoubtedly bring benefits – e.g. better coordination of work between formerly separate establishments, shorter communication lines, and increased overall reliability of the production process. But, Lange added, there were also readily evident limits on what concentration could achieve. Beyond a certain point, concentration would become a purely fictitious operation; it could not eliminate 'differences in the technical stages of production, the need to transfer an

9 E. Lipiński, 'O przedmiocie ekonomii . . . ,' *op. cit.*

unfinished product from one stage to the next, situations due to particular failures or other factors'. The problems of cooperation between the separate units of the united establishment would remain and even grow, as would a host of technical, informational and organizational problems.[10]

Answering to the partisans of centralization who asserted that all that was needed for setting the system aright was *adequate information,* the critics of centralization retorted that the latter's information-distorting elements could never be eradicated. What the center lacked was not information but rather *accurate* information; or, the quality of the information could not be improved so long as the center set binding enterprise targets which were at the same time used as standards for assessing performance and distributing rewards. Włodzimierz Brus pointed to the inevitable difference in perspective of the planner on the one hand and the enterprise manager on the other: the central planners were concerned with the national economy as a whole, while the manager was necessarily concerned only with his own enterprise.[11] Edward Lipiński held that the vital functions of organizing production processes and introducing technological progress belonged first of all to the enterprise; under centralized management, however, the center's incessant manipulations of prices and incentives had turned the enterprises into at best ineffective executors of the orders received, at worst cunning adversaries of any innovation which threatened to upset their routines.[12]

The most outstanding economists of Poland made, at the time, a clean break with a number of taboos then still in force – despite the continued presence of Russian troops in their country. The so-called 'theses' of the Polish Economic Council, adopted in 1957[13] (for discussion, not as a resolution), represent one of the *important landmarks* in the attempt to modify the basic premises of the economic mechanism forged under Stalin.

The theses stressed, first, that there was nothing immutable in the methods of management: they must change in accordance with changes in the production forces (i.e. in the technological level of the economy). The theses then went on to affirm that what mattered in planning was not

10 O. Lange (with A. Banasiński), *Introduction to Economic Cybernetics,* Oxford: Pergamon Press, 1970, p. 171.
11 W. Brus, 'Spór o role planu centralnego' (Controversy on the Role of the Central Plan) *Życie gospodarcze,* No. 12, 1957.
12 E. Lipiński, ' "Model" gospodarki socjalistycznej' (A 'Model' of the Socialist Economy), *Nowe drogi,* No. 11–12, 1956. In the same paper Lipiński dismisses as dysfunctional the formation of workers' councils, i.e. of collectives 'of unskilled administrators representing the interests of the whole [enterprise]'.
13 'Tezy Rady Ekonomicznej w sprawie kierunków zmian modelu gospodarczego (Theses of the Economic Council Concerning Certain Modifications of the Economic Model), in *Dyskusja o polskim modelu gospodarczym* (Discussion of the Polish Economic Model), Warsaw, Książka i Wiedza, 1957.

reducing the number of centralized indices, avoiding the details which encumbered existing plans, or finding better balancing methods (e.g. input–output or linear programming). Rather, what mattered was the analysis underlying the plan and the care with which its targets were determined. The analysis required studies of both consumption demand and the effectiveness of investments – two critical issues traditionally determined largely on political rather than economic grounds. As for the goals, the theses suggested the need to reappraise fundamental premises on the nature and forms of economic development under socialism – a direct contradiction of the Soviet view that the strategy of development had been determined once and for all, for all countries, by the conclusions reached in the Soviet debates of the 1920s. Finally, concerning plan implementation, the theses advocated both flexibility in the combination of incentives and directives – with emphasis on the former rather than on the latter – and an expanded scope for firms in drawing up their own production and investment plans.

Thus the authors of the Polish theses focused both on the rationale of the plan and on the center's instrumentalities. The issues considered were: the analytical foundations of the plan concerning consumption demand and investment effectiveness; the need periodically to review goals and priorities as the process of development unfolds; and the need for flexible combinations of incentives and directives, and for an expanded role for firms.

In short, the focus was on how to *combine the plan and the market in novel ways*. In some respects – e.g. in the discussions of prices – the theses were less innovative; they followed the traditional approach. But they did open new and promising directions in the overall analysis of the Soviet-type centralized system – directions which (as we shall see below) a number of Czechoslovak writers were subsequently to follow.

Many attempts at reform have been made in the socialist camp since those attacks on the single unified national enterprise; many writers have advocated since then the need of introducing 'economic methods in the enterprises' rather than 'enterprise methods in the economy'.[14] Yet nowhere – except in Yugoslavia from the mid 1950s to the early 1970s – have enterprises been truly upgraded from their subordinate role within the centralized single 'firm', the national economy as a whole. Freedom to plan outputs and to act somewhat independently of central supervision has been extended to most enterprises in various East European countries.

14 The very apt formulation can be found in B. Komenda and C. Kožušník's study, 'Některé základní otázky sdokonalení soustavy řízení socialistického narodního hospodářství', (Some Basic Questions on Improving the System of Management of the Socialist Economy'), *Politická ekonomie*, xii, No. 3, 1964, pp. 219ff.

But even in the most 'liberal' among them, in Hungary, enterprises still must fulfill an array of centrally determined tasks; in addition, they still lack control of their investments and remain emmeshed in a tight network of complex regulations concerning costs, prices, credits, incomes and the size and utilization of the funds left to the discretion of their managers.[15]

Concomitant with the debates on the conflict between the Marxian centralized system and the mounting need for decentralization, a germane issue came to the fore: that of the relation between costs and prices. Because this issue also involved several important Marxian theories and concepts, it eventually led to sharp confrontations between fundamentalist Marxists (so-called *dogmatists*) and the modernists (or *neo-revisionists*).

As we have already noted, in the early 1950s, Stalin had concluded that the law of value would be helpful to planners and managers alike for the rational conduct of production. The law would, however, not have a regulating function in the socialist sector: it would only exercise a certain narrowly prescribed influence on planners' and managers' decisions. But if the law was not to determine resource allocation in its essentials – if allocation was to be left to the discretion of the policy makers – how exactly would it influence planners' and managers' decisions on factor use and the pricing of goods? Would capital and land be recognized as productive and therefore be assigned prices which would enter cost calculations, as under capitalism? If so, would not such prices conflict with the oft-repeated contention of Engels that under socialism the means of production lose their previous quality of exploitative capital in order henceforth to be employed in 'direct association [with manpower] in production?' If not, how were the planners supposed to decide between alternative uses of the means of production, to find rational combinations of capital and other inputs, or to make optimal changes in techniques, without proper factor charges?

Under strong pressures for rationalization, both in Eastern Europe and in the Soviet Union, several changes in cost calculation and price formation, including interest payments on capital, were finally introduced in order to make relative prices correspond more closely to relative scarcities. In practice, these changes did little more than formalize the rough procedures which planners, managers, engineers, and technicians had used all along – for example, recoupment (or pay-back) periods on investment, and crude corrections of domestic prices based on comparisons with price structures prevailing in international markets. But the policy makers remained

15 See, for instance, I. Hetényi, 'National Economic Planning in the New System of Economic Control and Management' in *Reform of the Economic Mechanism in Hungary*, edited by I. Griss, Budapest: Akademiai Kiado, 1969, pp. 41ff.

adamant in refusing to specify whether the law of value functioned pervasively under socialism (as in any other commodity-producing, exchange economy), or whether it operated only intermittently and within carefully circumscribed limits. The unthinkability of breaking completely with the Marxian view that capital is not productive meant that the pressures for rationalizing the use of resources, however strong, resulted finally only in half-hearted, uneasy compromises concerning both cost calculation and price determination.

A small group of purists have advocated the open recognition that a socialist economy could not possibly achieve economic rationality without letting the law of value play an active role *within* the state sector, just as it did at the *periphery*. As happens to purists everywhere, their impact on actual economic policies has been negligible. A few economists and mathematicians, however – notably, Oskar Lange, Leonid Kantorovich, and V. V. Novozhilov – proposed solutions which would not only further the cause of rationalization, but could also help extricate the policy makers from their dilemma.

In the early 1960s, Lange attempted a peculiar synthesis of his Marxian predispositions and his perceptions as a theoretical economist schooled in Western economics. He first reasserted his full agreement with the Marxian analysis of capitalism, an analysis predicated on the postulate that labor is the sole source of value, while the owners of capital are only exploitative appropriators of surplus-value. He then argued that all rational human activity, whether in the economy or in other fields, whether under socialism or under capitalism, had nothing to do with this unique property of labor. Rational activity was concerned with such things as the ordering of goals, their quantification, and optimal choice. The last item, he continued, required the application of the *economic principle,* or the *principle of economic rationality,* derived from man's activities (*praxis*) in a variety of fields. This principle, that 'all human behavior is directed to the maximum realization of a given end', Lange concluded, was the greatest discovery of the science of rational activity called 'praxiology', a 'science which bourgeois economists like von Mises falsely identify with political economy'.

In short, Lange argued, praxiology formed a useful adjunct to the Marxian analysis of capitalism, and thus was appropriate as part of the foundation for socialism. Indeed, the peculiar success of socialism lay precisely in the hierarchical structuring of ends in a national plan, which expressed the social rationality made possible by a new mode of production. To achieve economic rationality, however, required that the labor theory of value not be used as a principle of allocation – a suggestion Lange had made some thirty years earlier. Rationality required a supplementary 'economic principle' based on such 'praxiological categories' as 'end and means, method, action, plan, effectiveness, efficiency, and so on'.[16]

In the late 1950s, Leonid Kantorovich made a less philosophical, yet no less decisive thrust against the prevailing misallocation of resources under socialism. His point of departure was his own pioneering work of the 1930s on a variant of linear programming, which focused on rational choices in narrowly limited cases – for instance, the optimal utilization of machinery for given tasks, optimal sowing patterns, and optimal patterns of freight shipment. Kantorovich now proposed to extend the use of his programming model and its resulting shadow prices ('objectively determined coefficients of standard efficiency') to all levels of plan calculation. By interconnecting entire sets of sectoral shadow prices, it would be possible to achieve an optimal (rational) plan for the entire economy. Thus he advocated that the existing cost-plus price be discarded and replaced with a shadow price structure reflecting true underlying relative scarcities.[17]

Thus, both Lange and Kantorovich offered a way round the ideological obstacles to economic efficiency in a Marxian system. Lange offered a philosophical rationale, Kantorovich a tool of calculation compatible with non-exploitative capital and centralized supervision. Nevertheless they were spurned and even harassed. Why? The Marxian system rejects any ideology-free criteria as downright heretical.

Efficiency, technological change and growth, vs. quasi-development

Massive socialization of the economy's commanding heights and their integration as it were into a single centrally directed enterprise, have not brought about even after decades of planning in the USSR the phenomenal upsurge in productivity predicted by the founders of modern socialism.

In a comparative study of productivity and efficiency in the USSR and the USA, Abram Bergson has convincingly demonstrated that, in the early 1970s, efficiency in the USSR was markedly below that in the USA. Bergson suggested that the relatively poor performance of the Soviet Union may be due primarily to the working arrangements of a socialist

16 Oskar Lange, *Political Economy*, trans. from Polish by A. H. Walker, New York, Macmillan, 1963, Vol. I, *General Problems*, pp. 148ff. See also the perceptive analysis of Lange's attempt at synthesis in R. L. Meek, *Economics and Ideology and Other Essays*, London, Chapman and Hall, 1967, pp. 215ff.

17 See L. V. Kantorovich, *Ekonomicheskii raschet nailushchego izpolzovaniia resursov* (Economic Calculation of Optimum Utilization of Resources), Moscow, Academia Nauk SSSR, 1960. See also the thoughtful comments of R. Pallu de la Barrière in his preface to the French translation of Kantorovich's *Calcul economique et utilisation des ressources*, trans. C. Sarthou, Paris, Dunod, 1963, pp. xxiff.

economy. The discussant of Bergson's study, Evsey D. Domar, argued that the differences can more readily be attributed to differences in stages of development – the USSR being at an earlier stage than the USA. Domar pointed out that problems of this type were usually solved by means of a multiple regression of, say, a productivity index for various countries against the relative stage of development and the presence or absence of socialism. In this case, however, such a procedure was precluded 'because just about every index of development, such as per capita income, productivity or the fraction of the labor force in nonfarm occupations depends to a considerable extent on the efficiency of the economy'.[18]

A number of studies published in Eastern Europe tend to support Bergson's view concerning the overwhelming impact on performance of the working arrangements of the socialist economies.[19] The transformation of a socialist economy into an integrated, centrally controlled enterprise does indeed allow the directors of the system to proceed rapidly toward vast structural changes no matter what the per capita income level is. Indeed, investment rates, employment structure, inter-industry flows, and sectoral output ratios soon exhibit the pattern familiar in advanced development: employment in industry generally and especially in priority industries increases very rapidly; the relative shares in interindustry flows of primary products and of manufactured goods fall and rise respectively; and the relative shares of agriculture and industry in total output shift in favor of the latter. And yet, in terms of productivity, technological progress, quality of goods produced, and marketability of these goods on international markets, the results have been exceedingly disappointing.[20] As we would expect, the massive shift of unskilled labor to industry, with scant regard to the available skills or to the profitability or quality of output, has led to an overall decline rather than an increase in productivity. Deliberate, unrelenting, priority expansion of certain sectors involves an increasingly skewed allocation of skilled manpower and capital, and corresponding deterioration and obsolescence in the nonpriority sectors; but it also involves an unceasing effort to push exports to the levels needed for growing imports of machinery and equipment. The catch is, however, that the export goods are of poor quality. Hence domestic expansion can

---

18 Abram Bergson, 'Comparative Productivity and Efficiency in the USA and the USSR', and Evsey D. Domar, 'On the Measurement of Comparative Efficiency', with a comment by A. Bergson, in *Comparison of Economic Systems*, edited by Alexander Eckstein, Berkeley, University of California Press, 1971, pp. 230 and 236.
19 See, for instance, Ferenc Jánossy, 'Gazdaságunk mai ellentmondásaink eredete és felszámolásuk útja' (The Origins of the Present Contradictions in Our Economy and How to Eliminate Them'), *Közgazdasági szemle*, July–August 1969.
20 See Michał Kalecki, *Introduction to the Theory of Growth in a Socialist Society*, Oxford: Blackwell, 1969, pp. 45 ff.

only occur on the basis of the goods (of equally low quality) obtained by barter from the other socialist countries, or on the basis of domestically produced equipment. In either case, expansion takes place only by increased capitalization, but without much technological progress. Simultaneously, the effort to push exports at all costs inhibits overall growth, as well as the capacity to import from countries with advanced technology. As Michał Kalecki put it:

At a certain rate of growth all efforts to equilibrate imports and exports cease to yield positive results. A further reduction in export prices does not serve any useful purpose, because it increases the volume of exports, but not its value (in foreign exchange) – the increase in volume being compensated by the decrease in price. Both less favorable markets and less profitable goods have been made use of to the limit. The same is true of feasible investment in import substitution. Thus, foreign trade difficulties resulting from limited foreign markets, along with the technological and organizational factors which hamper the development of particular industries, set a ceiling for the rate of growth.[21]

The effort to promote growth through taut plans and to stimulate enterprises to fulfill and overfulfill the physical plan indicators regardless of quality, breeds managerial resistance to changes in production methods and the introduction of new products. The result is that, in the limit, certain socialist economies resemble a huge Kafkaesque factory producing and using 'nothing but rejects'.[22]

With their highly-concentrated plants and ever-growing machine tool branches, certain socialist countries resemble the developed economies formally, but differ from them so far as results are concerned. They have all the characteristics of development but lack its substance:

In this connection, everything that is economically measurable and can be grouped with economic statistics is related to 'form' alone. The substance, which by its nature is qualitative, can thus be easily ignored. The 'how much' which we measure is only a form of the 'what' of the 'quantitatively' unmeasurable quality, that is of the substance. Here and there, so and so many workers are employed, so and so much is produced, invested, etc., – this is form. But what the quality of manpower is, what the products are like, what it is we invest – this is the hidden substance.[23]

The socialist economies are thus in fact 'quasi-developed' economies, whose basic feature is a marked discrepancy between form and substance.

The liquidation of the quasi-developed state economy – through the acquisition of the skills and technology in line with international standards, the modernization of equipment in the key branches of the economy and eventually in all branches, and emphasis on quality rather than on quantity – requires far-reaching changes in the 'working arrangements of

---

21 *Ibid.*, pp. 47–8.   22 Jánossy, 'Gazdaságunk . . . ', *op. cit.*   23 *Ibid.*

these economies, both in planning and in control over the results obtained. Nothing indicates that socialist policy makers are ready or willing to effect far reaching changes. Many of the Polish theses of 1957 have still not been carried out in practice in most of Eastern Europe or in the USSR. Departures from the key concept of the simple wholly unified country-wide enterprise operating under a highly centralized plan have more often than not been formalistic, and hedged round by provisions, reservations, and warnings against going too far too fast. Possible extensions of direct relations among enterprises within the centralized framework have been approached very gingerly. Exhortations to upgrade the information provided to the central organs, to improve enterprise incentives and performance criteria, and to promote ideological purity and social rather than individual interests continue to remain commonplace in the official Soviet and East European literature.

4 Determinants of the objectives of control

The frame of reference

According to Marx, answers to the basic economic questions: what is to be produced? how? and for whom? are determined by the conditions prevailing in *production*. These conditions include the following interacting elements: (a) the state and level of the *material forces of production* – i.e. the type and quality of both the instruments of production and of the labor force – and (b) the *social relations* — i.e. the relations between laborers and owners of the means of production both in the process of production and in the society at large. Since Marx's *Contribution to the Critique of Political Economy* (1859), emphasis on the primacy of production (and on the corresponding social relations) has become the hallmark of Marxian *economic* analysis.

The Marxists dismiss as subjectivist and ahistorical any attempt to analyze economic phenomena from the side of demand and market relations: 'the dynamics of the requirements [i.e. of demand] are determined by the requirements of production' and not the other way round.[1] By continuously changing the structure and the level of production, and therefore the relations among producers, the socialist system evolves ultimately into a 'cooperative commonwealth coextensive with the nation', producing 'all that is necessary for its preservation'.[2]

Who will determine how to restructure the economy and what is necessary to produce? Will conflicts of interest be avoided when decisions on what is deemed necessary are taken? What incentives will insure that outputs will be forthcoming in the required quantities and qualities, and, moreover, that the distribution of goods will conform to the wishes of all?

1 See K. Marx, *Capital*, Vol. III, *op. cit.*, p. 191, and K. Marx, 'Critique of the Gotha Programme' [1875], in K. Marx and F. Engels, *Selected Works* in three volumes, Moscow, Progress Publishers, 1970, Vol. III, pp. 19–20. See also Nikolai Bukharin, *The Economic Theory of the Leisure Class* [1914], New York, Greenwood Press, 1968, pp. 54ff.
2 Karl Kautsky, *The Class Struggle* (Erfurt Program) [1892], *op. cit.*, p. 103.

In Saint-Simon's Utopian schema of a future industrial society the directing organ of the system is a *Supreme Council of Industry* consisting of 'working bourgeois, manufacturers, merchants, bankers' advised by a *Council of the Learned*. The authority of this supreme organ will stem not from its place at the top of a hierarchy, but from its knowledge of 'what others are ignorant of'. Consequently, its actions will be devoid of arbitrariness. Following *la loi naturelle,* society will thus be in harmony with itself. The Supreme Council will not do merely what it wishes, but 'what fits the nature of things'. Moreover, since no one will wish to act 'other than in conformity with the nature of things', people will do as the Supreme Council says without having to be coerced.[3]

With Saint-Simon, Marx viewed true social consensus as entirely achievable. (According to him, however, this will occur only after the socialization of the means of production will generate such abundance as to fulfill everyone's needs.) He viewed a society not yet socialized as being torn apart by the antagonistic interests of the owners of the means of production, and of the workers who must sell them their labor power. Within such a society, the social condition of each class *uniquely* determines both its interests and the policies which serve it best. The *perception* of these interests and the formulation of the policies may, however, be obscured by a variety of elements. Consequently, a given individual – and indeed, a given class – may not readily perceive which interests or policies are basic or secondary, permanent or temporary, real or only apparent.

Under capitalism, in fact, the working class can scarcely rise above a trade-union mentality. Accordingly, Marx sternly advises workers involved in struggles over wages 'not to forget that they are fighting with effects and not with the causes of these effects', and that they would do better to replace their 'conservative motto: "A fair day's wages for a fair day's work" ' with the the 'revolutionary watchword: "Abolition of the wage system".'[4] (Communists, of course, claim that, as the workers' *avant garde,* they possess the class consciousness that most workers lack; hence, thanks to their Marxist training, Communists are always able to distinguish scientifically between the *objective* class interests [of the capitalists or of the workers] and the *subjective* reflection of these interests in the minds of the masses. Communist parties are therefore uniquely able to make the appropriate decisions in the 'intricacies of the class struggle'.[5])

The socialization of the means of production would change both the

3 Emile Durkheim, *Socialism and Saint-Simon (Le Socialisme),* edited by R. W. Gouldner and trans. by C. Sattler, Antioch, The Antioch Press, 1958, pp. 154–5.
4 Karl Marx, *Value, Price and Profit* [1865], edited by Eleanor Marx Aveling, New York, International Publishers, 1935, p. 61.
5 G. Glezerman, *Socialist Society: Scientific Principles of Development,* trans. from the Russian by L. Lampert, Moscow, Progress Publishers, 1971, pp. 72–3.

social framework and the conditions it generates. No antagonistic conflicts of interests are plausible thereafter: as collective owners of the means of production, the direct producers are henceforth presumed to have the same social interests and therefore to possess identical preferences concerning total output and its composition. Thus socialization is presumed to change the preference structure so that everybody has identical (social) preferences rather than distinct (individual) preferences over his own labor-consumption possibilities set. If, by some quirk, someone's preferences diverged from those of the collective, his error could be corrected merely by pointing out that his deviance conflicted with his own interests, which are necessarily those of the collective.

The foregoing argument, as much else in Marx's thought, was intended to apply to an industrially developed economy. In practice, of course, socialization has occurred primarily in less-developed countries, where palpable differences have been observed to persist between industrial workers, peasants, the 'intelligentsia', the permanent officials, managers and bureaucrats. Moreover, open conflicts and even upheavals have occurred in certain socialist countries. As a result, the possibility of a divergence of interests or contradictions under socialism is now acknowledged throughout the socialist camp. These contradictions are, however, held not to be antagonistic since most of the means of production already belong to the entire society. Social differentiation is usually presented only as a vestige of the past rather than as a characteristic of the future. For example, the eventual transformation of the collective farms into state farms in the USSR is supposed ultimately to erase the basic distinctions between the farmers and the workers, and to lead finally to the 'absorption by social interests . . . of all specific interests'.[6]

As supreme directors of the Soviet-type system, the Communist Party leaders – like Saint-Simon's *Supreme Council of Industry* – always claim to take decisions congruent with the workers' interests. They do so, however, not because they are following *la loi naturelle,* but because they embody the workers' *class consciousness.* Eventually, when all social differences have vanished entirely, the decisions of the system's trustees and the preferences of all the members of the society will be completely congruent.[7]

In the above schema, incentives occupy a rather awkward place. Communist writers affirm that social property engenders a new kind of interest, namely, a social material interest – the familiar *owner's interest* but directed to the expansion of *overall* production, the rise of social productivity, the increase of *national* income and the living standard of all. In

---

6 *Ibid.,* p. 86.   7 *Ibid.,* pp. 84–5.

turn, this social interest will eventually generate entirely new ideological, moral stimuli to work, the only stimuli which will ultimately persist under communism. In the meantime, though, especially in countries only beginning industrialization, people may have to be motivated primarily by self-interests. This means that material rather than moral stimuli will have to remain in use, perhaps indefinitely.

In short, the complex of economic issues involving preferences for the structure of the economy, for the allocation of resources, for the standard of living and for the nature and scope of incentives themselves hinge on the Marxist definition and perception of the workers' 'interests'. As von Mises has pointed out, interests are not understood in this connection as personal advantages 'chosen by men on the ground of judgments of value'. Rather, they are visualized as means to social ends, conditioned for everyone by the class position he occupies in a given historical framework, and by the ultimate ends themselves – namely, socialism and communism.[8]

Practical interrelations of production, interests and incentives

After a short period of economic recovery following the devastating years of World War I and the Civil War, the leaders of the Soviet regime in 1929 launched the USSR on the path of the planned reconstruction of industrial capacity and the socialist restructuring of agriculture. As the official text of the first Soviet five-year plan put it, the USSR embarked on a joint program of (1) *development,* carried out 'at the sacrifice of present needs for the sake of great historical achievements', and (2) *socialization,* aimed at the 'steady advance of the socialist elements in the economic system of the Soviet Union'.[9]

Planned economic development was meant to enable the USSR rapidly to 'catch up with and to surpass the highest indices of capitalism' (i.e. those of the United States) and to secure the country against any capitalist intervention.[10] The official economics textbook henceforth denounced as anti-Marxist and as a 'vulgarized, narrow consumers' approach' any questioning of 'the determining role of production in relation to consumption . . . [and of] the necessity for the priority growth of the production of means of production under socialism'.[11] The development of heavy indus-

8 Ludwig von Mises, *Theory and History, An Interpretation of Social and Economic Evolution,* New Haven, Yale University Press, 1957, p. 139.

9 *The Soviet Union Looks Ahead, The Five Year Plan for Economic Reconstruction* [English translation of the 'maximum variant' of the 1929 Soviet plan], New York, Horace Liveright, 1929, pp. 109 and 195.

10 See the textbook issued by the Institute of Economics of the Academy of Sciences of the USSR, *Political Economy,* trans. by C. P. Dutt and Andrew Rothstein, *op. cit.,* pp. 533–4.

11 *Ibid.,* p. 755.

try was counted the *prime prerequisite* for eventually providing the citizenry with abundant consumers' goods: 'The Soviet State carries out a system of measures to produce an abundance of industrial and food commodities in the country. *For these purposes* it develops heavy industry to the fullest extent and on this basis ensures a powerful rise of agriculture and of the production of goods for mass consumption.'[12] Economic expansion, defense capability, consumer wellbeing – all rested in this conception on the 'further strong development of heavy industry'.[13]

Upon close examination, the views of Stalin and other Soviet leaders on economic growth appear to have been based on their reading of the evolution of capitalism in the nineteenth century, and on a rather simplistic perception of developed capitalism in the early twentieth century. Like all other industrializing states trying to emulate its predecessors, from 1920 on the USSR copied, borrowed, adapted and internalized much of the modern technology in use in other countries. But success in overtaking one's predecessors does not hinge solely on technological transfers and adaptations. The United States and Germany overtook Britain in the nineteenth century, and Japan overtook Western Europe in the twentieth century, not by merely borrowing technology, but by also developing a whole series of other elements: flexible business institutions capable of effectively channelling and managing the resources invested; an economic framework in which innovative technological choices would be made at any level; the unimpeded application of science and technology; and a flair for organizing complex production processes to promote the efficient utilization of productive inputs. In the industrialized capitalist countries, the relative shares of industry to total output and the total labor force remained stationary or even declined, while industrial productivity increased along with that in all the other sectors. In the Soviet Union, by contrast, the leadership has adhered rigidly to its own *a priori* strategy of growth. Year after year, decade after decade, this leadership has unimaginatively pursued the vast mobilization of physical and human capital and the skewed allocation of resources to heavy industry.

The Soviet leadership presumes to know both the direction in which the economy must be steered to reach communism, and the Soviet workers' true interests. Yet, according to the ruling party dogma, once the means of production are socialized the *direct producers* themselves are supposed to know how to shape the economy to conform to their new, identical preferences with respect to output. An ambivalent situation is thus cre-

12 *Ibid.*, p. 539. Emphasis supplied.
13 *Gosudarstvennyi piatiletnii plan razvitiia narodnogo knoziaistva SSSR na 1971–1975 gody* (State Five-Year Plan for the Development of the USSR National Economy for the Period 1971–1975), Moscow, Politizdat, 1972, p. 22.

ated: the party, as the director of the system, claims for itself the right to formulate the basic decisions – the division of the national product between investment and consumption, the sectoral pattern of investment, and even the assortment of all outputs. The party also claims, however, that all the citizens can influence all the decisions taken, that they effectively participate in their formulation and determination, and that they are both the compilers of the economic plan and the administrators of its implementation. Here, for instance, are the words of the chairman of the Planning Commission of the USSR, N. Baibakov, in his preface to the Soviet 9th Five Year Plan:

The Five Year Plan for the 1971–1975 period is the result of collective work. It was compiled under the direct supervision of the Politburo of the [Central Committee of the Communist Party of the Soviet Union]. . . . The draft of the Directives for the Ninth Five Year Plan was widely discussed in the press, in party organizations, and the collectives of enterprises and institutions. Along with economic, planning, Soviet, and party bodies, the collectives of enterprises and civic associations, millions and millions of workers, take a direct part both in the compilation of plans and in performing the tasks set by them. Planning in our country has truly become the business of all the people and an important form of worker participation in administration of the state.[14]

The reality caricatures the ideal situation depicted by Baibakov. The Party leadership's Draft of Directives is published for discussion, but simultaneously it is transmitted down through the various ministerial administrations where the detailed *apportionment of tasks* for each plant is worked out. Within the limits set in the draft, key issues are negotiated within the planning–managerial pyramid – the growth pace of each industry or branch, the expansion or renewal of capacity, the introduction of new technology, and the determination of detailed output mixes. From the bottom up, that pyramid consists of operational plant managers, trusts (directorates of firms), ministries, the Planning Commission, the entire Council of Ministers, and finally the top decision-making body, the party Politburo. At no point, however, are the basic divisions of the national output, or the key choices concerning investment, open to discussion outside the Politburo. Only the apportioning of set tasks and the exact load to be imposed on any given plant or branch are matters of negotiation within the party–state bureaucracy. The workers' involvement in the compilation of the plan is ritualistic and perfunctory. Once the negotiated corrections are transmitted upward, they are adjusted, coordinated and consolidated in the final plan, which, after examination and approval by the Politburo, is transmitted to the state organs to be rubberstamped into

14 *Ibid.,* pp. 11–12.

law. The interests and preferences of the citizenry are expressed to some degree through the managerial hierarchy, but only on the assignment of production tasks rather than output mixes or the allocation of the national product. Any divergence between consumers' preferences and those of the policy makers at best finds expression in unplanned savings (through the refusal to buy products at state-fixed prices, or an unsatisfied demand for imported consumer goods) or in black markets.

As I pointed out, theoretically, under socialism, no divergence of interests can exist between the various social groups and strata of society or within any of these groups, because each and every individual is an owner of the means of production. The crucial Marxian contention that social harmony can be achieved through socialization, and through socialization alone, was supposed to become increasingly evident as socialism progressed, i.e. as both the material basis of the society and socialist relations in the sphere of production were expanded and consolidated. When, during the early years of his dictatorship, Stalin advanced the startling idea that class warfare was actually *increasing* with advance of Soviet socialism, it was viewed by some Marxists as a cunning aberration meant to justify the dictator's own purges and ruthless repressions.

After Stalin's death, the striking divergences of interests within and between the various groups and strata in every socialist country, along with the economic dislocations discussed earlier, led to the open recognition of contradictions under socialism – except in the USSR itself. The contradictions were, however, solemnly proclaimed to be non-antagonistic, susceptible of full harmonization, and in any event, in process of gradual disappearance. From Eastern Europe to China, economists, planners and even policy makers – including such diverse figures as Imre Nagy, Oskar Lange and Mao Tse-tung – competed to discover contradictions and to proclaim their own solutions to correct them. Nagy and his followers, as we saw, stressed above all the dislocations provoked by the Soviet strategy of development, and denounced their deleterious effect on the alleged worker–peasant alliance in violation of the law of the proportionate development of the national economy.[15] Lange emphasized the conflict between the productive forces and the relations of production, which he took as a contradiction between the level of development of the socialist economy and the antiquated methods of economic management used by its bureaucrats.[16] Finally, Mao, with traditional Chinese patience

15 See for instance A. Mód, 'A "nep" politika alkalmazásának néhány kérdésé pártunk politikájában', (Some Issues in the Application of the 'Nep' Policy in our Country), *Tarsadalmi szemle*, viii, Sept. 1953, pp. 811ff.
16 See for instance O. Lange, 'The Political Economy of Socialism' – his 1957 Belgrade lectures included in *Problems of Political Economy of Socialism* edited by O. Lange, Calcutta, People's Publishing House, 1962. See also O. Lange, *Papers in Economics and*

and exhaustiveness, drew up a long list of socialist contradictions – longer and more complex than that of any other socialist leader. He listed first the 'contradictions among the people', i.e. 'contradictions . . . within the working class . . . within the peasantry . . . within the intelligentsia . . . between the working class and the peasantry . . . between the workers and the peasants on the one hand and the intellectuals on the other . . . between the working class and other sections of the working people . . . and so on'. He added secondly 'the contradictions between the government and the people', which include contradictions among the interests of the state, collectives and individuals, and between democracy and centralism, the leaders and the led, the bureaucrats and the masses, and so on. He concluded finally that 'contradictions and struggles are universal and absolute' and that all that mattered was to handle them properly.[17]

From then on, every socio-economic or political upheaval in the socialist camp brought to the fore new harvests of contradictions along with new proposals for coping with them. Finally, a Soviet writer, Glezerman, has suggested that endless fragmentation of interests indeed exists under socialism because of the division of labor among the workers – a fact recognized by Marx himself. (Actually, Marx had contended that this fragmentation existed under capitalism and would vanish under socialism because of job rotation and the vanishing differences between intellectual and manual work.) Glezerman affirms that socialization leads not to the disappearance of this fragmentation but to a successful harmonization by the state of the divergences of interests it generates.[18]

Besides the contradictions and their sources, the question of incentives and their interrelations with material interests has also recieved ambiguous treatment in the socialist economic literature and in the pronouncements of socialist policy makers. In the years just prior to the Bolshevik revolution, Lenin alloted no place for material incentives in his conception of socialism. In *State and Revolution*, he wrote that, under socialism, 'all that is required is that they [the citizens] should work equally, do their proper share of work, and get equal pay'.[19] The question of motivating managers and workers seemed irrelevant within a centrally run, smoothly operating socialized economy. Early socialist practice turned out to be surprising and disconcerting, but Lenin had no qualms about adapting his

Sociology, 1930—1960, Oxford, Pergamon Press, 1970, particularly pp. 418ff. and *passim.*
17 *Quotations from Chairman Mao Tse-tung* (the 'Little Red Book') New York, Bantam, 1967, Ch. IV, pp. 25–6, 31.
18 See for instance G. Glezerman, *Socialist Society . . . , op. cit.,* pp. 84ff, and, more extensive but less accessible to the Western readers, N. N. Constantinescu, *Problema Contradicţiei in economia socialistă* (The Problem of Contradiction in the Socialist Economy), Bucharest, Editura Politica, 1973.   19 Lenin, *State and Revolution, op. cit.,* p. 473.

views to the new conditions. As I have already noted, soon after the formation of the Soviet state, Lenin conceded the inevitability of some decentralization of decisions within the state-wide unified centralized economy; of granting (within certain limits) some authority to the operational manager; and of using various forms of rewards, in money and in kind, for both managers and workers. In time, however, this concession evolved into a complex system of prizes and privileges based squarely on political considerations, and only tenuously on economic criteria. Today, the system consists of extensive, well-differentiated privileges, according to one's rank in the party–state hierarchy: not only salaries but access to different types of shops, goods (imported and domestic), housing and other services at differentiated prices, and job appointments and promotions only remotely related to technical competence. In principle, at the lowest rungs of this hierarchy, the operational manager's behavior is primarily determined by carefully graded bonuses granted him according to his degree of fulfillment of plan targets. In fact, the bonuses are only part of the story: the operational manager partakes of some of the hierarchy's manifold and diversified privileges and rewards. So also do the shock workers, the skilled technicians and specialists, the foremen – although they never accede to the privileges of the high members of this intricate system of patronage, control, and rewards. Soviet wage differentials, bonuses, premia, and other apparent material incentives have been officially justified as so-called 'considerable survivals of the old division of labor' (allegedly 'being overcome gradually as the material forces of socialism develop and the material production basis of communism is created').[20] Nevertheless, the hidden privileges have continued to grow and diversify, rather than diminish, as the Soviet production capacity has expanded.

This combined system of open, relatively limited wage differentials and of hidden, extensively differentiated privileges and controls has been emulated without significant variations by all the European socialist countries and Cuba. At various times in various countries, proposals have been made to amend or discard this system. Thus, in Eastern Europe, as early as the 1950s there were specific suggestions (largely ignored) to tie rewards more directly to economic performance and less to political influence.[21] In Cuba, Che Guevara recommended in the mid 1960s that the highest

20 Academy of Sciences of the USSR, *Political Economy, op. cit.,* p. 565.
21 Oskar Lange described as follows the wide-ranging implications of the Soviet-type system of incentives with reference to Poland's experience in the mid 1950s: 'appropriate steps to increase the material interest of workers are an integral part of the reconversion of the national economy. However, the problem regarding the attitude towards work should not be restricted to the question of direct material incentives. It is also related to a series of questions of a general character such as that of the standard of living, the conditions of promotion, the problem of [workers'] participation in the direction of the enterprise, as

financial rewards be extended to those who work hardest physically – e.g. the sugar cane cutters. This proposal was dismissed in most socialist quarters as a naive interpretation of the labor theory of value. Fidel Castro himself also stressed at the time the great importance of social rather than material stimuli, castigating those who assumed that 'in every Cuban man or woman there is a potential Sancho Panza'.[22] Ultimately, however, the Cuban Communists fell in line and faithfully adopted the Soviet system: the party in full command of the distribution of rewards according to position in the hierarchy, and tightly controlling each person's job and standard of living.

Moral incentives and modest material rewards directly tied to performance have been utilized in China. Stinging criticism of the Soviet system of incentives, along with continuous exhortations to 'selflessness, frugality and anti-economism', have abounded in China.[23] Wage differentials have indeed been kept there far narrower than anywhere else in the socialist camp. Moreover, the Chinese have developed effective collective controls and pressures on each individual in both urban and rural areas. And, the Cultural Revolution of the 1960s helped, temporarily at least, to keep differences in rewards in check. Yet, as everywhere else in the socialist camp, in a system devoid of built-in checks and balances, the system's top directors alone are the dispensers of bounties and the supreme decision makers as to what the standard of living of each official, technician, specialist, shock worker, foreman or simple worker must be.

The critique of aims and of their rationale

It was the probing of the fundamental Marxian tenet that all citizens have identical interests under socialism that opened the door in Czechoslovakia in the early 1960s, to one of the most penetrating critiques of the Soviet

well as the people's confidence as to the rational character of the economic policy of the state. The nihilistic attitude of a great part of the workers is a result both of their bad living conditions, and of the lack of conviction that the economic policy which calls for such great sacrifice on the part of the workers is appropriate and justified. . . . For several years it has become characteristic of our economy that there is no relation between the results attained by workers in their work, on the one hand, and the possibilities of promotion on the other. The personnel policy has been generally unrelated to the efficiency of any given worker. . . . In order to eliminate the nihilistic attitude towards work, it is necessary to establish and strictly to observe the principles according to which the right to operate selection and grant promotion should rest with the directors responsible for the work of the enterprises or institutions ('Wsprawie doraźnego programu' ('On immediate programs'), *Życie gospodarcze,* July 16, 1956.

22 Castro's address 'On the Sixth Anniversary of the Committee for the Defense of the Revolution', Havana radio dispatch of Sept. 29, 1966.

23 See for instance 'On Khruschev's Phoney Communism and Its Historical Lessons for the World', in *The Polemic on the General Line of the International Communist Movement,* Peking, Foreign Languages Press, 1965, pp. 438ff.

economic mechanism. A new perception of the distinctiveness and significance of individual and small-group interests, as opposed to the interests of the society as formulated by the governing body, led Czechoslovak economists, planners, and eventually even policy makers to question and finally to reject Marxian assertions about the primacy of production over demand; of central planning over the market; and of bureaucratic commands over economic incentives.

The implications of the nature, origin, determinants and impact of interests were not, of course, immediately clear to all. While the conviction grew in the early 1960s that the economic system needed to be reformed, consensus ended when it came to the point of deciding the what, why and how of the reforms. But the widening discussions of interests eventually came to serve as a forum for launching attacks on the established theoretical positions, for asserting the need for change, and (in the end) for giving the Czechoslovak reform drive an unmistakable character of its own.

As rates of economic growth declined in the early 1960s, the official party press placed the blame on the workers' anachronistic ideas about their individual interests; the reeling economy could be righted if only the workers would develop the habit of working for the general good.[24] This was a familiar story. But this time, there was a strong counter-attack against the contention that individual interests were but holdovers of bourgeois prejudices in the people's minds, and that the direct producers, by working for the society, were also working for themselves. The counter attack was opened by Ota Šik, in a book destined to have a profound influence during the next few years – *Economy, Interests, Politics*.[25] In that book, Šik argued that at any point in time in any society and at any level of socio-economic development, there is a varied and complex interplay between the objectively determined production relations and the subjectively determined material interests of individuals. Striking close to home, Šik pointed out that even in state, military and corporate bureaucracies, unavoidable differences of interest exist between the upper layers of decision takers, directors and controllers, and the lower layers which must submit to commands, injunctions and supervision.

The idea that conflicts of interest were inevitable was seized upon with increasing boldness, not only by Šik himself but also by a number of his followers, in order first to develop a searching critique of the prevailing

24 See for instance *Plánované hospodářství*, II, 1961, pp. 961ff; *Politická ekonomie*, 9, 1961, pp. 841ff; *Rudé právo*, Jan. 19, 1963, etc.
25 Ota Šik, *Ekonomika, zájmy, politika* (Economy, Interests, Politics) [1962]. (The edition available to us and referred to here is the German translation of the work, *Ökonomie, Interessen, Politik*, Berlin, Dietzverlag, 1966.)

system, and then to work out proposals for a new system. The so called non-traditionalists, or anti-dogmatists – O. Šik, R. Kocanda, B. Komenda, C. Kožušník, O. Kýn, L. Matejka, and many others – in time came to question the very logic of determining objectives under socialism, the feasibility of improving economic performance while maintaining the primacy of the plan, and the rationale of the prevailing system of instructions and incentives for fulfilling the centrally selected targets.

Concerning social aims, the non-traditionalists stressed that if only common interests are recognized as legitimate under socialism, personal or group interests must be sacrificed and branded as antisocial. In a penetrating critique of the so-called 'personality cult era', A. Lantay noted that 'behind the veil of the dogmatic interpretation of social interests the human being with his needs and wishes became lost'.[26] The dogmatic approach to the identity of interests inevitably created an atmosphere of indifference to the people which eventually led to 'actively hurting personal interests and infringing citizens' own rights'. This engendered, in turn, increased individualism, covert assertions of individual and group interests without regard for (or even against) social interests, and indifference toward the preservation and expansion of the nation's wealth.

Hostility to the dogma of the 'identity of interests' was manifested in many forms throughout the period up through the 'Prague Spring' of 1968. As Jan Zoubek caustically put it,

Up till now our system has been built on comprehensive national ownership which asserted verbally that we are all owners, and that factories belong to all of us. Thus we are all interested in production; everything concerning it is in the interest of society and thus in our interest. If, by chance, our interest is not identical with it, then we have to adapt our interest to the national interest. We even reached the point where everything was in the national interest, while the interests of almost all members of society were something quite different from the declared national interest.[27]

The motto of 'Prague Spring', *socialism with a human face,* came to mean a new variant of socialism, a socialism concerned with and responsive to the diverse needs and wants of individuals, in opposition to the traditional variant in which all interests are identical and are correctly perceived by the system's top directors.

The leaders of the Communist party became increasingly alarmed in the early 1960s at the incapacity of its administrators to control the behavior of the enterprises. The latter were reacting defensively to the deteriorating economic situation by raising their demand for imports, expanding their

26 Andrey Lantay, 'Problémy jednoty záumov v socialistickej spoločnosti' (Problems of the Identity of Interests in Socialist Society), *Ekonomický časopis*, xi, No. 6, 1963.
27 *Reporter* (Prague), No. 30, 1968.

requests for new investments and construction, hoarding materials, and employing manpower far in excess of the official provisions. In response, the party itself commissioned a group of economists to formulate proposals for change. Within this very group, the non-traditionalist faction led by Šik took shape. In time, Šik and his associates developed a position consisting of two parts: a critical analysis of the existing system and of the limits to improving it; and a set of proposals embodying a resolute shift from shamefaced borrowing of market mechanisms to a clear recognition of the necessity for their widespread use.

The non-traditionalists contended, first of all, that socialist commodity relations existed because the state enterprises continued to act as relatively independent units, because the socialist division of labor could not and did not differ radically from that prevailing under capitalism, and because, finally, the center could not, try as it might, determine more than the basic proportions of that structure and of outputs of the economy. Accordingly, it would be to the center's own advantage to guide the interests of the enterprises themselves toward an optimum development of production. To that end, the managers should obey not 'one-sided quantitative indicators that have the character of directives from above' but the stimuli of demand. Both short-term and current enterprise production plans must be determined by the managers themselves, guided by demand:

It is precisely to arouse the interest of enterprises in an optimum development of production and in making their own detailed decisions on this development, not only in accordance with the narrow production interests, but also in accordance with consumer interests, that the interest of the enterprise in merely fulfilling one-sided quantitative and often very subjectively set targets must go, and there must be an *interest in increasing income*. This development of earnings by the enterprise must not, again, be conceived of as a quantitative norm determined for the enterprise from above as part of a plan, but as the actual effect of its own management, realized in the process of production and sale of goods to consumers.[28]

From the mid 1960s on, Šik and his followers harped incessantly on the idea that so long as commodity production existed – or so long as market relations existed both within and outside the state complex – production must develop in accordance with market trends. If it does not, either 'production is not satisfying or stimulating demand efficiently, or . . . part of production is useless because there is no demand for it'.[29] The center cannot decide which decisions – techniques, prices, output mixes – should

28 Ota Šik, 'Problems of the New System of Planned Management', *Czechoslovak Economic Papers*, Vol. 5, 1967, p. 17. See also Ota Šik, *Plan and Market under Socialism* [1967], trans. by Eleanor Wheeler, White Plains, NY, International Arts and Sciences Press, 1967, pp. 123–4.   29 Ota Šik, 'Problems . . . ', p. 20.

be left to the lower bodies. Consumers do not have a *general* demand for shoes, textiles or cars, but *specific* desires for certain styles, sizes, colors, and other attributes. No amount of centralized planning can bridge the discrepancies that will result if orders are given for prescribed behavior:

when production of these goods does not correspond generally to the demand for the product, the consumers feel this as a shortage, although there is a sufficiency of other kinds of shoes. Or, for instance, it is not enough to balance production and consumption of textiles in general without ascertaining precisely the necessary amount of each kind and range of textile materials. If, on the one hand, there is a surplus of cotton material in relation to demand, and, on the other hand, there is a lack of certain woolen or silk material that is in greater demand, then it is useless to explain that we are producing the planned amount of textiles. As soon as disproportions arise in the production of textiles the figures for total production will not mean anything.[30]

Accordingly, the policy-making planning center should shift its focus from arbitrary determinations of operating details to the broad appraisal of demand patterns in both the domestic and foreign markets, the evaluation of the changes in macro-structure which future trends in demand may entail, and the proper study of the effectiveness of investment alternatives which these changes may involve. This, the reformers stressed, requires enterprise participation in planning right from the start, along with the proper functioning (i.e. market-determination) of prices. In the vision of the Czechoslovak anti-dogmatists, economic reform implied not only theoretical justifications for discarding this or that element of the Soviet-type economic system, but also the development of detailed practical proposals for an alternative system. Their proposals involved re-establishing the primacy of the market, methodically adjusting production to consumers' demand, and the systematic use of enterprises' and individuals' material interests for the benefit of all. The reformers did not advocate altering the social ownership of the means of production. But they did go further than any other reformers in Eastern Europe towards destroying the role of the partyarchy in economic planning and management. They sought to remove the partyarchs' control not only over the setting of goals, the allocation of investment, and the determination of detailed production assignments – as the Yugoslavs had done – but aimed also at divorcing the party from the business of appointing, shuffling and promoting managerial–technical personnel. They wanted to put an end to the manipulation of the 'direct producers' through either arbitrarily set goals or covert but pervasive patronage and distorted incentives. In no small measure, it was the Czechoslovak reformers' clearly stated program

30 Ota Šik, *Plan and Market . . .* , *op. cit.*, p. 129.

for ending the party's role as 'universal administrator of society'[31] that provoked the ire of the Soviet leaders and finally led to their smashing the Czechoslovak attempt at reform with Soviet tanks.

Primacy of plan or market?

In the 1950s and 1960s, the emerging national leaderships of Yugoslavia, Hungary, Poland and Czechoslovakia attempted, as we have seen, to disentangle their countries from the all-pervasive influence and control of the USSR. In the attempt they worked out significantly different interpretations of the planning principle and of the role of market relations under socialism. In all cases, through their critiques of centralized administrative management and the various combinations of planning and market mechanisms proposed or implemented, they moved firmly away from the cardinal idea of an all-embracing directive plan as the hallmark of socialism. Whenever possible and feasible, they even questioned the more sacred *primacy* of the plan over any market relations – that is, the concept that the plan was the instrument *par excellence* of socialism.

In the early 1950s, following the enactment of the Law on Planned Management on Enterprises (1951), the Yugoslav leadership was the first Communist establishment actually to dismantle the central planning of production details typical of Soviet directive planning *à la* Stalin; to return production decisions to the enterprises; and to confine central planning to the control of the volume and structure of investment.[32] Also in the 1950s, during the New Course in Hungary (1953–55) and the debate on the economic model in Poland (1956–57), the role and scope of the central plan as overall economic regulator came under scrutiny. Yet none of the top Hungarian or Polish politicians and economists went as far as the Yugoslavs. The overall conception of the economic system implicit in their search for alternatives to Stalinist centralized command planning might be called central guidance of a socialist economy under the undisputed primacy of a central plan. (In Poland, only two little known economists, S. J. Kurowski and J. Popkiewicz, openly questioned the policy makers' priorities and their rationale in the late 1950s.)[33]

By the early 1960s, however, the perception of the appropriate scope and function of the central plan under socialism had changed appreciably throughout Eastern Europe; this was particularly true in Yugoslavia,

31 Dubček's speech of Feb. 22, at the meeting on the 20th anniversary of Feb. 1948 events, *Rudé právo*, Feb. 23, 1968.

32 Deborah D. Milenkovitch, *Plan and Market in Yugoslav Economic Thought*, New Haven, Yale University Press, 1971, pp. 121, 177.

33 Włodzimierz Brus, 'Spór o role planu centralnego' (Controversy on the Role of the Central Plan), in *Życie gospodarcze*, No. 12, 1957.

Hungary and Czechoslovakia. But the reasons for the change in thinking varied from country to country, as did the results.

In Yugoslavia, an open conflict erupted in the 1960s between so-called centralizers and decentralizers. The first group, led by N. Čobeljić and R. Stojanović, advocated greater central control over development strategy. The second group, led by A. Bajt, R. Bićanić, B. Horvat, and others, called for fewer central controls and further decentralization in favor of enterprises and local authorities. The debate between the centralizers and decentralizers involved the respective merits of the plan and the market, but also regional policy issues of crucial significance in that deeply divided multinational state. In the mid 1960s the central government finally decided to abandon the central planning of investments. The reason was not, though, the persuasive arguments of the 'decentralizers', but the fact that no agreement could be reached among the country's centrifugal regional leaderships on what the overall rate of investment should be and what the pattern of sectoral and regional allocation investment should be. Central priorities had become both unattainable and unenforceable.[34] Yugoslavia thus became the first and only *market-directed* socialist economy largely *by default*. Along with decentralized economic institutions, each regional Communist leadership was firmly in control of appointments and patronage in its own bailiwick. Only later did the core of the national party grouped around Tito manage to regain the upper hand to curb the centrifugal regional tendencies, and to move back toward a power balance in the partyarchy which would again allow central decisions to be enforced throughout the entire country.

In contrast to both the Soviet Union and Yugoslavia, Hungary became, throughout the decade of the 1960s, the socialist paragon of the *guided* (rather than *administered*) socialist economy – a model of what can be done *under the primacy of the plan* to enforce a limited number of central priorities, particularly with respect to investment. Moving a step at a time, the Hungarians first reduced the detailed central planning of production minutiae. Then they extended the sphere of direct contacts between sellers and buyers, and decontrolled the price system. Simultaneously, they introduced indirect economic instruments into the planning of agriculture and foreign trade. The Hungarians adroitly combined *centrally planned control* (i.e. the central plan itself, central regulations, and centralized guidance of certain activities by the ministries and banks) with greater freedom to respond to market forces at the enterprise level. In this way, the Hungarian leaders avoided a slide (like that in Yugoslavia) of the economy towards the decentralization of investment and of technological change. In

---

34 See the competent and detailed account of this debate in Milenkovitch, *Plan and Market*
    . . . , *op. cit.*, pp. 177ff.

short, by retaining overall coordination of the national economy, the Hungarian party sought to increase economic efficiency without sacrificing its own power monopoly in the process. Even the Communist Party, though, cannot get something for nothing: the centralized investments and regulations, plus a reluctance to suit rewards to performance, impeded the success of the Hungarian management reforms.

Finally, by the end of the 1960s, the Czechoslovak reformers attempted to move from the Soviet-model further than did any of the other East European reformers. They attempted to both install a market-directed economy and remove the party from its patronage and manipulations behind the scene. Their drive for a truly market-guided economy expressed less their unbounded confidence in market forces as such, than their implacable distrust of the party's capacity to keep its own interference in the economy under control. Early in the decisive year 1968, the anti-dogmatists, including the new party leader, Dubček himself, saw the crux of the matter in the 'very concept of [the party's] directing the society and the practical execution of this concept'. In the past, the party's interference had 'deprived . . . economic, and social institutions of a substantial part of the core of their activity and responsibility'.[35] The anti-dogmatist prescriptions – expanding the role of state, economic and social institutions; increasing the responsibility and the scope of action of managers at all levels; recognizing merit and competence, and truly keying rewards throughout the economy to the quantity and quality of the work done – implied a sharp curtailment of the party's functions and a reliance on the market to *an extent not yet seen in the socialist camp.*

The Czechoslovak notion of socialism with a human face and of a weakened partyarchy, must have struck the Soviet partyarchs as much more dangerous than any mere experimentation with market mechanisms. In any event, in August 1968 Soviet military power was used to substitute for it what the Austrian Marxist philosopher Ernst Fischer has aptly called '*Panzerkommunismus*' (Communism of the tanks) – a version of Communism which Stalin himself would have readily accepted as being truly his own.

35 Dubček's speech of Feb. 22, *loc. cit.*, and a speech at Kladno, *Rudé právo*, March 5, 1968.

5 Critical appraisals of the variants, and further searches

On the fleeting revivals of economic science

We have seen that the search for an economic model different from that of the USSR has led to the greater use of the market mechanism under socialism. The partisans of the market have argued their case from the standpoint of *economic rationality*. In contrast, the partisans of centralized administration and the primacy of the plan have argued their case on *political* grounds, using Marx's socio-economic categories and premises. They have viewed economic issues as being predominantly political and social in character, capable of solution through socio-political means with the help of some simple accounting devices and technical–engineering concepts. As a result, much of the discussion of the Soviet model both inside and outside the socialist camp has been conducted on two different logical planes. Furthermore, suggestions for improving that model have been misinterpreted, particularly outside the socialist camp, as implying shifts toward economic rationality or a Western-type economy, and as decisive departures from traditional Soviet principles of economic organization.

In this concluding chapter, I propose to show, first, that any revival of *economic science* (as economics is called in the East) can take place only at moments of deep political strain, will necessarily be short-lived, and will usually disappear without leaving any appreciable impact. Second, I propose to indicate the basis on which partisans of the Stalinist model continue to reject any systematic use of economic principles in investment allocation, pricing, and planning. Third, I intend to demonstrate how the partisans of market primacy argue that the Soviet model cannot be improved but must be discarded if the economy is to operate efficiently. Fourth and finally, I shall show that further searches for alternatives to the Soviet model will necessarily conflict with the basic Marxian prescriptions concerning the organization of a socialist society.

In normal times, polemics between partisans and adversaries of the Soviet model do not find their way into official Communist publications.

They surface only during deep socio-economic and political upheavals – e.g. following the death of Stalin in 1953 and his denunciation by Khrushchev in 1956, or the East European crises of the 1950s and 1960s. Economic science has a lowly position in socialist countries, strictly subordinated to party decisions. The economists are not the interpreters or analyzers of these decisions, but only their implementers and (occasionally) apologists.

With the triumph under Stalin of a completely monolithic party, exercising full control over the path of development, rules of operation, and organizational structure of the economy, Soviet economics lost the vitality and significance it had during the NEP, when opposite policies and solutions could be aired openly. Since 1929, economics textbooks and teaching have merely translated the policies defined by the party leaders into formal language and presented them as emerging scientifically from Marx's descriptions of the stages of economic history. It is this peculiar embodiment of Soviet Union national policy that has been passed on to the East Europeans as the economics of socialism.

During the thaw which followed Stalin's death, the East Europeans began to perceive the peculiarities of their own experiences. As their own opinions crystallized, many East European economists tried to redefine the scope of socialist economics. They started to question the key elements of Stalin's legacy and labored to find new approaches in a variety of fields, from planning and investment to the theory of the firm and foreign trade. Given the tendency of the socialist countries to insulate themselves from one another, the impact of these discussions varied substantially from country to country. They were felt, however, throughout the socialist camp – even as far away as China, as we shall see. Perhaps least affected by the winds of change was the Soviet Union itself. Soviet economics retained its Stalinist essentials, even though the Soviets eventually made some limited changes in organizational structures and economic instruments.

The East European critics of the Soviets' economics of socialism rebelled in particular against the confinement of economics to sheer apologetics – for example, the glorification of the Soviet methods of economic administration, the exaltation of Stalin's laws, platitudinous vulgarizations of Soviet (and their own governments') policies, and dogmatic and schematic repetitions of Marxist–Leninist theses. They objected further to reducing economists to mere incense-bearers for the policy makers, barred from direct access to economic data and prevented from carrying out any meaningful (let alone innovative) work. As the crises and upheavals erupted, many of the critics believed that they had finally succeeded in breaking through official resistance, and that a true rebirth of socialist economics was close at hand – if not throughout the entire bloc, at least in their own countries.

In June 1956 at the Second Congress of Polish Economists a large number of participants felt free to defy their dogmatists and to announce the rebirth of their discipline. They denounced the absence of theory in policy making and analysis, the poverty of economic writings, the carefully cultivated custom of quoting from Marx or from official pronouncements, the lack of access to economic data, and the servility of economics teachers. One of the younger Polish critics, Stefan Kurowski, condemned the prevailing economic science as 'court "science" hailing every act of economic policy'.[1] Summarizing the congress, Oskar Lange noted that the Congress had unanimously recognized that economics had indeed 'sunk to the depth of apologetics' and had become 'entangled in stagnating dogmatism and schematism'; henceforth, however, it was dialectically evident that the old distortions could be overcome and that a rebirth of Marxist economic thought would undoubtedly ensue.[2] Eventually, Lange himself cautiously defined this rebirth as encompassing the mathematization of economic investigations, the adoption of a new planning methodology, the use of more rational approaches to prices and resource allocation – in short, the evolving of a more 'systematic science of management of the socialist economy'.[3]

In the end, the renewal of socialist economics as a discipline, the disen-

---

1 As quoted in the offical report signed: H. Ch. and A. L., 'Dyskusja na II Zjeździe Ekonomistów Polskich' (Discussion at the Second Congress of Polish Economists), in *Ekonomista*, No. 5, 1956, p. 98.
2 'Końcowe przemówienie prof. Oskara Langego na II Zjeździe Ekonomistów Polskich w Warszawie' (Concluding Speech by Prof. Oskar Lange at the Second Congress of Polish Economists), *Ekonomista*, No. 5, 1956, pp. 145–9 *passim*.

    It is interesting to note that at the time, very similar points of view were propounded in China by a group of six economists headed by Professor Chen Chien-han of the University of Peking. Perhaps under the influence of Lange, the six affirmed in an article entitled 'Our Views of the Present Economic Work in China' (published in *Ching-chi yen-chiu* [*Economic Research*], No. 5, 1957), that the country's economic policies, blindly copied on those of the USSR, were applied in a 'subjectively confident mood' in defiance of economic principles and rules. The six recommended the end of the official self-satisfied dogmatism and experimentalism and the appropriate use of 'bourgeois economics after its being criticized and corrected'. The same issue of *Economic Research* contains a series of sharp rebuttals of this 'rightist-bourgeois clique' and of its 'fallacies'. The official economic orthodoxy was again questioned openly in 1961, after China's break with the USSR. But even then, the anti-orthodox ideas concerning prices and accounting, enterprise management and central planning, were summarily dismissed as anti-Marxist and the official Stalinist orthodoxy was strongly reaffirmed. See the documents translated in *The Short-Lived Liberal Phase in Economic Thinking in Communist China*, published in June 1963 by the Office of Research and Reports of the US Central Intelligence Agency, CIA/RR ER 63–14.
3 Oskar Lange, 'Nauka na zakręcie: Ekonomia' (Science at the Turning Point: Economics), *Przegląd Kulturalny*, No. 15, Warsaw, 1961.

tanglement of economics from apologetics and from dogmatism and schematism, never took place. The East European upheavals of the 1950s spurred a search for ways only to *improve*, not to *discard*, the prevailing system of centralized economic administration, more or less along lines suggested by Lange.[4] This was thought possible by borrowing, naturalizing and fitting to specific tasks the techniques and approaches recently developed in the Western decision sciences; it did *not* require calling into question the established Marxian premises on which the official science rested.

It is interesting to recall that the changes were hailed in the West as a clear shift in management, or at least as a drift toward economic rationality. As the harbingers of further moves toward market-socialism, the economic reforms were held to be the true beginnings of a new era in *both* Soviet economic concepts and Soviet-type economic administration. The limited introduction of input–output and linear-programming techniques into Soviet-type planning and project-making, along with the introduction of capital charges and changes in enterprises' performance criteria or *success indicators*, were taken as proof that (in Wassily Leontief's words) 'the Soviets are about to adopt . . . Western economic science'.[5] Leontief foresaw the rise of a new Soviet economic science from the depths of sterility to the heights of advanced scientific inquiry into the problems of the optimal allocation of resources.

Leontief's interpretation would imply that, by using some of the results of Western economics, Soviet and East European economists had adopted its premises, rationale, or corpus of knowledge, and in the process discarded their own premises and methods. In fact, they merely attempted – reluctantly and clumsily, as we shall see below – to weave into the fabric of their own economics certain threads from Western techniques. Predictably, the results in terms of enhanced economic efficiency were limited; indeed, it was the usefulness of precisely this kind of tinkering that the Czechoslovak critics boldly questioned and finally rejected in the 1960s.

The Czechoslovaks openly proclaimed their dissatisfaction with the fundamental, immutable characteristics of Soviet-type economic management: central party control of structure and aims; the rules of economic order and the alleged reflection of objective economic laws; the preference for command instruments; and the imposition of specific requirements on the enterprises. About the time the Russians proclaimed the introduction of a series of administrative improvements styled as a system of 'New Management', in 1968, the Czechoslovak reformers proclaimed that the

4 See above, Ch. 4.
5 Wassily Leontief, 'The Decline and Rise of Soviet Economic Science', *Foreign Affairs*, XXXVIII, Jan. 1960, p. 265.

Stalinist system was intrinsically immune to improvement. In the words of R. Selucky:

No economic theoretician alone can present a proposal for improving the entire system and for solving all the problems with which socialist economy is coping. He cannot do so especially under the present model of socialism and economic management. This would exceed his ability, it would be simply impossible. During the fifty years of the development of socialism, all possible forms and combinations have been tested, while the *quality of the model itself* has not changed.[6]

Eventually, as their own proposals gained a wider public audience, the Czechoslovak anti-dogmatists fell victim to the heady illusion that the rebirth of economics under socialism was in the making, that their economists were already leading the way, and that the immutable barriers of the past were actually crumbling. In a revealing review of several anti-dogmatist publications, Antonín Červinka wrote as follows:

Šik's work, *Problems of Socialist Commodity Relations,* undoubtedly has an eminent place in the creative development of the political economy of socialism and, together with a large number of articles, treatises and discussions, appears as a broader treatment of the subject which significantly contributes to the clarification of the theoretical foundations of the new management system. Thus theoretical economists march today, not *ex post,* but one step in front, showing their work, and thus they reap the first fruit of that life-giving direction in the development of economic theory, which starts from economic life and throws light on the road to its improvement. It is even possible to say that economic theory talks with so strong a voice to practice that it has started to din into the ears of some practical workers and has become disagreeably bothersome . . . I would not like to exaggerate but I think we are on the threshold of a rebirth of economic theory. Practical workers begin to appreciate the results of our work.[7]

The rebirth – like all those announced before it in the other socialist countries – was stillborn. The dogmatist theorists and practitioners waited out the storm, changed nothing in their basic framework, eventually regained the upper hand, and then carried on exactly as before. It is on the same old basis – administrative *à la* Lenin, voluntarist and dogmatic *à la* Stalin – that Soviet and East European officials continue to approach economic science, and that policy makers, planners and economists continue to reject the premises, rationale, and most of the findings of Western economics. Ultimately, all revivals of economics are but fleeting occurrences in the socialist camp. Inevitably, they suggest possibilities which

6 See in this connection the entire discussion 'Against Dogmatism, For a Creative Development of Economic Science', (held at the Prague Conference of Economists under the sponsorship of the editors of *Hospodářské noviny*), *Hospodářské noviny*, November 8, 1963, Vol. 7, No. 45, pp. 1, 6, and 7, and November 15, 1963, No. 46, pp. 6 and 7.
7 *Politická ekonomie,* No. 3, 1965.

conflict with the basic Soviet contention that a given, historically evolved alternative, the Soviet model, has been and remains the only one possible, the only scientifically selected and characteristic road to socialism.[8]

Objections to market-oriented deviations

The active, unrelenting opposition of all Communist leaderships, except in Yugoslavia, to the extensive use of market mechanisms – and *a fortiori* to the possible primacy of the market under socialism – has three principal sources. It expresses, first of all, a commitment to the traditional Marxist–Leninist vision of the transition to communism. It embodies, secondly, overt and covert interests in maintaining a central party role and its multiple functions in administering the state and managing the economy. It reflects, finally, deep-seated fears about the impact of market forces on production and demand, on overall resource utilization, and above all on the structure of society.

The Russians have long since mended fences with the Yugoslavs, and the Chinese have come to support the independence of Yugoslavia from the Soviet Union. Yet pride of place in the economic literature of practically the entire socialist bloc is held by rejections of deviations from the Soviet model, especially of the market-oriented variety. Relentless attacks against market socialism are viewed not only as part of the traditional Marxist–Leninist fight against reformism, but also as protection against any broader deviationism.

The arguments used in the fight against revisionism do not fit easily into an economic framework. They are an unlikely blend of doctrinaire assertions, politico-sociological contentions and economic propositions – a blend, moreover, which cannot be decanted into the separate categories since the ingredients intermingle with each other. We shall consider here only a subset of the arguments – those referring to what we have defined as the management structures, rules of operation, requirements on the enterprises, and determinants of the system's goals.

The management structure developed in the USSR is based on the postulate that the party controls the state, and the state in turn runs the economy *in the name* of the working class. Any tampering with that structure is an attack upon the dominant role of the latter. It is a reaction-

---

8 See András Hegedüs, 'Alternatives of Social Development', *Kortras*, June 1968, trans. by A. H. Whitney in *Studies in Comparative Communism*, Vol. 2, No. 2, April 1969, pp. 128ff. See also the all-out attack against all forms of market socialism developed in the collective work *Razvitoe sotsialisticheskoe obschchestvo: Sushchnost', kriterii zrelosti, kritika revizionistskikh kontseptsii* (The Developed Socialist Society: Essence, Criteria of Maturity, Critique of the Revisionist Conceptions), Moscow, Mysl', 1973, particularly pp. 372 and 373.

ary move that conflicts with the defense of socialism and with the scientific and technical revolution of our era. Finally, it is a deviation from Marx's own schema of historical change.

Yugoslav economists have argued that *de-etatization* – separating state from economic administration, limiting the partyarchy's economic functions, devolving various central powers upon operating economic units – is a means of decentralizing planning methods and controlling bureaucratization. For certain Chinese or Soviet critics of the Yugoslav deviation, however, de-etatization is incompatible with socialism, and hence must be summarily dismissed.[9] 'How can the working class as a whole be organized as a class, so that it can play its role in the construction of socialism on the basis of common, fundamental class interests', asks a Soviet critic, Yu. Georgiev, on the basis of 'nihilistic appraisals and anarchic attitudes toward the state' exhibited by those who want to 'artificially accelerate' the processes of the state's 'withering away?' Fragmentation and self-management, he adds, go against the need to strengthen the state in every conceivable way at a time when technological changes at the level of the economy as a whole require 'the regulatory levers of state rule'.[10]

The Yugoslavs argue that decentralization necessarily supersedes the totalitarian centralization characteristic of any Soviet-type regime. It emerges from a more democratic form of ownership – by collectives rather than by the state – and thus represents a decisive and necessary step in the process of de-bureaucratization. This is a false and misleading deviation, the critics respond: Soviet-type centralization is based on Lenin's concept of *democratic centralism* – the highest attainable democracy, embodying the workers' own desiderata translated by the party into decisions for action. 'Collective ownership' is nowhere to be found in Marx's discussions of ownership after socialization. Therefore the Yugoslavs are guilty of the grievous Marxian sin of attempting to work out a new 'periodization' of history. The Yugoslav system, the critics add, is not truly socialist, because the variations in size, endowment and incomes of the collectives confer different benefits on the members of different collectives. Finally, decisive steps toward de-bureaucratization are only possible after a long and complicated path of development, leading to high levels of culture and prosperity, which can be attained only far in the future.

9 See for instance the pamphlet edited by the Editorial Departments of *People's Daily* and *Red Flag, Is Yugoslavia a Socialist Country?*, Peking, Foreign Languages Publishing House, 1963. See also Yu. Georgiev, 'Yugoslavia: New Variant of Socialism?', *Kommunist*, No. 15, October 1968, trans. in the *Current Digest of the Soviet Press*, Jan. 15, 1969, pp. 3ff, and P. Kostin, 'State Rule and Self-Government under Socialism, On Some Erroneous Concepts of the Political and Legal Development of Socialist Society', *Sovetskoe gosudarstvo i pravo*, No. 2, 1969, trans. in the *Current Digest of the Soviet Press*, April 30, 1969, pp. 3ff.   10 Yu. Georgiev, 'Yugoslavia . . . ', *op. cit.* pp. 4 and *passim*.

Turning to the rules of operation of a socialist economy, it is here that economic considerations tend to outweigh doctrine, even if the economic considerations themselves must be placed in the usual Marxian frame of reference. To start with, Soviet and other critics of pro-market reformers reject the idea of relying permanently on markets, or on plan–market combinations, under socialism; they view market mechanisms as transitional by definition. A policy of perpetuating limited nationalization along the lines of the Soviet NEP is regarded as a retreat from socialization, a hybrid system which in time will lead to the rebirth of capitalism. Put differently, giving a permanent role to markets is equated with the re-emergence of the law of value as an economic regulator that encroaches on the true regulator of a socialist economy, the planning principle embodied in the socialist state itself.

The critical Soviet argument against market socialism, either in the Yugoslav version from 1951 on, or in the Czechoslovak version of 1968, is that it tends to replace the centrality of the state with centrality of collectives and communes (Yugoslavia) or of the enterprise (Czechoslovakia).[11] It does not matter that, in Šik's variant of market socialism, the state still owns the enterprise's means of production. What is crucial is that the enterprise manager, freed of the tutelage of the partyarchy, would be able to determine its own activities and plans: it would respond primarily to market signals, engage in competition, pay its taxes and fight for its own place in the sun. But this, the Soviet critics assert, posits a conflict between the state and the enterprise that does not exist. To adopt such a method of management would destroy the mutual support of state and enterprise, fragment the economy, lead to the closing down of non-competitive firms, generate unemployment, and cause the 'degeneration of the entire public sector'.[12] The Soviet critique unwittingly concedes, of course, that the form of ownership does not really matter. Rather, the fundamental issue is the framework within which the enterprise operates: how, by whom and for what purpose managerial functions are discharged.

Contentions of the partisans of market socialism that the market signals consumer preferences, which must be obeyed by producers in order to allocate resources efficiently, are dismissed out of hand by Soviet critics and their East European followers. According to these critics, such contentions 'contradict the elementary fact that the process of production always takes place in the interest of the owners of the means of production', and that accordingly the objective of capitalist production is maximal profit,

11 *Ibid.*, p. 5, and P. Kostin, 'State Rule . . . ', *loc. cit.*
12 See in the collection *Razvitoe . . . , op. cit.*, particularly the essay of the East German professor G. Nik, 'Kritika modeli rynochnogo sotsializma' (Critique of the Model of Market-Socialism), Ch. 16, pp. 376 and 377.

while that of socialism is the fulfillment of everyone's needs. In the name of higher efficiency, the critics continue, the adherents of market socialism attack the system of centralized planning under party guidance; but it is precisely such guidance that is 'the political, economic and material technological "spine" of the socialist order'.[13]

Following the crushing of the 'Prague Spring', the Soviet campaign against all variants of market socialism moved into high gear. Any and all market-oriented socialist models were denounced as warmed-over concoctions of revisionist theories.[14] The object of such models was to emasculate the revolutionary substance of Marxism–Leninism and to 'liquidate the Leninist principles of socialist construction which have universal significance and express all the laws of transition from capitalism to communism'.[15] Socialism with a human face was attacked as false humanism masking the class struggle and thus preparing for the annihilation of socialism. In short, as an East German critic put it, 'there is no socialist alternative whatever' to the system 'based on the classics of Marxism–Leninism and confirmed by the experience of the Soviet Union and of the other socialist countries'.[16] Clearly, to be acceptable to the directors of that system, changes must not endanger the partyarchy's centralized control over the combined administration of state and economy.

During crises, however, the partyarchy (along with the administrative and the managerial pyramid) can split wide open. According to András Hegedüs – the former Stalinist premier of Hungary who is now an avowed reformist – the anti-reform centralizers are usually central planners and managers of heavy industry, who would be affected adversely by decentralization and the freer play of market forces. The decentralizers are to be found among the leaders of state financial institutions, other branches of industry, and cooperatives, who would derive substantial advantages from the expansion of market forces.[17] Most workers, particularly in heavy industry, and the leaders of the trade unions, are distinctly unsympathetic toward intellectual schemes which, if implemented, could close

13 *Ibid.,* pp. 367–8 and 371.
14 This includes also those traceable to the old or new Western 'reformist' tendencies. See for instance F. Ia. Polianskii, *Sotsializm i sovremennyi reformism* (Socialism and Contemporary Reformism), Moscow, Moscow University Press, 1972 – which indeed places the fight against the 'reformist conception of market-socialism' in the context of the past and present ideologies of Western social-democratic currents. (See particularly, Ch. II, pp. 123ff.)
15 See in the collection *Razvitoe . . . , op. cit.,* the essay of professors R. Gavlichek and L. Grzal of Czechoslovakia, 'Revizionizm pod maskoi "Sotsializma s chelovecheskim litsom"' (Revisionism under the Mask of 'Socialism with a Human face'), Ch. 15, p. 347.
16 Essay of G. Nik in *Razvitoe . . . , op. cit.,* p. 373.
17 See 'Perché è in crisi l'economia dell'Est europeo' (Why is the East European economy in crisis), an interview with András Hegedüs, by Carlo Boffito, *Corriere della sera,* July 9, 1976.

down unproductive enterprises and create unemployment. (In 1968, the anti-Dubček forces in Czechoslovakia eventually capitalized on anti-intellectual, anti-reform feelings among workers.)

While operational managers and technicians would benefit from greater enterprise autonomy, they seem ambivalent about far-reaching reforms. They would not, of course, oppose reductions in the volume and scope of centralized instructions, the modernization of planning techniques, and other similar measures. But they may well oppose radical transformations of the undemanding environment to which they have become accustomed, and in which, after all, they have prospered. It would be understandable if they preferred to bargain with the planners within the safety of the bureaucracy rather than having to confront the risks of a market environment. What they would like – as a Czechoslovak economist told this author – is 'the market system's freedom with the administrative system's advantages'. Ideas of basic reform thus remain alien to large segments of socialist societies, while proposals for improving the prevailing mechanism still evoke sympathy, even though past experiences with improvements have proven ineffective.

The limits of improvement of centralized economic management

How have the directors of Soviet-type systems envisaged improvements? Which changes have been considered compatible or incompatible with the system, and why? To what extent have the compatible changes, when implemented, pushed these economies closer to a market-directed system? Finally, what criticisms have been levelled against these changes by would-be reformers of the Soviet-type system, in particular by advocates of the primacy of the market over the plan?

Every reform which has taken place in the 1960s in the Soviet Union and Eastern Europe (excluding Yugoslavia) under the generic name of New Economic Management (NEM) has emphasized improving the *methods of directing the economy*. In practice, this meant improving plan formulation and implementation, since the plan is viewed as the major instrument of centralized economic management in these economies. Changes in methods of direction did *not* involve fundamental alterations in the place and function of the partyarchy in guiding and controlling the economy. They did, however, involve re-evaluations, if not actual changes, of the *scope* of the plan and the *methods* of preparing and implementing it.

Only one country, Hungary, actually reduced the scope of central planning by delegating a significant role to enterprises in the preparation of their own production programs. The other countries which introduced the NEM, in contrast, focused on reducing both the number of central instructions contained in enterprise plans, and the amount of central monitoring of their implementation.[18] With respect to plan preparation, the number of product balances in the hard core of the plan was reduced. Moreover, the exchange of information between the center and the enterprises was simplified, and preliminary attempts, at least, were made to rationalize the price system. Within the streamlined structure, however, these countries continued to rely heavily on the traditional methods of setting up and adjusting each material and monetary balance, seeking in each case to achieve precise equivalence between available resources and planned allocations.

Extensive changes were also made in plan implementation. These changes have involved both the *instructions* issued by the central authorities concerning inputs, outputs, costs, financing, and marketing, and *monitoring* the carrying out of these instructions. Concomitantly, a variety of measures altered the distribution of authority between upper and lower managerial levels.

Everywhere, including the USSR, the plan coefficients imposed on the enterprises were significantly reduced in number, simplified, and better coordinated. The methods and instruments in monitoring performance were also trimmed and somewhat changed. Innovations were introduced in fiscal and credit controls: charges were assessed on enterprise assets; the role of credit in the financing of working capital was expanded; and new rules were devised for increasing the national interestedness of enterprises in the fulfillment of their plans and in the size of their bonuses. At the same time, the primary standard of performance (the enterprise's success indicator) was shifted from gross production to volume of sales. It was, however, only a symbolic change because the sales in question continued to be made just as in the past, to designated purchasers (who have no alternate suppliers) at fixed prices and at predetermined profit markups.

The issue of the possible limits to improving the existing methods of economic direction was extensively examined and criticized in the various socialist countries as the above measures were being discussed and implemented. To understand the critics' objections, one should recall the basic assumptions of Soviet-type economic administration: that harmonious, proportionate economic development can be achieved only through detailed centralized planning using a set of material balances; and that the operational tasks implied by these balances can be translated into precise tasks having the force of law. It is these basic assumptions that the partisans of the primacy of the market have continually questioned. Ota

18 For a very detailed, country by country survey, see: Hans Hermann Höhmann, Michael C. Kaser, Karl C. Talheim (eds.), *The New Economic Systems of Eastern Europe*, London, C. Hurst & Co., 1975.

Šik, in particular, pointed out that all the centralized directives and norms can do is to determine the *quantitative* aspects of production: total output, numbers of workers, output per worker, and so forth; they *cannot*, however, determine the *qualitative* aspects of production: what specific commodities to produce; how to produce them; how to introduce new products, new techniques, or specialization in production; how to change manpower skills; and so on.[19] The critics argued not only that the policy makers and planners could not achieve proportionate economic development, but also that, inevitably, a series of distortions were bound to arise both inside and outside the framework of balances and norms, and the indicators and surveillance devices based on them.

The critics conceded that the introduction of input–output and other mathematical models into plan formulation can give policy makers and planners a clearer view than before of inter-relations between economic goals, instruments, and economic structures. But these methods are of little help, in their view, in carrying out the concrete managerial–administrative tasks implicit in a central directive plan.[20] Among the many drawbacks of input–output analysis, the worst are the linearity of the assumed relations, the complexity encountered in expanding the tableau beyond several hundred sectors, and the quality of the technical coefficients. Mathematical models do not allow for the conflicts which arise in hierarchical systems between the preferences of the center, superimposed on lower managerial levels, and the perception of the specific tasks to be performed by the executants at these levels.[21] Furthermore, like the traditional balance system, the mathematical models are static; rendering them dynamic raises complex and as yet unresolved technical questions. Finally, and above all, with or without input–output techniques, Soviet type planning remains centered on the requirements of *production* as a function of investment–military targets and interindustry requirements; *consumption* and *foreign trade* are treated as a kind of residual.

The scope and effectiveness of information processing can undoubtedly be increased by simplifying information flows within the economic and managerial administration, and by creating an integrated, perhaps computerized, system of record-keeping, accounting and communication. But

19 Ota Šik, 'Problems of the New System of Planned Management', *op. cit.*, p. 12.
20 See for instance Vladimir Strnad, Zdeněk Tlustý, 'K současnym možnostem použití matematických modelů ekonomického růstu v plánování' (Contemporary Possibilities of Using Mathematical Models of Economic Growth in Planning) *Politická ekonomie*, xv, No. 9, 1967, pp. 801–6. All this echoes some very familiar discussions in the West. See T. C. Koopmans, *Three Essays on the State of Economic Science*, McGraw-Hill, New York, 1957, pp. 189ff.
21 For a critical review of the models that explicitly reflect organization structure, see Timothy W. Ruefli, 'Analytic Models of Resource Allocation in Hierarchical Multi-level Systems', *Socio-Economic Planning Sciences*, Vol. 8, 1974, pp. 353–63.

computers cannot replace the market, which is a continuous process incessantly generating new information and reshuffling it in unexpected ways. Prices are rationalized under NEM not via market impulses – except to a limited extent in Hungary – but via bureaucratic rules defined according to Marxian concepts. The bureaucratic prices are certainly more sophisticated now than before; as I have pointed out, they now include material and labor costs, overhead costs, depreciation, interest on fixed and working capital, and profits related to total outlays. But these prices do not reflect how and why goods are exchanged in either production or trade, and thus do not contribute to the harmony of supply and demand. They do not influence production to respond to trends in social needs – quite the contrary. On the one hand they encourage wasteful investment and the expansion of the budgets for capital investment, since such use of more capital increases the accounting measure of gross production on which a number of important indicators, viz. the productivity of labor, and therefore wages and premia are based. On the other hand, they continuously accentuate discrepancies between the purchasing power created, the consumer goods produced, and the consumer goods sought after by the consumers. Since producers are, to a considerable degree, given incentives to engage in productive activities that run counter to demand, perpetual shortages and an attendant parallel (or second) economy operating through black markets have become the hallmarks of the Soviet-type economies.[22]

In these conditions, the critics are understandably skeptical that anything less than a marked shift away from direct centralized appropriations and grants can have a measurable, positive impact. Under the NEM, accounting and effectiveness remain tied to defective prices, the administrative distribution of products, the rigid monitoring of capacity expansion and technological innovations, and perverse incentives on input use and output assortment. Furthermore, wages are linked not to production and sales satisfying consumer demands, but to state regulations. While many reformers do not oppose the regulation of wages or of enterprise incentives funds, they do advocate that the incomes earned be spent on goods the consumers prefer.[23]

In spite of claims about the scientific nature of Marxian socialism, the various reorganizations of economic administration undertaken in the Soviet bloc have often been more the outcome of subjective ideas about organization than the result of objective analysis of the best framework for enhancing enterprise performance. The Soviet administrative structure

22 Ota Šik, 'Problems of the New System of Planned Management', *op. cit.*, pp. 18–19.
23 Šik, *loc. cit.* and Zdìyslav Šulc, 'Creative Development of Marxist Economic Thinking', *World Marxist Review*, June 1965, p. 38.

has fluctuated from organization along ministerial lines (typical under Stalin) to regional organizations (typical under Khrushchev), and back again to ministerial centralization. A major cause of the fluctuations are the strong, at times almost irresistible, tendencies toward autonomy and self-sufficiency, whether within ministries or regions. Partitioning and repartitioning centralized structures do not lead to decentralization down to the enterprise level. Where autonomy has been given to large enterprises, as in Hungary, the enterprises continue to occupy monopoly positions in their branches, just as they did under the tutelage of a ministry or regional administration. Such changes do not encourage specialization and cooperation among enterprises, nor do they improve central accounting for resources used and results obtained.

No matter how much the methods of direction in a centralized planning system may be modernized or simplified, the system remains extremely complicated and cumbersome. This being so, either many economic activities are bound to occur independently of the system – generating black or gray markets – or the planners must attempt to change their plans to take account of unceasing disproportions and disturbances. But the planning machinery is so complex, and its adjustment so laborious and time-consuming that when plan changes are finally effected the real conditions may call for a *different* centralized response.

Old assumptions and new options

The basic Marxian prescriptions for the socialist organization of society and the economy have been implemented in practice by the Bolsheviks. The owners of the means of production have been expropriated in the USSR and in the other socialist countries. The social and economic control structures have been highly centralized. Directive planning has displaced market mechanisms. Interrelations between the components of the economy and the rules of the economic order have been transformed. Finally, social and economic objectives have been set by the directors of the system in accordance with what they claim to be the long-run interests of the working class.

It is well known that the socialization carried out in the USSR and Eastern Europe (with the exception of East Germany and Czechoslovakia) unfolded in *backward,* less developed societies, not in the advanced capitalist surroundings Marx forecast. Socialization did not immediately penetrate the countryside and did not permanently modify it, although (except for Yugoslavia and Poland) the peasantry was forced into cooperatives and most land was consolidated into large agricultural units. The commanding heights of the economy – the modern sectors of industry, banking, transport, and communication – were, however, rapidly occupied by socialism, and have since been run, for all practical purposes, as a single, state-owned enterprise.

Further, while the former state power was indeed shattered and new structures involving workers' councils (Soviets) erected in its place – as Marx said they would be – the workers did not as a result achieve the self government of the producers they were supposed to. The blame for this may be placed (in the USSR) on the backwardness of Russia or (in Eastern Europe) on Soviet armed interventions. Whatever the origins of state-directed socialism, instead of a government of direct producers, the positions of command in the Soviet bloc are held by a vast and sprawling bureaucracy. This bureaucracy has emerged not only from the Communist party but from the Soviets themselves. Pious claims that the socialist bureaucracy is merely a transient phenomenon, and will eventually wither away, can be dismissed as self-serving blather.

Central planning (based on massive socialization) was established on a statewide scale in every socialist country, and capital and manpower were reallocated to production needs rather than 'values' – as Marx and Engels said they would be. But confounding Marx and Engels, these measures did not bring about higher productivity than under capitalism or uninterrupted growth, or the overthrow of the law of value. Indeed, the law of value continued to operate not only openly and unashamedly at the periphery of the state complex, but also unexpectedly, pervasively, and embarrassingly, within this complex itself. Planning could have taken many other forms, including combinations with market mechanisms. But the Soviets and their East European satellites followed Marx and Engels themselves quite literally: under socialism, 'plan-conforming, conscious organization' would definitely supplant the market, and the economic laws of capitalism would then necessarily die out.

The Communist parties which assumed control of both the state and the economy – in accordance with Lenin's particular interpretation of Marx – claimed to express the long-term interests of the workers. It must be pointed out, however, that in a classless (one-class) society, in which most if not all of the means of production are jointly owned, it would matter little *who* actually formulated the operational objectives and tasks of the society. By definition, all preferences would be identical with respect to all the possible choices confronting the community. In actual fact, it matters very much to Soviet and East European Communists that *they* determine the objectives and tasks of the society. Some Communists continue devoutly to uphold the validity of the mechanism devised by Stalin, but blame the poor results on Stalin's *modus operandi*. Another group, particularly outside the USSR, places the blame on Russian backwardness, its Asian

traditions and Mongolian habits. Still others, within and outside the
socialist camp, have begun to question the validity of the premises themselves.

The attempts in Eastern Europe to devise new management structures,
to limit the scope of nationalization, to reappraise the scope and character
of the central plan, to recognize conflicts of interest in socialist societies
have all implied re-evaluations and reconsiderations of the underlying
Marxian assumptions. The searches for new roads to socialism have thus
entailed not only defiance of Soviet theories alleging the unique scientific
character of Soviet policies and institutions, but also direct challenges to
the Marxian premises on which these theories are based. The efforts to
probe those premises have been thwarted in Eastern Europe by the vested
interests which the system itself generates, and by the actual or imminent
intervention of Soviet troops. But if the implications of the clashes over
organizational alternatives have been suppressed in Eastern Europe, fer-
ment has continued in Communist parties outside direct Soviet control
and not yet burdened by having to manage Soviet-type societies.

The leaders of the Italian and Spanish Communist parties, for instance,
apparently are also searching for alternative routes to socialist development. The East European experiences suggest that their options can be
increased only by relaxing the Marxian assumptions about management,
the scope and impact of socialization, the nature and role of the plan, and
the ways in which social and economic objectives are determined. Only by
understanding that the economic failures of the Soviet-type economies
stem not from their *overlooking* the postulates of Marx and Engels but
from the *faithful* implementation of those postulates, can new organizational alternatives and options emerge.

The Soviet doctrinaires are probably right that the revisionist rethinking
of what a socialist society can or should be, which first developed in
Eastern Europe and which now extends outside the Soviet orbit, is essentially similar to the so-called traditional revisionism which had developed
in the European Social Democratic parties before World War I. There is
indeed a significant correspondence between the ideas of the Communist
partisans of change in Eastern Europe and the ideas propounded by Social
Democrat thinkers such as Karl Kautsky, Otto Bauer, Friedrich Adler – all
of whom Lenin reviled. Revisionism towards Marxian fundamentals is
equivalent to heresy in the Leninist catechism. Yet, ironically, it appears
today as the only possible way to achieve more workable, more efficient
institutions under socialism.

SELECTED ESSAYS

I   Bureaucracy and the economy

Introductory note

Bureaucracy in the state administration, in the military and in industry, is anathema to the Marxists. In the Marxist–Leninist conception, the capitalist society is both supported and controlled by a bureaucratic–military apparatus, which upholds the dominance of capital over the workers. Marx sees this apparatus as a parasite and recommends that it be destroyed by a workers' revolution. After the revolution he suggests that this apparatus would be replaced by organization of the workers as the ruling class. An important feature of the Marxist reorganization of the society is that the workers in arms hire specialized state officials, managers, technicians or engineers as the need may be and pay them workers' wages. True democracy would thus ensue because the majority is assumed to be in control. The entire population is seen as being eventually involved in the administration and management of the state and the economy. (See below the excerpts from Lenin's study of the state.)

Unexpectedly, an immense bureaucracy arose in the USSR as well as in the other socialist countries combining everywhere the apparatus of the Communist party, the state administration (emerging from the Soviets) and the managerial hierarchy. This development eventually prompted the Yugoslav leaders to try to debureaucratize their economy and to democratize their own regime after their break with the Russians. Perhaps on the suggestion of Milovan Djilas (who was later labelled a heretic) the Yugoslav leaders decided to achieve this democratization through a sharp reduction of the *economic functions* of the state. (See below, J. B. Tito's Report of April 1960.) Accordingly, each Yugoslav collective of employees of an industrial enterprise (or of any other state-owned enterprise) was invited to assume directly the functions of management. A series of other measures, such as reduction in the scope of central planning, increased reliance on indirect rather than on direct economic instruments, the freeing of the market forces with respect to prices and interfirm transactions, etc., aimed to strengthen and support the basic effort of overall debureaucratization.

Within a decade after the launching of the reform, however, a disagreement developed between official claims and the assessment of some Yugoslav academics as to what the experiment actually indicated. According to the official claims, the reform had successfully replaced the Soviet-type bureaucratic *statist* mechanism with a system in which management was developing as a social service and as the 'collective organizer of the working man at his place of work and in his free creative endeavour'. Within this framework, the interests of the technical experts and of the unskilled workers were alleged to be interacting *non-antagonistically* thanks to the distribution of income according to work. (See E. Kardelj's paper.) According to the academics, the collectives were actually unable to exercise any meaningful control over the technical and professional decisions of the technical managerial staff. Therefore, the collectives were advised to concentrate their attention primarily on programmes and requirements regarding income earning – i.e. on output programs and on income distribution – rather than on technical entrepreneurial issues. (See D. Bilandžić's essay.)

In addition, one may note that within each large-scale plant, within the state administration, and within the economy, the collectives are never able to exercise power directly, but only through delegation. The delegates are usually selected precisely from among the technicians and from the skilled workers (not from the unskilled) and tend to be fairly independent of their mandators. Thus, what proved impossible with Lenin's recommendations on the scale of the socialist economy – viz. reversion to primitive democracy – proves equally impossible with Tito's recommendations on the scale of each and every collectively-controlled enterprise.

The pre-revolution program of smashing the old bureaucracy and of abolishing it altogether, as well as efforts to revert to primitive democracy, are unable to suppress the *functions* of (and therefore the need for) specialized bureaucratic–expert–technical staff. The Soviets have indeed erected an immense, interlocking state and economic administration under party control. But the main challenge to this system, the Yugoslav-type self-management has also failed either to organize the unskilled workers into the ruling administrative–managerial strata, or to rid the socialist economy of bureaucracy and bureaucratic–technical leadership.

V. I. LENIN

Reversion to primitive democracy*

... The only 'correction' Marx thought it necessary to make to the *Communist Manifesto* he made on the basis of the revolutionary experience of the Paris Communards.

The last preface to the new German edition of the *Communist Manifesto* signed by both its authors, is dated June 24, 1872. In this preface the authors, Karl Marx and Frederick Engels, say that the program of the *Communist Manifesto* 'has in some details become out-of-date', and they go on to say:

'... One thing especially was proved by the Commune, viz., that "the working class cannot simply lay hold of the ready-made state machinery and wield it for its own purposes" ...'

The authors took the words that are in double quotation marks in this passage from Marx's book, *The Civil War in France*.

Thus, Marx and Engels regarded one principal and fundamental lesson of the Paris Commune as being of such enormous importance that they introduced it as an important correction into the *Communist Manifesto*.

Most characteristically, it is this important correction that has been distorted by the opportunists, and its meaning probably is not known to nine-tenths, if not ninety-nine-hundredths, of the readers of the *Communist Manifesto*. We shall deal with this distortion more fully farther on, in a chapter devoted specially to distortions. Here it will be sufficient to note that the current, vulgar 'interpretation' of Marx's famous statement just quoted is that Marx here allegedly emphasizes the idea of slow development in contradistinction to the seizure of power, and so on.

As a matter of fact, *the exact opposite is the case*. Marx's idea is that the working class must break up, smash the 'ready-made state machinery', and not confine itself merely to laying hold of it.

On April 12, 1871, i.e., just at the time of the Commune, Marx wrote to Kugelmann:

If you look up the last chapter of my *Eighteenth Brumaire*, you will find that I declare that the next attempt of the French Revolution will be no longer, as before, to transfer the bureaucratic–military machine from one hand to another, but to *smash* it (Marx's italics – the original is *zerbrechen*), and this is the precondition for every real people's revolution on the Continent. And this is what our heroic Party comrades in Paris are attempting (*Neue Zeit*, Vol. xx, 1, 1901–02, p. 709).

* Excerpts from Lenin's 'The State and Revolution', *Collected Works*, June–September 1917, Vol. 25, Moscow, Progress Publishers, 1964, pp. 414–21; 425–7.

The words, 'to smash the bureaucratic–military machine', briefly express the principal lesson of Marxism regarding the tasks of the proletariat during a revolution in relation to the state. And it is this lesson that has been not only completely ignored but positively distorted by the prevailing, Kautskyite, 'interpretation' of Marxism! . . .

Secondly, particular attention should be paid to Marx's extremely profound remark that the destruction of the bureaucratic–military state machine is 'the precondition for every real *people's* revolution'.

. . . In Europe, in 1871, the proletariat did not constitute the majority of the people in any country on the Continent. A 'people's' revolution, one actually sweeping the majority into its stream, could be such only if it embraced both the proletariat and the peasants. These two classes then constituted the 'people'. These two classes are united by the fact that the 'bureaucratic–military state machine' oppresses, crushes, exploits them. To *smash* this machine, *to break it up,* is truly in the interest of the 'people', of their majority, of the workers and most of the peasants, is 'the precondition' for a free alliance of the poor peasants and the proletarians, whereas without such an alliance democracy is unstable and socialist transformation is impossible. . . .

What is to replace the smashed state machine?

In 1847, in the *Communist Manifesto* Marx's answer to this question was as yet a purely abstract one; to be exact, it was an answer that indicated the tasks, but not the ways of accomplishing them. The answer given in the *Communist Manifesto* was that this machine was to be replaced by 'the proletariat organised as the ruling class', by the 'winning of the battle of democracy'.

Marx did not indulge in utopias; he expected the *experience* of the mass movement to provide the reply to the question as to the specific forms this organization of the proletariat as the ruling class would assume and as to the exact manner in which this organization would be combined with the most complete, most consistent 'winning of the battle of democracy'.

Marx subjected the experience of the Commune, meagre as it was, to the most careful analysis in *The Civil War in France.* Let us quote the most important passages of this work.

Originating from the Middle Ages, there developed in the nineteenth century 'the centralised state power, with its ubiquitous organs of standing army, police, bureaucracy, clergy, and judicature'. With the development of class antagonisms between capital and labour, 'state power assumed more and more the character of a public force for the suppression of the working class, of a machine of class rule. After every revolution which marks an advance in the class struggle, the purely coercive character of the state power stands out in bolder and bolder relief.' After the revolution of 1848–49, state power became 'the national war instrument of capital against labour'. The Second Empire consolidated this.

'The direct antithesis to the empire was the Commune.' It was the 'specific form' of 'a republic that was not only to remove the monarchical form of class rule, but class rule itself . . . '

What was this 'specific' form of the proletarian, socialist republic? What was the state it began to create?

. . . The first decree of the Commune . . . was the suppression of the standing army, and its replacement by the armed people . . .

This demand now figures in the program of every party calling itself socialist. The real worth of their programs, however, is best shown by the behavior of our Socialist-Revolutionaries and Mensheviks, who, right after the revolution of February 27, 1917, actually refused to carry out this demand!

The Commune was formed of the municipal councillors, chosen by universal suffrage in the various wards of Paris, responsible and revocable at any time. The majority of its members were naturally working men, or acknowledged representatives of the working class . . . The police, which until then had been the instrument of the Government, was at once stripped of its political attributes, and turned into the responsible and at all times revocable instrument of the Commune. So were the officials of all other branches of the administration. From the members of the Commune downwards, public service had to be done at workmen's wages. The privileges and the representation allowances of the high dignitaries of state disappeared along with the dignitaries themselves . . . Having once got rid of the standing army and the police, the instruments of the physical force of the old Government, the Commune proceeded at once to break the instrument of spiritual suppression the power of the priests . . . The judicial functionaries lost that sham independence . . . they were thenceforward to be elective, responsible, and revocable . . . '

The Commune, therefore, appears to have replaced the smashed state machine 'only' by fuller democracy: abolition of the standing army; all officials to be elected and subject to recall. But as a matter of fact this 'only' signifies a gigantic replacement of certain institutions by other institutions of a fundamentally different type. This is exactly a case of 'quantity being transformed into quality': democracy, introduced as fully and consistently as is at all conceivable, is transformed from bourgeois into proletarian democracy; from the state (= a special force for the suppression of a particular class) into something which is no longer the state proper.

It is still necessary to suppress the bourgeoisie and crush their resistance. This was particularly necessary for the Commune; and one of the reasons for its defeat was that it did not do this with sufficient determination. The organ of suppression, however, is here the majority of the population, and not a minority, as was always the case under slavery, serfdom and wage slavery. And since the majority of the people *itself* suppresses its oppressors, a 'special force' for suppression *is no longer necessary*! In this sense, the state *begins to wither away*. Instead of the special institutions of a privileged minority (privileged officialdom, the chiefs of the standing army), the majority itself can directly fulfil all these functions, and the more the functions of state power are performed by the people as a whole, the less need there is for the existence of this power.

In this connection, the following measures of the Commune, emphasized by Marx, are particularly noteworthy: the abolition of all representation allowances, and of all monetary privileges to officials, the reduction of the remuneration of *all* servants of the state to the level of *'workmen's wages'*. This shows more clearly than anything else the *turn* from bourgeois to proletarian democracy, from the democracy of the oppressors to that of the oppressed classes, from the state as a *'special force'* for the suppression of a particular class to the suppression of the oppressors by the *general force* of the majority of the people – the workers and the peasants. And it is on this particularly striking point, perhaps the most important as far as the problem of the state is concerned, that the ideas of Marx have been most completely ignored! In popular commentaries, the number of which is legion, this is not mentioned. The thing done is to keep silent about it as if it were a piece of old-fashioned 'naïveté', just as Christians, after their religion had been given the status of a state religion 'forgot' the 'naïveté' of primitive Christianity with its democratic revolutionary spirit.

The reduction of the remuneration of high state officials seems to be 'simply' a demand of naïve, primitive democracy. One of the 'founders' of modern opportunism, the ex-Social-Democrat Eduard Bernstein, has more than once repeated the vulgar bourgeois jeers at 'primitive' democracy. Like all opportunists, and like the present Kautskyites, he did not understand at all that, first of all, the transition from capitalism to socialism is *impossible* without a certain 'reversion' to 'primitive' democracy (for how else can the majority, and then the whole population without exception, proceed to discharge state functions?); and that, secondly, 'primitive democracy' based on capitalism and capitalist culture is not the same as primitive democracy in prehistoric or pre-capitalist times. Capitalist culture has *created* large-scale production, factories, railways, the postal service, telephones, etc., and *on this basis* the great majority of the functions of the old 'state power' have become so simplified and can be reduced to such exceedingly simple operations of registration, filing and checking that they can be easily performed by every literate person, can quite easily be performed for ordinary 'workmen's wages', and that these functions can (and must) be stripped of every shadow of privilege, of every semblance of 'official grandeur'.

All officials, without exception, elected and subject to recall *at any time*, their salaries reduced to the level of ordinary 'workmen's wages' – these simple and 'self-evident' democratic measures, while completely uniting the interests of the workers and the majority of the peasants, at the same time serve as a bridge leading from capitalism to socialism. These measures concern the reorganization of the state, the purely political reorganization of society; but, of course, they acquire their full meaning and significance only in connection with the 'expropriation of the expropriators' either being accomplished or in preparation, i.e., with the transformation of capitalist private ownership of the means of production into social ownership.

'The Commune,' Marx wrote, 'made that catchword of all bourgeois revolutions, cheap government, a reality by abolishing the two greatest sources of expenditure – the army and the officialdom.'

From the peasants, as from other sections of the petty bourgeoisie, only an insignificant few 'rise to the top', 'get on in the world' in the bourgeois sense, i.e., become either well to do, bourgeois, or officials in secure and privileged positions. In every capitalist country where there are peasants (as there are in most capitalist countries), the vast majority of them are oppressed by the government and long for its overthrow, long for 'cheap' government. This can be achieved *only* by the proletariat; and by achieving it, the proletariat at the same time takes a step towards the socialist reorganization of the state.

. . . There is no trace of utopianism in Marx, in the sense that he made up or invented a 'new' society. No, he studied the *birth* of the new society *out of* the old, and the forms of transition from the latter to the former, as a natural–historical process. He examined the actual experience of a mass of proletarian movements and tried to draw practical lessons from it. He 'learned' from the Commune, just as all the great revolutionary thinkers learned unhesitatingly from the experience of great movements of the oppressed classes, and never addressed them with pedantic 'homilies' (such as Plekhanov's: 'They should not have taken up arms' or Tsereteli's: 'A class must limit itself').

Abolishing the bureaucracy at once, everywhere and completely, is out of the question. It is a utopia. But to *smash* the old bureaucratic machine at once and to begin immediately to construct a new one that will make possible the gradual abolition of all bureaucracy – this is *not* a utopia, it is the experience of the Commune, the direct and immediate task of the revolutionary proletariat.

Capitalism simplifies the functions of 'state' administrations; it makes it possible to cast 'bossing' aside and to confine the whole matter to the organization of the proletarians (as the ruling class), which will hire 'workers, foremen and accountants' in the name of the whole of society.

We are not utopians, we do not 'dream' of dispensing *at once* with all administration, with all subordination. These anarchist dreams, based upon incomprehension of the tasks of the proletarian dictatorship, are totally alien to Marxism, and, as a matter of fact, serve only to postpone the socialist revolution until people are different. No, we want the socialist revolution with people as they are now, with people who cannot dispense with subordination, control and 'foremen and accountants'.

The subordination, however, must be to the armed vanguard of all the exploited and working people, i.e., to the proletariat. A beginning can and must be made at once, overnight, to replace the specific 'bossing' of state officials by the simple functions of 'foremen and accountants', functions which are already fully within the ability of the average town dweller and can well be performed for 'workmen's wages'.

We, the workers, shall organize large-scale production on the basis of what capitalism has already created, relying on our own experience as workers, establishing strict, iron discipline backed up by the state power of the armed workers. We shall reduce the role of state officials to that of simply carrying out our instructions as responsible, revocable, modestly paid 'foremen and accountants' (of course, with the aid of technicians of all sorts, types and degrees). This is *our* proletarian task, this is what we can and *must* start with in accomplishing the proletarian revolution. Such a beginning, on the basis of large-scale production, will of itself lead to the gradual 'withering away' of all bureaucracy, to the gradual creation of an order – an order without inverted commas, an order bearing no similarity to wage slavery – an order under which the functions of control and accounting, becoming more and more simple, will be performed by each in turn, will then become a habit and will finally die out as the *special* functions of a special section of the population.

A witty German Social-Democrat of the seventies of the last century called the *postal service* an example of the socialist economic system. This is very true. At present the postal service is a business organized on the lines of state-*capitalist* monopoly. Imperialism is gradually transforming all trusts into organizations of a similar type, in which, standing over the 'common' people, who are over-worked and starved, one has the same bourgeois bureaucracy. But the mechanism of social management is here already to hand. Once we have overthrown the capitalists, crushed the resistance of these exploiters with the iron hand of the armed workers, and smashed the bureaucratic machine of the modern state, we shall have a splendidly equipped mechanism, freed from the 'parasite', a mechanism which can very well be set going by the united workers themselves, who will hire technicians, foremen and accountants, and pay them *all*, as indeed *all* 'state' officials in general, workmen's wages. Here is a concrete, practical task which can immediately be fulfilled in relation to all trusts, a task whose fulfilment will rid the working people of exploitation, a task which takes account of what the Commune had already begun to practise (particularly in building up the state).

To organize the *whole* economy on the lines of the postal service so that the technicians, foremen and accountants, as well as *all* officials, shall receive salaries no higher than 'a workman's wage', all under the control and leadership of the armed proletariat – this is our immediate aim. This is the state and this is the economic foundation we need. This is what will bring about the abolition of parliamentarism and the preservation of representative institutions. This is what will rid the laboring classes of the bourgeoisie's prostitution of these institutions.

J. B. TITO

On workers' management in economic enterprises*

The National Assembly has now before it a draft Law which is one of the most important acts of socialist Yugoslavia. This is the Bill of a Basic Law concerning the Management of National Enterprises and Principal Productive associations by the workers engaged in them. The passing of this Law will be the most important act of the National Assembly after the passing of the Law for the Nationalization of the Means of Production. That workers' watchword 'The factories to the workers' was not achieved by mere nationalization of the means of production, for that watchword, or the watchword 'The land to the peasants' were not abstract propaganda phrases, but contained a profound purpose. This watchword contains itself the whole program of a socialist relationship in production, regarding national property, regarding the rights and duties of the workers – and so it must be made a reality, if we really mean to achieve socialism . . .

Our workers have already been able to see for themselves that the people's regime in our country has full confidence in them. On the other hand, our workers are in their daily work showing themselves ready to master even the greatest of difficulties. So are we going to say that the

* Excerpts from 'O radničkom upravljanju u privrednim preduzećima', speech of June 26, 1950 at the special session of the Yugoslav National Assembly, in J. B. Tito: *Govori i članci*, (Vol. v, November 18, 1950–November, 9, 1951, pp. 205–35) Zagreb, Naprijed, 1959.

workers who make such efforts, and with such elan and self-sacrifice make every effort to produce the maximum, who with such drive build new factories, new public buildings, new railways, and so forth, who reveal their deep attachment to the factories they have built, who by countless improvements of machinery do all they can to perfect our means of production – are we going to say that such men and women are not capable also of managing their factories? Of course they are, they are capable of managing them – and the new hands now entering factory, mine and other enterprises will learn all that from their comrades.

There may be some who think that this Law will be premature, that the workers will not be capable of mastering the complicated technique of managing factories and other enterprises. Whoever thinks that, is mistaken, and such a view of the matter would amount to lack of confidence in our workers, would amount to a failure to grasp what tremendous creative forces that management of our enterprises will develop in our workers, for this Law is going to open up for our workers still greater future prospects for themselves and for our whole community.

So, not only is this not premature, it is even a measure that is a little late, and the reasons for that lateness are to be found in the fact that our Party, prior to the notorious Cominform Resolution [ostracizing Yugoslavia] cultivated too many illusions and accepted and tried to transplant in our country with too little criticism, what was being done and the way it was being done, in the Soviet Union, even things not in harmony with our own specific conditions, or in the spirit of the teachings of Marxism–Leninism. There was a certain wish for ready-made formulae, which were pressed on us, where we ourselves did not aspire after them; there was a tendency to follow the line of least resistance.

But today we are building up socialism in our own country without the use of any ready-made forms, guided solely by the science of Marxism, and we are following our own road, taking account of the specific conditions which exist in our own country . . . At a late hour we took steps to put a stop to that way of doing things, in every field, and that is why with every day we achieve greater successes in our work of construction. Marx, Engels and Lenin contain mainly answers to questions of basic principle. The elaboration and application of those principles in any country can be accomplished only by those who have grown out of the bosom of that country, who know its problems inside-out, who know its history, its customs, its weaknesses and its strong points, who are in a position to follow every development closely, on the spot, but who at the same time are instructed in the Marxist approach, that is to say, have grasped the spirit of Marxism and are able to apply it in reality . . .

As I said earlier the Law which we are to adopt here is of great importance for the future correct development of our socialist country, but, it still does not settle this question completely; it is merely another step forward towards communism. The functions of the State in the administration of the economy have not yet completely ceased, but they are no longer exclusive. They are diminishing as the result of workers being drawn into management. The workers are beginning to take up their right as producers to manage production, but gradually, not all at once. Why is this happening gradually, and not all at once? Will this take a long time, and if so how long? One cannot tell how long this will take, because it depends on various circumstances. It depends on the speed of cultural development, that is, the all-round training of the workers to make them capable of carrying out the management of factories, mines, transport, etc. efficiently and for the benefit of the community, because otherwise the workers will not be able to exercise supervision and control. Without a rise in their educational standards workers will not be able to acquire complete mastery over the techniques of management. And that, again, depends on the speed of development of the productive forces, etc. . . .

. . . According to Lenin, it can be seen that bureaucracy flourishes particularly where there is a greater degree of backwardness. These words make it quite plain where we must seek the roots of bureaucracy. Does not this show that bureaucracy flourishes precisely where people are not aware of their right to control, and to wage a decisive struggle against every bureaucratic procedure, where people are not yet aware that the presence of bureaucracy is detrimental to socialism, and it cannot be extirpated merely by decrees from above, but every conscious individual should fight against it in his everyday life. It should not be imagined that bureaucracy can only prevail in the higher institutions and that it is more difficult for it to prevail on a lower level. No, bureaucracy penetrates to a lower level too, down to the lowest state and economic administrative institutions, if we do not fight against it. It goes without saying, it is a tragedy for a socialist country if bureaucracy takes root in the administration from top to bottom, if the people at the top do not, or will not, see the harm it can do. In order to counter bureaucracy successfully, it is not enough to take measures against it only on a top level, on the highest official level, and to consider, on a lower level, that it is, allegedly, not dangerous. How really dangerous it is on lower levels practical experience has shown us. Consequently, bureaucracy is a danger, whether in the administration of the republics, or in the administration of the regions, or in the administration of the districts and local bodies, or in the administration of the various commercial and other economic institutions; and it is imperative that we enlist the assistance of the broadest masses to fight against it and not allow this menace to socialism to get under way.

Today, when not only the state administration but the entire economy is in the hands of the people, the people are competent to exercise a vigilant supervision over the work of those who are placed in the administration to carry out their duties for the benefit of the socialist community. The working collectives and their councils, which are going to manage the factories and mines etc., will have a very important task in preventing bureaucratic methods in the management.

J. B. TITO

Significance of workers' and social self-management*

It is ten years now since the introduction of workers' self-management, which has ushered in a new stage of socialist social relations and socialist democracy in this country. Today, at this Congress, we can be proud of our work collectives and the really tremendous results and successes to their credit.

. . . During the past ten-year period of workers' self-management the rights of the workers' councils have been constantly expanding, in line with the process of improvement of our social system and with the strengthening of the material basis of the country. On the basis of the very good results, and the experience gained, in industry and on agricultural estates, the principle of self-management was also introduced into all other branches of the economy. In some branches the system of self-management is still incomplete, as for example on the railways, in the postal service and in the electric power industry; and for this reason it is necessary to decide as soon as possible how these branches can be brought into line with the tasks, or rather the needs, of the powerful driving force behind our economy.

From the very outset of the transfer of the enterprises to the management of working collectives we have constantly borne in mind that this is no mere organizational measure nor merely a change in the mechanism of management, but a revolutionary measure of social transformation which is creating for the producers such rights and a position in economic relations that the entire economic system must be adjusted to the new relations in production. In this period of development in workers' self-

* Excerpts from the Report to the Fifth Congress of the Socialist Alliance of the Working People of Yugoslavia, April 1960. Published in J. B. Tito: *Govori i članci*, (Vol. xv, September 17, 1959 – September 11, 1960), Zagreb, Naprijed, 1962, pp. 176ff.

management there have been instances of insufficient respect and under-standing for the rights of workers as producers on the part of certain higher officials in the enterprises who have been slow to rid themselves of administrative dead-weight. But today this is on the decrease, and it is up to the collectives themselves to see that it disappears altogether.

Parallel with the decentralization of management, that is to say, with the reduction of the economic functions of the machinery of state, our economic measures have, to an increasing extent, ceased to have an administrative character and have gradually assumed an economic-regulatory character; we have abolished the system of state plans and introduced a new system of social plans in which the basic proportions are laid down. This shows the absurdity of the allegations of certain of our critics abroad, for example those in the East, who allege that the abolition of centralistic state planning and the introduction of workers' self-management is tantamount to anarchy, or those in the West, who allege that workers' self-management is not in fact real self-management, but a fiction, an illusion, to get the workers to work harder, and so on and so forth. We are not trying to impose our system of workers' self-management and social self-government upon anyone else, but we do consider that instead of making abstract criticisms it would be much better to find out how the system works. Perhaps then these critics would change their minds about the significance of workers' and social self-management.

We, too, had at the beginning a system of centralized state management of the economy, and we do not consider that was a mistake. But as soon as we realized that such a system did not provide incentives to the forces of production, but was beginning to act as a brake, and as soon as we saw that the existence of social property was still not the equivalent of new economic relations founded on socialist democracy, we decided to change the prevailing system of management. In so doing, it was essential to make a fundamental change in the attitude of the producers towards the means of production and the social product created. This process, which is to an increasing extent becoming the dominant factor in the development of the economic and social system in our country, actually started with the introduction of workers' councils. . .

The new economic–political social system

Any discussion today about the withering away and non-withering away of the State has – as a theme – already been overtaken by events, because, from theoretical premises, this theme is relentlessly forging ahead towards socialism in practice, and not only in this country but elsewhere. . .

The State is most certainly essential in the conditions of the transitional, socialist society. First, it plays a significant role in the defense of the socialist system from the internal and external enemies of socialism. Secondly, at the time of the appropriation of the means of production, and at a time of low accumulation it plays an important role in the concentration and distribution of funds in the first period of the development of the socialist economy and this is particularly the case with underdeveloped countries. Thirdly, its role, particularly in the initial stages, is important for building up and channelling socialist elements in society. But its functions gradually decrease, accordingly as they are taken over by society. It would be wrong to lay down a time limit for the withering away of the State, or rather the functions of the State. Because that depends on society itself, on the higher or lower rate of development of socialist social relations, on social consciousness and the conditions which obtain, above all the material and moral–political conditions. Consequently, it would be foolish and unrealistic to assert that after the proletariat has assumed power it has no further need of the State. But in accordance with the basic aim of socialism, the liberation of man and labor, it is also foolish to consider that the State, even a socialist one, can arrogate to itself for all time all the political and economic functions of the progressive forces of society and be the sole interpreter of the consciousness and interests of the working class, in other words that in spite of Marxist theory it must even in a socialist society continue to exist as a sort of superstructure of society. Consequently, the criticism directed against us in this respect is either the result of a complete lack of knowledge of Marxist science on the development of the socialist society or is the expression of a deliberate distortion of the facts – and a calumny.

Distribution of income

. . . Social intervention has been reduced to planning and economic methods of guiding economic development, thus leaving enough room for self-initiative and independence in the activities of the economic organizations. Every participant in the distribution of income, from the producer up to the Federation, is assured of a place and in this way becomes capable of exercising self-initiative in development. With the development of production relations in the distribution of the social product changed, with a tendency towards steady growth in the resources of the economic organizations and other bodies of social management.

The basic principle by which we have been guided in the establishment and elaboration of the system and its instruments has been to secure a system of remuneration according to work. In the same way it was essential to ensure that every participant in distribution, while respecting the rights of the work collective and the bodies of social self-management, should be free to dispose as he wishes of the means which result from his activities and the results achieved, or from his participation in distribution as laid down by law.

In every country moving towards socialist social transformation, elements of the old society make themselves strongly felt during the transitional period; and this slows down the normal process of development. And underdeveloped countries, such as ours used to be, still suffer from the consequences of underdeveloped productive forces. We, for that reason, considered an increase in the productive forces to be an essential prerequisite for more rapid general social development. It was only possible to achieve this aim by implementing the principle of remuneration according to the labor effect, as reflected, in the form of financial remuneration, i.e., personal income. Instead of introducing such an equality which does not stimulate but puts a brake on the development of the productivity of labor, we are compelled to apply the principle of remuneration according to work and the kind of 'inequality' based on the principle 'to each according to his ability and works', which in the present stage gives the greatest possible impetus to the development of productive forces. Thus, we are advancing along a path leading to full equality, which can be achieved when there is an abundance of products, when it becomes possible to realize the principle 'to each according to his needs'. For these reasons, in the present stage of development, competition for a greater share of work becomes the only means of determining the individual material conditions of life, a means of achieving a higher rate of development of productivity and of productive forces.

Experience to date, however, shows that various tendencies come to the surface in the practical application of these principles. Some find expression in the trend towards egalitarianism and in underestimating the objective laws of economic development, others in underestimating the role of the conscious factor in production, and in a technocratic approach to the role of individuals or groups as well as in their attempt to secure privileges for themselves and disproportionate scales of personal income, which has sometimes happened when pay-scale regulations were being drawn up, bonuses distributed, etc. The roots of these tendencies are often found to be survivals of bureaucratic practices and survivals of the still unemancipated mentality of the hired worker and insufficiently enlightened producer, tendencies mainly to be found among the new workers coming from the villages. Regardless of their source, these tendencies virtually amount to stumbling blocks in the way of a wider application of the basic principle of our economic system – remuneration according to work – thus slowing down the rate of growth of production. For this reason, in the next period, too, one of our basic tasks will be to eliminate these harmful tendencies, in order to bring more consistency to the application of the basic principles of the economic system, in order to improve further the individual instruments of the system and to develop further workers' self-management, so that the principle of remuneration according to work, or rather according to labor results, should be implemented more fully. . . .

EDWARD KARDELJ

The main dilemma: self-management or statism*

. . . In our social life today there are many sets of problems, dilemmas, interests and contradictions, on which its further course depends.

. . . Let us take, for example, the dilemma between self-management and centralized technocratic–statist management, with all the bureaucratic deformations it brings in its wake. Engels once wrote that the expropriation of the expropriator was the first and last independent step taken by the State of the revolutionary proletariat. Today, this thought of Engels seems to many Marxists too optimistic, unrealistic and unscientific. In actual fact, however, Engels definitely anticipated those very contradictions and dilemmas in the development of social relations founded on social ownership of means of production, which we are discussing today. That dilemma does not live only in the minds of individuals 'at the top' – as is usually said. It begins in every factory and in each of its working units, and ends in the relationships between the entire social process of labor and the State.

The dilemma lies in whether – within the framework of the system of self-management – the mechanism of social management is being increasingly developed, so to say as a 'service' and collective organizer of the working man at his place of work and in his free creative endeavor – and through him as a service of the working class and the people as a whole – or whether State and social management persist and grow stronger as a mechanism of power over man, over his place of work, over accumulation, over suplus labor, turning the working man, in fact, into a tool, a wage laborer, uninterested and politically inert. This is, in my opinion, the main dilemma of socialist development at its present stage. Answers to this crucial issue are given by people according to the difference of interests to be found at the present level of the development of the productive forces

* Excerpted from a report published in *Socialist Thought and Practice*, No. 24, Oct.–Dec. 1966 (pp. 3–29), pp. 15–20.

and of the social structure. These are not necessarily antagonistic interests; on the contrary, they are mostly mutually dependent, but they have their own logic.

For instance, when we speak of the interests of technical experts and unskilled workers, of the span of personal incomes, of division of labor, we cannot say that what we are dealing with are antagonistic interests. As I said, these interests are, essentially, mutually dependent within an integral system of distribution of income according to work. But when each of them acts haphazardly, various conflicts occur, which in turn give rise to different attitudes towards the dilemmas our society is faced with today. Consequently, the main thing is not whether there is somebody in an executive committee who maintains a sceptical or even antagonistic attitude toward the promotion of social self-management, for such people can be found everywhere. We come across them in every enterprise, every institution, and especially among other social strata, outside direct production, who live on budgetary resources and the social concentration of accumulation, and often press for greater State concentration of resources for various justified or unjustified social needs; in other words, these are the sources of direct pressure aimed at narrowing down the base of self-management and strengthening bureaucratic monopoly.

The point I really wish to make is that resistance or hesitation with regard to self-management do not depend only on the subjective mood of Communists, neither do they spring up only in a typical 'bureaucratic' environment – but appear in the social structure itself. If, therefore, we wish to anticipate phenomena and react to them in an adequate manner, we must pay more attention, above all, to that structure, and primarily, within it coordinate actions and reactions through an appropriate democratic mechanism.

It is a fact, that we Communists, have been acting for years under the pressure of narrow practicality connected with the material construction of our society, and have hence neglected many questions related to the ideological and political struggle. Since the League of Communists was not sufficiently active in this field, a profusion of consultations, symposia etc., were held by most diverse institutions in Yugoslavia, which often dealt with the fundamental issues of our social development without taking into consideration the socialist practice of the League of Communists. Since the League of Communists has not, to an adequate extent, performed the function of linking up all the creative forces in the country, we cannot be surprised if in the activities that are now evolving beyond the reach of the League of Communists or on its fringes, sundry questionable theses or even quite open anti-socialist influences should sometimes gain the upper hand.

Naturally, I do not mean to say that various symposia and consultations should not be held. On the contrary, it seems to me that this practice provides a useful indication to the League of Communists as to how it should proceed in investigating and discussing the basic issues of social life and development. However, notwithstanding all this, the League must act as a factor of active ideological and political struggle, not on the lines of 'agit-prop' control, but as a protagonist of the practical synthesis of the whole of society's creative endeavor, with the purpose of guiding and formulating the specific tasks of day-to-day conscious socialist action.

The pressure of economic and political practicality has – contrary to the principles of our program – led to the further merging of Party and State leaderships and leaderships of economic management. In consequence, the action of Communists has, to a certain extent, been subordinated to the constellation of interests that prevailed at the moment, and prevented them from acting, in all the dilemmas of social development, as the representatives of the social–historical interests of the working class, i.e., the protagonists of the social efforts to emancipate human labor and creativity from relations and factors which alienate man from the possibility to control the conditions, means and products of his labor.

Hence it happens that sometimes the interest of the working people in the League of Communists wanes. The working people often find that Party committees or Party organizations do not tell them anything else but what they hear from State organs, the manager, the board of management, the president of the commune, etc. Therefore, they have the feeling that Party committees often even hamper them in the assertion of their rights of self-management.

A similar statement could be made concerning the problems related to the system of distribution of income according to work performed. The entire system of distribution is, namely, exposed to the pressure of two extremes: the tendency to level out incomes and the striving for privileges. This gives rise to conflicts of sorts and engenders various political and ideological trends.

With regard to this question, too, we Communists were quite explicit in declarations of principles; in actual practice, however, we often let things take their own course; there is hardly any enterprise, let alone non-economic organizations, where the problems of the distribution of income according to work performed has been solved in such a satisfactory manner as to prevent deformations in the sense of a levelling out of all incomes or deformations reflected in excessive differences and too large spans in distribution, which verge on privileges.

Let us take, further, the set of problems in the sphere of our political system. All the programmatic documents of the League of Communists stipulate that the democratic political system is the integral part of the struggle for socialist social relations. They also emphasize that one of the most important tasks of the League of Communists in its struggle for social progress is to increase democratization in all fields of social life, and that the entire development of the system of democratic institutions and relations in our society must be founded on socio-economic relations proper to self-management and must ensure the unimpeded advancement of these relations.

However, this policy was incessantly exposed to the pressure of two contrasting trends: on the one hand, the tendencies of political absolutism and glorification of the policy of the 'firm hand', stemming from statist and bureaucratic–technocratic concepts based on state ownership; on the other hand, to trends, partly engendered by the remnants of the old system and partly by the ambitions of various petty politicians, by the lust for power, etc., which found expression in various demands for a multiparty system of the bourgeois-representative type. Although the protagonists of the first tendency advocate the 'firm hand', and the others freedom, both, in actual fact, aspire to political monopoly over social management, and mean the expropriation of the working man of his rights to self-management, and his alienation from the conditions, means and products of his own labor.

Despite the fact that we condemned both tendencies, they nevertheless made their influence felt in our social life. One of the consequences of this influence has been the slow development of appropriate democratic institutions, means and relations. This, naturally, hampered the entire development of self-management and fostered the very tendencies I have just mentioned. Accordingly, in this respect too, we are faced with a whole series of extremely important and urgent tasks . . .

DUŠAN BILANDŽIĆ

Workers' management of factories*

. . . A wealth of experience from all spheres of life has been accumulated in the course of almost eighteen years of development of workers' management. During this time both minor and far-reaching changes have taken place in social relationships, the economic system, technology, etc., changes which have enabled us to gain significant experience, particularly with regard to workers' possibilities and limitations in factory management.

* *Socialist Thought and Practice*, No. 28, Oct.–Dec. 1967.

I

. . . Critics of self-management who maintain that workers would 'eat up' the newly-created value, even the machines, if they were allowed to dispose freely of social resources, point to the historical tendency of workers to go on demanding higher wages until they have swallowed the entire disposable revenue of their respective enterprises.

As regards this historical tendency of workers to press for higher wages, the critics of workers' management are evidently right. But their claim that capital formation depends on the 'free will' of the workers is neither original nor new. Marx had similar discussions regarding 'free will' with vulgar bourgeois economists who maintained that every capitalist was 'free' to apportion part of the profit for personal consumption and part for capital formation. In this great work, Marx proved that the accumulation of capital was the economic necessity of every society and that it did not depend on the free will of people. Capitalist social–economic relations, the law of value, the law of profit, etc., all compelled the capitalists to allocate part of their profit to capital formation. The accumulation of capital was a *conditio sine qua non* for profit, a condition for survival – for victory or defeat – in the sharp competition among capitalist commodity producers.

Any discussion of the 'free will' of workers is plainly senseless since no such will exists. But one can ask whether and to what extent there exists in reality an objective economic necessity, i.e., social–economic relations which determine the 'free will' of the workers in their decision-making on the distribution of the income of the enterprises they manage. For Yugoslav experience has shown that unless appropriate social–economic relations are created to make the workers' position dependent on the capital formation they themselves have determined, the latter will show a tendency to 'eat up' the enterprise's development funds. If, for a moment, we assume the possibility of their being given full freedom in distributing the entire value they have newly-created in the factory of their employer (the capitalist or the State, be it capitalist or socialist), the workers would most likely decide to 'eat up' the entire income. This is easy to understand, since under such social–economic relations of production, it is not the workers who manage production and distribution, nor does their material position depend on the way they manage the enterprise.

If, however, relations of production are such that the amount of earnings they need for their personal and common expenditure (housing, social services, etc.), i.e., for the satisfaction of their needs, depends on the income earned by the enterprise they manage, the workers will naturally be interested in securing the highest possible revenue for their organization knowing that the higher this revenue is, the higher will their personal earnings be and the greater their possibilities to satisfy their needs. Since in such cases, the revenue of the enterprise depends directly on the productivity of their labor, and that productivity depends on capital intensity, then capital formation, as a condition for achieving the desired effects, becomes for the workers just as important as their direct personal income. Such an immediate material interest in ensuring the optimal expansion of production and in business efficiency in general, cannot be expected from social agencies outside production, i.e., from the state apparatus, regardless of the latter's ability to find the most opportune and rational solutions, since their own material interests do not hinge on the success or failure of the enterprise's operation.

II

. . . Another question that is frequently coming up in discussions may be summed up as follows: how can all workers take part in the management of their respective enterprises, especially today when a series of technological changes are under way and when the enterprises have to fight a fierce struggle under conditions of a market economy and in face of sharp competition both at home and abroad.

Those who carefully follow what is understood in relevant discussions in Yugoslavia by the concept of workers' management of enterprises, will have certainly noted that there are differences in positions and views, most frequently depending on the social status and knowledge of the people concerned. A serious enquiry in an enterprise with a complex occupational structure would be enough to show that self-management is differently experienced and understood by the director, engineer, book-keeper, worker, technologist, etc. Of course, there are also differences in views both among directors and workers. There are also differences in views among individual political functionaries, scholars, lawyers, sociologists, politicians, etc.

There are those who see the essence of workers' management in an arrangement where the entire collective of an enterprise, that is, every worker in it, is called upon to participate in self-management and express views and opinions on almost every question and decision taken by the enterprise. In line with this view, demands are not infrequently voiced that workers operating machines should in a competent way discuss market analyses presented to the meetings of the workers' council by the enterprise market research service. According to those holding this view, the worker should be a greater expert than the economist, the economist a greater expert than the technologist, the technologist a greater expert than · the commercialist, and vice versa, and the workers' council should be more conversant with expert and technical matters than the directors and administrative staff, for how else could they appraise the soundness of the expert analyses and reports submitted to them? The corollary would be that workers' management has been introduced in order to have the organs of self-management concern themselves with expert and technical problems, instead of having the workers control production relations.

Views such as these would give no cause for concern, were it not for their adverse social consequences. For these views and the practice they entail, as we shall try to prove, tend to lead workers' management astray, and thus discredit the very idea of self-management, blunt the responsibility of the executive staff and experts and allow incompetent personnel to evade responsibility for their own lack of knowledge and skill and shift it on to the workers' council under the proverbial excuse: 'Comrades, it is you who have taken the decision, I am only an expert here.' Such relationships obstruct the creative endeavors of experts and organizers of business, and also make it more difficult for most members of the collective, and even the workers' council, to enter into the sphere of real management.

In contrast to this romantic conception, and partly also as a reaction to it, we come across views according to which a conflict between rational management of modern industrial establishments and workers' management is inevitable.

Proceeding from some true aspects of today's sociological, economic and technological realities, but overlooking the other side of the problem, some critics find arguments in favor of their thesis in the antinomy, as they see it, between self-management and the streamlined economy.

Here are some of the arguments used:

(a) Technological and economic results in a modern economy depend less on the skill, ingenuity, initiative and will of 'ordinary' people taking part in production, and far more on the scientific organization of work, with science and modern technology increasingly forming the basis of rational processes and behaviors in modern society. Part of this thesis cannot really be refuted – science has indeed become a direct material productive force, the most powerful at that, but from this fact an erroneous conclusion is drawn about the role man plays in this process, as we shall try to show below.

(b) The participation of large numbers of workers in discussions and decision-making in lower echelons and at enterprise level, becomes under conditions of a scientific organization of work both unnecessary and superfluous, or at least, it is not warranted by the results it can yield. By resorting to scientific methods it is possible to build up adequate subsystems and systems in an enterprise which ensure a considerable measure of auto-regulation, so that any amateurish interference, which brings along the artisan or any similar mentality, would only impede the creativity of true experts and specialists.

(c) Modern industrial production, especially the increasing role science plays in all spheres of work, tends to widen the occupational gap among individuals and groups of workers. In enterprises with a relatively small labor force the manual worker cooperates with the technologist, the locksmith with the nuclear physicist, the time clerk with the cybernetics specialist, etc., a fact which inevitably gives rise to increased clashes of ideas, views and conceptions, where experts are often called upon to prove that black is black and white white. All this leads to social tensions, dehumanization of relationships, squandering of energy, time, nerves, and so on and so forth.

The criticism of workers' management based on such and similar arguments correctly perceives certain aspects of social processes, certain phenomena, but seems unable to bring the entirety of social and economic flows into the focus of its analyses. These critics forget the centuries-old experience of past and contemporary societies that progress in material production is directly proportional to the interest of the masses in creative endeavor.

We have presented here two, in our opinion, erroneous views. They both, each in its own way, hinder the realization of workers' management in enterprises.

These discussions clearly show that the real problem lies in determining the right relations between the administrative staff and workers, that is, the workers' council.

We shall try to give here a short analysis of the basic tendencies noted in the way workers take part in the process of self-management.

In a modern enterprise there are hundreds of extremely varied jobs and functions. This is seen in the thousands of occupations exercised on the basis of expert knowledge and skills. It is not necessary to try to prove that people cannot objectively 'interfere' in other people's occupations, they simply do not have the necessary knowledge for it.

People of most varied occupations cooperate in a modern enterprise: the unskilled and semi-literate worker and the top researcher, the locksmith and the nuclear physicist, the time clerk and the cybernetics specialist, the economic analyst and the technologist, etc. All are grouped in individual sectors of work such as market research, the economic-analytical service, the technological-development service, production units, etc., and are all united in a common organization of work which enables them through their combined action to achieve the best results and earn the highest possible income.

Naturally, this description of the occupational division of labor cannot itself explain self-management relations, since action must be combined regardless of production relations, but the occupational division, organization and authority are very relevant factors in the determination of self-management relations in an enterprise.

As a result of the division of labor in an enterprise, individual members of the collective are objectively placed into very different positions regarding the extent to which they can influence the business policy of their enterprise. *On the basis of the occupational division of labor some members of the collective exercise a decisive influence on business policy, while the influence of some others is so small that it can almost be overlooked.* Those occupying key technological and administrative positions have incomparably greater opportunities to shape business policies than those who are more or less responsible for the actual execution of individual operations. This conclusion is of exceptional significance for the possibility and mode of putting self-management into effect. The next relevant factor is the role played by science. A modern industrial enterprise is inconceivable without scientific management. In an enterprise based on advanced principles of organization things cannot be dealt with at random and in a haphazard way, since such a method of work would adversely affect those who resort to it. The solution of any major operational problem in an enterprise must be preceded by scientific research and a detailed scientific and expert analysis of all the conditions and elements affecting the relevant decisions. In fact a rational decision can be taken only on the basis of an analysis of relevant factors from various scientific aspects – technical–technological, economic, demographic, legal, sociological, etc. Scientific projections of the results of decisions to be taken are made with mathematical precision. Science has been integrated into all social processes to such an extent that it has now become the basis and condition for any rational decision.

Because of this, scientific, expert and technical staff must be ensured as much authority as they objectively can have, or else there will be no rationality and no economy of operation in the enterprises. As the role of science grows in importance – a fact which is generally recognized both as a reality and tendency – those in charge of organizing the process of social labor will objectively exercise a growing influence on the projection of decisions and decision-making and on the selection of the most appropriate means for the implementation of decisions taken on the basis of self-management.

This role of scientific and expert staff and of those responsible for organizing material production is present in almost all phases of the decision-making cycle in an enterprise. Executives and experts are as a rule, always and in every situation, in a better position to formulate and realize their views, since they hold key positions in the production process and in management, their general and professional education is markedly higher than that of the so-called ordinary worker, they are usually able to grasp problems more fully, to see all the intricacies involved and the ways and means of resolving them.

The influence of the workers' council on managing the enterprise's production processes and business policy is restricted, on the one hand, by the fact that its members are mainly workers engaged in jobs which do not allow them to keep abreast of numerous particulars on which decisions depend, since by the nature of their jobs they cannot 'memorize' the many technical and economic problems.

Those in charge of the management of the enterprise are best able to develop business initiative and action since it is they in fact who work out a given policy and propose concrete measures for its realization.

It is quite natural that the executive staff and specialized services are objectively the most important factors in running business. It is well known that an incapable, unskilled, inert, petrified and unenterprising technical and executive staff is most frequently exclusively responsible for operating losses, low personal income and empty enterprise funds. And conversely: under the same given conditions a good management will pull the enterprise out of a hopeless situation. There are, of course, exceptions where the actual situation is such that even the most capable management will find it difficult to get the enterprise out of its plight.

Because of the prime role and importance of the executive and technical staff in every economic organization, the question often arises as to how to activate and encourage their enterprising spirit still further, while preventing technocratic–bureaucratic tendencies from assuming a predominant role, and at the same time enabling every worker in the enterprise to take part in self-management.

Firstly, in some enterprises, neither the executive staff nor the organs of self-management, nor, for that matter the workers themselves, are any longer satisfied with certain aspects of self-management relations prevailing in them. This serious statement necessarily calls for an explanation.

What is the essence of the problem?

In many enterprises, the meetings of the workers' council are presented with expert and technical reports previously discussed in detail by the expert staff and by the enterprise managing board and on which positions and views regarding the decisions to be made have already been taken. If a worker trained to operate his machine would want to discuss these highly technical reports he would have to be a better economist than the economist of the enterprise, a better legal specialist than the enterprise's legal adviser, a better technologist than its technologist. And since in fact he cannot be, nor does he need to be all this, such meetings are dominated by those who have written the reports. Occasional discussion points coming from 'laymen' do not change this situation. Apart from this, certain minor current questions relating to the life of the collective, are raised at these same meetings which in a way, divert the workers' attention from the central, principal problems affecting social–economic relations. Feeling that under such unequal conditions they cannot competently discuss the enterprise's strategy, the workers try to wage their 'battles' with the administration on minor tactical points. A considerable section of the workers feel that this is not the essence of self-managing decision-making.

On the other hand, executive staff and specialized services in enterprises tend to complain that their freedom of action is very often restricted, that they are not given the chance to show what they really know and what they could do to increase production and income.

Thus in some enterprises both good workers and capable executive staff find such self-management relations unsatisfactory.

In contrast to this many self-styled experts endorse these relations as they allow them to lay the blame for their business failures on the workers' council and collective, which formally decide and are formally responsible for their decisions.

Self-management is not that state of relationships where there is no respect for the organization of work, the established working regime and procedure, professional responsibility, obligations and rights stemming from and corresponding to individual areas of production, or individual jobs. Rather it is the contrary that is true. Self-management practice has shown that since they share the fate of the enterprise, the workers want to know exactly who does what, how he does it and for what he is responsible. Consequently, the aim of self-management is not to try to abolish the division of labor in a primitive, anarchic and disintegrating way, and even less to teach workers all of the many skills and specialized jobs that exist in a factory.

Self-management will accomplish its democratic assertion not by encroaching upon the professional behavior of a man at his work, but by changing his social and economic position based on labor, i.e., by changing production relationships. And these are two essentially different things.

The bureaucratic organization of social production cannot be resisted nor can bureaucracy be overcome by negating and ignoring technical and professional standards of behavior, since this would only tend to strengthen bureaucracy in the social organization of labor, and would naturally compromise workers' self-management.

III

If we accept as approximately accurate the above considerations of the professional division of labor and of the mode of implementing self-management in work organizations, the question arises as to how to ensure the next step in the realization of self-management and in the expansion of business efficiency.

Experience has shown that attempts to have all workers in an enterprise participate in decision-making on all problems, even on those of a professional nature, have failed. The question is therefore how to enable all workers in a factory to manage their enterprise efficiently.

In seeking an answer to this question one could, on the basis of the above-mentioned criticism and considerations, conclude that workers' councils and workers generally should not discuss technical and professional reports containing proposals for decisions by self-management bodies. But this cannot be the answer. On the contrary, they must discuss these matters, but in a way that will enable them to exercise their self-management rights, that is in a way deriving from the class nature of workers' management itself. For it should not be forgotten that workers' self-management has not been introduced so that all workers should be trained to discuss all the numerous technical and professional problems of their enterprises, but in order to enable them to manage production relations, to change and determine these relations in their enterprise. And therefore any attempt to deflect working people from this basic road, from the road of determining production relations, is in fact an attempt to lead self-management astray, no matter under what pretext it is done. Management by the workers must be understood as a basic social relationship of production, as the power the working class exercises over the conditions and results of associated labor. Workers' management is not to be sought in the sphere of technical problems concerning the promotion of production, but in the sphere of the realization of the personal and social interests of producers.

In the name of this, and proceeding, on the one hand, from the inexorable logic of the social and technical divisions of labor and the character and mode of operation under conditions of a market economy, and the real content and essence of self-management, on the other, the basic relationships in work organizations must be so arranged that, regardless of the jobs they perform in the enterprise, all workers should determine the framework and lay down the targets, programs and requirements regarding income earning – personal earnings and capital formation – while the executive and expert staff should propose material–technical, technological, financial, organizational and other solutions as a means of fulfilling the jointly established programs and targets. There is surely no need to prove that in this way no member of a working collective is placed in an unequal position with regard to the right to take part in the determination of working programs and targets.

Such relationships practically mean that by participating in self-management, the working man is able on the basis of facts, scientifically and expertly established, to consider and decide, among other things, primarily upon the social–economic and financial effects one or another decision or program will have on him personally, on his working community, and finally on the social community as a whole.

This means that self-management does not imply the right and duty of the workers to 'declare themselves' on the validity of individual technical–economic, investment, financial, and other similar studies and reports which would require them to possess expert knowledge in order to be able to approve or reject them.

Let us repeat: self-management means deciding on the social–economic implications of these expert reports, analyses and programs, and here we have two different things.

Workers and their councils exercise self-management when they demand to hear the proposals for a particular production program, reconstruction project, modernization scheme, etc., and discuss these primarily from the aspect of what personal earnings and what income for their enterprise the proposed programs or projects will ensure.

It is quite possible for a workers' council to hire experts outside its enterprise to help it appraise whether or not a proposed project can really ensure the desired effects for their personal income and the enterprise's funds, or by the same logic, to appraise if a project already realized could have produced better results.

In other words, working people demand and seek those roads and those ways and means which will ensure them a certain amount of personal earnings and income for their enterprise within a specified time. This then becomes the task, obligation and aim of all and everyone in the enterprise. It is on such 'militant' tasks that the executive staff and workers' council pass or fail the test of their ability. And this means that those executives and specialists vested with the highest responsibilities will be the first to be called to account for any possible business failure.

Self-management decision-making at all levels presupposes a discussion of the social–economic and social–political implications of individual technical, financial, economic, organizational, and other variants for the solution of individual problems, and establishment of tasks and targets. It further implies the full professional and scientific 'independence' and responsibility of experts for the data, estimates, proposals and arguments offered in such discussions. Moreover, it presupposes team work and the supplying of workers with reliable information on all aspects of consequences that one or another solution adopted might realistically have . . .

II Interplay between socialization, resource shifts and the economy's laws

Introductory note

For the Marxists the socio-economic framework of the society *determines* the economic principles which operate within it. Forces which interact in a market economy – e.g. supply and demand – will not affect a socialist economy in the same way. Indeed, the Marxists see political economy as a historical science, and the role of the economist as that of an investigator of the *'special laws* of each individual stage in the evolution of production and exchange' (Engels). Since, however, with the end of capitalism, marketing and exchange of goods are supposed to be replaced by a system of free distribution of goods, Rosa Luxemburg – and after her the Bolsheviks Nikolai Bukharin and Eugenii Preobrazhenskii – proclaimed that 'the last chapter of economics will be the social revolution of the world proletariat'. A special connection is thus alleged to exist between a particular distribution of ownership and the interplay of economic forces.

After the Bolshevik revolution, and especially after the inauguration of markets during the NEP, the Bolsheviks started to ask themselves which particular economic laws were henceforth ruling the interrelations between the socialized and the non-socialized sectors, what role if any was now played by the law of value, and whether markets would finally be superseded by centralized planning. These questions became even more disturbing after the complete collectivization of the peasantry, the launching of comprehensive planning, and the official proclamation of the 'completion of the construction of socialism in the USSR' (1937). Money, values, and markets instead of receding into history had indeed become in the meantime part and parcel of everyday life.

Cutting through the tangled mass of conflicting interpretations concerning economic laws, Stalin finally proclaimed, in 1952, that the economic laws of socialism were simply the obverse of those ruling capitalism, viz. maximum welfare for all instead of maximum individual profit, and planned proportionate economic development instead of market spontaneity. Stalin added, however, that the law of value continued to function under socialism, but in a subsidiary way; it was now so to speak kept under the control of the socialist government and could, accordingly, be put to beneficial uses by it. (See Stalin's introductory study.)

Whenever any given policy needed legitimization, a reference to the operation of this or that economic law became *de rigueur* throughout the socialist camp. When, in 1953, the new premier of Hungary, Imre Nagy, attempted a decisive political reversal, namely the return of his country to the NEP – i.e. to a system involving a marked reduction in the scope of socialization, the revitalization of small-holder agriculture, the slowing down of the pace of industrialization and the systematic increase of the standard of living – he naturally claimed that all this was necessary in order to conform to the socialist law of balanced, proportionate economic development discovered by Stalin. (See I. Nagy's paper.) Espousing in various respects Bukharin's formulae of the mid 1920s, Nagy aimed thus to breathe new life into a system discarded by the Russians, and turn it into an alternative to Stalin's own economic model.

After Nagy's fall from power, a number of East European economists pointed out that all these alleged laws were often *declaration of intent* serving, as the case may be, as political instruments or as convenient alibis for the policy makers' and planners' preferences and decisions. The question of laws, amply debated in Hungary (see the papers of Tamas Nagy – no relation of Imre Nagy – and of Peter Erdös) was eventually also taken up by various Polish economists (among them, Lipiński and Lange). All these East European commentators stressed that no economy – capitalist or socialist – could function otherwise than as 'commodity producing and exchange economies', i.e. as economies relying extensively on market relations and on market mechanisms.

After the crushing of the Hungarian revolt of 1956, and after the end of the Polish upheaval of 1956–57, the critique of economic laws subsided in Eastern Europe. To this day, Stalin's interpretation of the laws of socialism remains enshrined in all Soviet economic textbooks. This interpretation embodies the officially accepted view on the interplay between *socialization, resources shifts,* and *economic regularities* during the period of transition from capitalism to communism.

J. V. STALIN

Remarks on economic questions*

. . . Character of economic laws under socialism

Some comrades deny the objective character of laws of science, and of laws of political economy particularly, under socialism. They deny that the laws of political economy reflect processes, governed by objective law, which operate independently of the will of man. They believe that in view of the specific role assigned to the Soviet state by history, the Soviet state and its leaders can abolish existing laws of political economy and can 'form', 'create', new laws.

These comrades are profoundly mistaken. It is evident that they confuse laws of science, which reflect objective processes in nature or society, processes which take place independently of the will of man, with the laws which are issued by governments, which are made by the will of man, and which have only juridical validity. But they must not be confused.

. . . It is said that economic laws are elemental in character, that their action is inavertible and that society is powerless against them. That is not true. It is making a fetish of laws, and oneself the slave of laws. It has been demonstrated that society is not powerless against laws, that, having come to know economic laws and relying upon them, society can restrict their sphere of action, utilize them in the interests of society and 'harness' them, just as in the case of the forces of nature and their laws, just as in the case of the overflow of big rivers . . .

Reference is made to the specific role of the Soviet government in building socialism, which allegedly enables it to abolish existing laws of economic development and to 'form' new ones. That also is untrue.

The specific role of the Soviet government was due to two circumstances: first, that what the Soviet government had to do was not to replace one form of exploitation by another, as was the case in earlier revolutions, but to abolish exploitation altogether; second, that in view of the absence in the country of any ready-made rudiments of a socialist economy, it had to create new, socialist forms of economy, 'starting from scratch', so to speak.

That was undoubtedly a difficult, complex and unprecedented task. Nevertheless, the Soviet government accomplished this task with credit. But it accomplished it not because it supposedly destroyed the existing

Economic Problems of Socialism in the USSR, New York, International Publishers, 1952, pp. 7–12; 18–22; 31–4.

economic laws and 'formed' new ones, but only because it relied on the economic law that the relations of production must necessarily conform with the character of the productive forces. The productive forces of our country, especially in industry, were social in character, the form of ownership, on the other hand, was private, capitalistic. Relying on the economic law that the relations of production must necessarily conform with the character of the productive forces, the Soviet government socialized the means of production, made them the property of the whole people, and thereby abolished the exploiting system and created socialist forms of economy. Had it not been for this law, and had the Soviet government not relied upon it, it could not have accomplished its mission.

... It is said that the necessity for balanced (proportionate) development of the national economy in our country enables the Soviet government to abolish existing economic laws and to create new ones. That is absolutely untrue. Our yearly and five-yearly plans must not be confused with the objective economic law of balanced, proportionate development of the national economy. The law of balanced development of the national economy arose in opposition to the law of competition and anarchy of production under capitalism. It arose from the socialization of the means of production, after the law of competition and anarchy of production had lost its validity. It became operative because a socialist economy can be conducted only on the basis of the economic law of balanced development of the national economy. That means that the law of balanced development of the national economy makes it possible for our planning bodies to plan social production correctly. But possibility must not be confused with actuality. They are two different things. In order to turn the possibility into actuality, it is necessary to study this economic law, to master it, to learn to apply it with full understanding, and to compile such plans as fully reflect the requirements of this law. It cannot be said that the requirements of this economic law are fully reflected by our yearly and five-yearly plans.

It is said that some of the economic laws operating in our country under socialism, including the law of value, have been 'transformed', on the basis of planned economy. That is likewise untrue. Laws cannot be 'transformed', still less 'radically' transformed. If they can be transformed, then they can be abolished and replaced by other laws. The thesis that laws can be 'transformed' is a relic of the incorrect formula that laws can be 'abolished' or 'formed'. Although the formula that economic laws can be transformed has already been current in our country for a long time, it must be abandoned for the sake of accuracy. The sphere of action of this or that economic law may be restricted, its destructive action – that is, of course, if it is liable to be destructive – may be averted, but it cannot be 'transformed' or 'abolished'.

Consequently, when we speak of 'subjugating' natural forces or economic forces, of 'dominating' them, etc., this does not mean that man can 'abolish' or 'form' scientific laws. On the contrary, it only means that man can discover laws, get to know them and master them, learn to apply them with full understanding, utilize them in the interests of society, and thus subjugate them, secure mastery over them.

Hence, the laws of political economy under socialism are objective laws, which reflect the fact that the processes of economic life have their own laws and operate independently of our will. People who deny this postulate are in point of fact denying science, and, by denying science, they are denying all possibility of prognostication – and, consequently, are denying the possibility of directing economic activity.

. . . The law of value under socialism

It is sometimes asked whether the law of value exists and operates in our country, under the socialist system.

Yes, it does exist and does operate. Wherever commodities and commodity production exist, there the law of value must also exist.

In our country, the sphere of operation of the law of value extends, first of all, to commodity circulation, to the exchange of commodities through purchase and sale, the exchange, chiefly, of articles of personal consumption. Here, in this sphere, the law of value preserves, within certain limits, of course, the function of a regulator.

But the operation of the law of value is not confined to the sphere of commodity circulation. It also extends to production. True, the law of value has no regulating function in our socialist production, but it nevertheless influences production, and this fact cannot be ignored when directing production. As a matter of fact, consumer goods, which are needed to compensate the labor power expended in the process of production, are produced and realized in our country as commodities coming under the operation of the law of value. It is precisely here that the law of value exercises its influence on production. In this connection, such things as cost accounting and profitableness, production costs, prices, etc., are of actual importance in our enterprises. Consequently, our enterprises cannot, and must not, function without taking the law of value into account.

Is this a good thing? It is not a bad thing. Under present conditions, it really is not a bad thing, since it trains our business executives to conduct production on rational lines and disciplines them. It is not a bad thing because it teaches our executives to count production magnitudes, to count them accurately, and also to calculate the real things in production precisely, and not to talk non-sense about 'approximate figures', spun out of thin air. It is not a bad thing because it teaches our executives to look for, find and utilize hidden reserves latent in production, and not to trample them underfoot. It is not a bad thing because it teaches our executives systematically to improve methods of production, to lower production costs, to practice cost accounting, and to make their enterprises pay. It is a good practical school which accelerates the development of our executive personnel and their growth into genuine leaders of socialist production at the present stage of development.

. . . It is said that the law of value is a permanent law, binding upon all periods of historical development, and that if it does lose its function as a regulator of exchange relations in the second phase of communist society it retains at this phase of development its function as a regulator of the relations between the various branches of production, as a regulator of the distribution of labor among them.

That is quite untrue. Value, like the law of value, is a historical category connected with the existence of commodity production. With the disappearance of commodity production, value and its forms and the law of value also disappear.

In the second phase of communist society, the amount of labor expended on the production of goods will be measured not in a roundabout way, not through value and its forms, as is the case under commodity production, but directly and immediately – by the amount of time, the number of hours, expended on the production of goods. As to the distribution of labor, its distribution among the branches of production will be regulated not by the law of value, which will have ceased to function by that time, but by the growth of society's demand for goods. It will be a society in which production will be regulated by the requirements of society, and computation of the requirements of society will acquire paramount importance for the planning bodies.

Totally incorrect, too, is the assertion that under our present economic system, in the first phase of development of communist society, the law of value regulates the 'proportions' of labor distributed among the various branches of production.

. . . These comrades forget that the law of value can be a regulator of production only under capitalism, with private ownership of the means of production, and competition, anarchy of production, and crises of overproduction. They forget that in our country the sphere of operation of the law of value is limited by the social ownership of the means of production, and by the law of balanced development of the national economy, and is consequently also limited by our yearly and five-yearly plans, which are an approximate reflection of the requirements of this law.

Some comrades draw the conclusion from this that the law of balanced development of the national economy and economic planning annul the principle of profitableness of production. That is quite untrue. It is just the other way round. If profitableness is considered not from the standpoint of individual plants or industries, and not over a period of one year, but from the standpoint of the entire national economy and over a period of, say, ten or fifteen years, which is the only correct approach to the question, then the temporary and unstable profitableness of some plants or industries is beneath all comparison with that higher form of stable and permanent profitableness which we get from the operation of the law of balanced development of the national economy and from economic planning, which save us from periodical economic crises disruptive to the national economy and causing tremendous material damage to society, and which ensure a continuous and high rate of expansion of our national economy.

In brief, there can be no doubt that under our present socialist conditions of production, the law of value cannot be a 'regulator of the proportions' of labor distributed among the various branches of production.

... The basic economic laws of modern capitalism and of socialism

... Is there a basic economic law of capitalism? Yes, there is. What is this law, and what are its characteristic features? The basic economic law of capitalism is a law that determines not some particular aspect or particular processes of the development of capitalist production, but all the principal aspects and all the principal processes of its development – one, consequently, which determines the essence of capitalist production, its essential nature.

Is the law of value the basic economic law of capitalism? No. The law of value is primarily a law of commodity production. It existed before capitalism, and, like commodity production, will continue to exist after the overthrow of capitalism, as it does, for instance, in our country, although, it is true, with a restricted sphere of operation. Having a wide sphere of operation in capitalist conditions, the law of value, of course, plays a big part in the development of capitalist production. But not only does it not determine the essence of capitalist production and the principles of capitalist profit; it does not even pose these problems. Therefore, it cannot be the basic economic law of modern capitalism.

For the same reasons, the law of competition and anarchy of production, or the law of uneven development of capitalism in the various countries cannot be the basic economic law of capitalism either.

It is said that the law of the average rate of profit is the basic economic law of modern capitalism. That is not true. Modern capitalism, monopoly capitalism, cannot content itself with the average profit, which moreover has a tendency to decline, in view of the increasing organic composition of capital. It is not the average profit, but the maximum profit that modern monopoly capitalism demands, which it needs for more or less regular extended reproduction.

Most appropriate to the concept of a basic economic law of capitalism is the law of surplus value, the law of the origin and growth of capitalist profit. It really does determine the basic features of capitalist production. But the law of surplus value is too general a law; it does not cover the problem of the highest rate of profit, the securing of which is a condition for the development of monopoly capitalism. In order to fill this hiatus, the law of surplus value must be made more concrete and developed further in adaptation to the conditions of monopoly capitalism, at the same time bearing in mind that monopoly capitalism demands not any sort of profit, but precisely the maximum profit. That will be the basic economic law of modern capitalism.

. . . Is there a basic economic law of socialism? Yes, there is. What are the essential features and requirements of this law? The essential features and requirements of the basic law of socialism might be formulated roughly in this way: the securing of the maximum satisfaction of the constantly rising material and cultural requirements of the whole of society through the continuous expansion and perfection of socialist production on the basis of higher techniques.

Consequently: instead of maximum profits – maximum satisfaction of the material and cultural requirements of society; instead of development of production with breaks in continuity from boom to crisis and from crisis to boom – unbroken expansion of production; instead of periodic breaks in technical development, accompanied by destruction of the productive forces of society – an unbroken process of perfecting production on the basis of higher techniques.

It is said that the law of the balanced, proportionate development of the national economy is the basic economic law of socialism. That is not true. Balanced development of the national economy, and, hence, economic planning, which is a more or less faithful reflection of this law, can yield nothing by themselves, if it is not known for what purpose economic development is planned, or if that purpose is not clear. The law of balanced development of the national economy can yield the desired result only if there is a purpose for the sake of which economic development is planned. The purpose the law of balanced development of the national economy cannot itself provide. Still less can economic planning provide it. This purpose is inherent in the basic economic law of socialism, in the shape of its requirements, as expounded above. Consequently, the law of balanced development of the national economy can operate to its full scope only if its operation rests on the basic economic law of socialism.

As to economic planning, it can achieve positive results only if two conditions are observed: (a) if it correctly reflects the requirements of the law of balanced development of the national economy, and (b) if it conforms in every way to the requirements of the basic economic law of socialism.

IMRE NAGY

The role and significance of the NEP*

The March, 1955, resolution of the Central Committee did not deal with the question of the NEP,[1] its role and its significance, and not even with those problems in this field that the Party and the government had to resolve. Thus the March resolution of the Central Committee did not commit the Party to the NEP policy, although it pointed out that the June 27–28, 1953 resolution of the Central Committee, which opened up a new phase in the application of the NEP, was still in effect without change and constituted the basis of the March resolution. In reality, matters were different. Since the March resolution, it was precisely in the field of the NEP that there had been the most extensive return to pre-June, 1953 conditions.

. . . According to Lenin's teachings the guiding policy of the NEP is to ensure victory over the capitalist elements to the proletariat in power, and the building of socialism through economic solidarity based on the exchange of goods between the working class and the small peasants. In the interest of the latter, the economy uses even the capitalist elements, so that they will be overcome and a socialist economy be built through the market and by use of the market rather than of barter, or without a market simply to avoid a market.

Thus the NEP is the specific means and form for building socialism, and is absolutely necessary in every country where there is a significantly large number of small peasants. Consequently, during the transitional period, the NEP is the basis for our entire economic policy. This means that the elements of the NEP are not operative to the same extent throughout the

* *Imre Nagy on Communism. In Defense of the New Course*, New York, Frederick A. Praeger, 1957, pp. 194–201.
1 The New Economic Policy was launched in the Soviet Union in April, 1921. According to Imre Nagy, a similar policy was allegedly inaugurated in Hungary, in the early post World War II years.

entire transitional period, but wither away to the extent that the building of socialism proceeds and to the extent that the socialist sectors of the economy develop.

The question that must be asked is whether the NEP was utilized [in Hungary] in the spirit of Marxist–Leninist teachings.

A. During the period of the Three-Year Plan, the main task of the NEP – to establish the economic solidarity of socialist big industry and the small peasants – was on the whole successfully accomplished despite some smaller or larger mistakes in the field of free-market sale and trade.

B. The second period of NEP, from the beginning of the Five-Year Plan to June, 1953, was characterized by the liquidation of private retail trade, i.e., the substantial elimination of private small industry, and also by increasingly serious violations of the basic principles of NEP in the economic consolidation of socialist industry and the small peasants, particularly after December 1, 1951. The origin of the errors was the excessive rate of industrialization and the extraordinary speed aimed at creating an integrated socialist national economy. This showed up first in agricultural production, and principally in the neglect of aid to private peasant farmers; frankly speaking, in antipeasant policies. It turned out that with the too rapid development of heavy industry, the material resources of the country did not prove sufficient to give new impetus to agricultural production.

. . . At that time, my opponents justified the rapid rate of development of heavy industry mainly on the basis of mechanization of agriculture. In actual fact, however, agricultural machine production did not keep pace with the large-scale development of our machine building as a whole; the ratio of agricultural machine production to machine production as a whole was reduced considerably. Tractor production, for example, was reduced to such an extent that in 1952 it did not cover replacement needs. Consequently, the agricultural tractors available not only failed to increase but decreased.

C. During the period before June, 1953, NEP was seriously violated by accelerated collectivization, which shattered the security of peasant production; less and less help was provided for the peasantry; the ever increasing state deliveries reduced sharply the quantity of goods that could be sold by the peasantry on the free market, thereby simultaneously reducing the actual material interest of the peasantry in producing as well as their desire to produce. As has already been mentioned, this loosened considerably the economic basis of the worker–peasant alliance, which is the main force for building socialism. Added to this, similar errors were committed in the field of retail trade and small industry; errors that similarly restricted the NEP and even eliminated it in numerous fields.

During the period between 1950 and June, 1953, the economic policy of our Party came into sharp conflict with the NEP, which is the basis of building socialism during the transitional period. This policy repeatedly violated NEP principles so seriously that in this period, especially in the year 1952, preceding the June resolution, in contradiction to Marxist–Leninist teachings, building of socialism in our country continued essentially without NEP. And yet Lenin had told us, with strong self-criticism, the errors committed in the Soviet Union with respect to the NEP:

We, who were raised high by waves of enthusiasm, who aroused the fervor of the people, first in the general political field and later in the military field, thought that we could also solve equally great economic problems directly and with enthusiasm. We counted on the fact – or perhaps more correctly, we took it for granted without sufficient consideration – that the proletarian state could directly, by command, organize in our country of small peasants all state production and state distribution of products on the basis of Communist principles. Experience showed that we were mistaken. There is a need for many transitional periods, during which state capitalism and socialism are needed to prepare – through long years of work – for the actual transition to Communism. Let us work first of all to build sturdy little bridges that will lead our small-peasant country to socialism through state capitalism: otherwise we will not arrive at Communism.

The conduct and views manifested among the highest leadership of our party in regard to the application of the NEP and in the matter of correcting the serious errors committed in this field is leading to renewal of old mistakes, instead of better understanding the lessons of the past, and is downright foreign to the spirit of Lenin's teachings and the system of self-criticism. Taking all this into consideration, we can rightfully say that the June, 1953, resolution of the Central Committee also opened a new period in the application of the NEP in Hungary. Of course this did not go easily. The opposition was very strong in this area also, but we achieved important results anyhow. Without enumerating the results that were achieved through use of the New Economic Policy during the following one and a half to two years, we can conclude that the reinstatement of the NEP was the most significant fact of the June economic policy from the viewpoint of principle and practice. We will understand this if we know that, in accordance with the teachings of Leninism, the fundamental question in building socialism is the economic association of the working class and the working peasantry, primarily through the exchange of goods. This is the essence of the NEP.

Inasmuch as the NEP is the basis of economic policy during the transitional period, the collaboration of the working class and the working peasantry is of necessity the focal point of the NEP.

In connection with the NEP, Lenin unequivocally expressed his view that in order to be victorious, we must secure the relations between the working class and the peasantry, and between socialist industry and the peasantry, through trade between city and village developed in every way possible – because, as Lenin frequently said, the small commodity producers will tolerate no economic ties to socialist industry except through merchandise, which normally result in trade. This arises from the fact that the peasantry wants to deal entirely freely with as much of its produce as possible. The peasantry wants to accomplish this not through direct exchange of goods but through the market.

According to Lenin's teachings, the NEP represents a certain degree of compromise, but a compromise without which socialism cannot be victorious. This is the kind of compromise, as Lenin said, that is necessary because it is the only guarantee of slower, but at the same time surer, progress.

Lenin also pointed out very often that the utilization of the NEP requires unusually varied and most distinct methods, which must be developed on the basis of experience. 'The more varied our methods are, the better and richer our experience will be, and the surer and quicker the success of socialism.'

On the basis of the June, 1953, resolution of the Central Committee, we successfully utilized these Leninist guides for a year and a half to two years in every field of the national economy to which they apply: in economic relations between the workers and the peasantry, in socialist industry and the production of small peasantry, in private trade, artisan trade, the turnover of goods, and the market.

The resolutions passed since the June, 1953, session of the Central Committee took a basically correct position on the questions of the practical application of the NEP, and had results too. Essentially, we corrected the serious errors committed in the earlier period. Nevertheless, the failure to clarify completely the theoretical problems of the NEP, along with the special circumstances and methods under which they would be put into effect in Hungary during the transitional period, was a serious omission and one for which we paid dearly later.

In wide circles, principally in the ranks of the Party membership, there was and remains a high degree of ignorance and confusion on this matter.

The March resolution of the Central Committee does not even mention NEP, which is the fundamental instrument of building socialism during the transition period. The criticism, moreover, which was directed against NEP's most important economic and political precepts, and described by them as opportunist right-wing deviationism, promoted within the Party leadership the rise of anti-Marxist views, which also appeared in disguised form in Party resolutions and according to which application of the NEP was an opportunist right-wing policy and a 'distortion' of Leninism—Marxism. This explains why the 'rectification' of the supposed 'distortion' and right-wing deviationism committed in various areas of the national economy is directed essentially and primarily against the application of the NEP. Actually, instead of making baseless accusations, it would have been more proper to learn from past experience, to search for the roots of the errors, and to listen to Lenin, who as we see courageously revealed the errors in economic policy and pointed to the need for courageous application of the NEP. Lenin dealt a great deal with questions of the NEP. 'The small farmer, as long as he remains a small farmer,' writes Lenin, 'has need for such stimulation, prodding, and encouragement as will conform with his economic basis or that of a small-scale independent farm.'

Elsewhere Lenin points to the fact that the NEP's 'significant and main task above all others is to establish solidarity between the new economy which we have begun to build and the peasant economy which is the basis of subsistence of millions and millions of peasants'.

Lenin also emphatically called our attention to the fact that 'we must be free to use, and we must be able to use, every form of economic transition whatsoever if it is at all needed to strengthen the relations between the peasantry and the proletariat . . . for the promotion of industry and for the facilitation of other large-scale or more important moves such as electrification, for example'.

From the above, we can see that our party leadership did not apply, in the spirit of Leninism, and at present applies even less, the NEP policy, which constitutes the basis for building socialism.

Fear of the free market, fear of the development of the peasant farms, fear of the revival of capitalism as a result of the NEP policy – in other words, underestimation of the power of authority of the People's Democratic government, a disguised lack of faith in the concept of federation between peasants and workers – this is characteristic of the representatives of the extreme 'left-wing' agrarian policy, who incline somewhat more toward 'militant Communism' than toward a properly developed and continued NEP policy. Yet, in Lenin's words, the most dangerous fault of the 'left-wingers' is that 'they think of their desires as objective truth'.

Unfortunately, it appears that our 'left-wing' extremists are suffering from the same dangerous error. It is worth calling attention to the warning Lenin gave on May 27, 1919, to the Hungarian workers, especially to Hungarian workers having leftist tendencies. Lenin spoke of a rather prolonged transition period from capitalism to socialism. This period was necessary to break the power of habits of a petit bourgeois economy. This warning should not be forgotten, as it was in 1919 that an attempt was made to make socialized agriculture the predominant sector of agriculture within a period of four or five years.

These facts indicate that, in putting into effect certain theoretical precepts of Marxism–Leninism, some extremists ignore not only the special characteristics of the development of the Soviet Union, but of their own country as well. Yet Marxism is not a dogma but a guide to action.

Even before the March resolution of the Central Committee, opinions were being expressed to the effect that the practice of NEP should be curtailed. The old, incorrect, anti-Marxist thesis that in the worker–peasant alliance the economic link between worker and peasant should be strengthened during the transition period through the socialization of agriculture, rather than through a broadening of market connections, came into prominence again. This false, anti-Marxist theory is nothing but the theoretical formulation of the liquidation of NEP. It means that they want to lay the foundations of socialism by restricting market connections, or actually NEP at first, and finally by eliminating it altogether. It means further that socialism can and must be built without the political cooperation, alliance, and agreement of the working peasants and the peasant masses. But it means also that they intend to split apart the two interdependent main tasks of agriculture which are required by the basic law of socialism, as well as by the law of systematic, well-proportioned development as applied to the development of agriculture. These two interdependent tasks are: the simultaneous development of the production of the independent peasants, and the organization and development of the production of the producer cooperatives. By splitting these tasks, they intend instead to force the development of the producer cooperatives alone, at an increased speed and in excessive number. The attacks on NEP appearing in articles in the Party press since the March resolution of the Central Committee, plus a whole series of economic measures initiated since then by the government and the economic organs, all show that the actual implementation of the anti-NEP, anti-Marxist–Leninist, extreme leftist line that has become predominant in the Party leadership is being rapidly carried out. This seriously endangers the entire future of our building of socialism . . .

TAMAS NAGY

Some issues of political economy*

... We have discussed, at the Institute of Economics Studies, in a small group with the participation of several university teachers, the chapters dealing with capitalism and socialism of the second edition of the political economy textbook.[1] The debate was very instructive and stimulating for all participants. The present article has been written on the basis of this discussion, using some of the ideas brought up during the debate; it also deals with questions that have not been brought up at the discussion. The views expressed in the article were not shared by all participants.

Since the publication of Stalin's last work more than three years have passed. With perhaps a little exaggeration we could say that in these three years it became clear that it was not wise to bring up the concept of the fundamental economic law of individual modes of production, and the majority of Soviet economists, who participated in the discussion over the textbook, were right when – as Stalin writes – 'they reacted weakly' to this thought. It is not correct to formulate in one single law all those fundamental connections that determine the essence and the process of development of a mode of production. It turned out that the formulation of the fundamental economic law of certain methods of production did not bring us any closer to the understanding of the internal connections of that particular mode of production. An entire legal scholasticism has developed around the fundamental law, and since it tried to emphasize the exceptional importance of the fundamental law, several formulas have spread, such as the fundamental law has a 'leading role' in the system of laws, the fundamental law 'determines' the other economic laws, the other economic laws are 'subordinated' to the fundamental law. But let us suppose that every mode of production does have its own fundamental

---

* 'A politikai gazdaságtan néhány kérdéséről', *Közgazdasági szemle*, III, No. 6 (June, 1956), pp. 657–75.
1 The textbook in question is *Politicheskaia ekonomiia, uchebnik (Political economy, a manual)*, Gospolitizdat, Moscow, 1954 – a fundamental text of basic economics used throughout the socialist camp. It was written by a collective of Soviet economists and published under the auspices of the Institute of Economics of the Soviet Academy of Science. The Soviet authors relied heavily on the theoretical formulations elaborated during the economics conference organized in November 1951 by the Central Committee of the Communist Party of the USSR, commented upon by Stalin in his last work, *Economic Problems of Socialism in the USSR*, published in 1952.
   The first Soviet edition was published in Hungary twice; the second Soviet edition corresponds therefore to the *third* enlarged Hungarian edition. All quotations refer to the latter text [Ed.].

law, and that it is possible and purposeful to formulate the different fundamental laws. Even then, the Stalinist formulation of the fundamental economic law of present day capitalism is definitely incorrect, and the same is true of the attempt to apply to the conditions of monopoly capitalism the theory of surplus value as the theory of maximum profit. For not only in its imperialistic stage does capitalist production aim (objectively and subjectively) to reach maximum profit, maximum surplus value, but it had the same aim also in its pre-monopoly stage. Therefore it is not correct to consider that maximum profit was the goal of capitalism, only in its imperialist stage. For the designation of the profit of monopolies, much more suitable than 'maximum profit' are the expressions 'high monopolistic profit' or 'monopolistic extra-profit' used by Lenin. Also, the formulation is incorrect, for it does not mention the means of increasing production (although it correctly appears in the textbook among the main characteristics of the law of surplus value) and thus supports the incorrect view that the systematic increasing of the production is no more applicable in the case of modern capitalism. Finally, the Stalinist version of the fundamental law completely neglects the non-monopolized areas of capitalist industry and agriculture, although these are not negligible. Therefore, the textbook should not apply the theory of surplus value to modern capitalism for otherwise all kinds of scholasticisms and misunderstandings would arise. Instead, it should treat more thoroughly and in detail the sources and ways of acquiring of the huge monopolist profits.

... The greatest merit of the textbook is its being the first systematic study of socialist political economy – in the part dealing with socialism. This part arouses the greatest interest, and gives the most help to the Marxist–Leninist political economic education and propagandist work. But naturally, most problems appear in connection with this part.

Those circumstances which were unfavorable to the further development of Marxist political economy, and which I have mentioned before, have strongly influenced the development of political economy's treatment of socialism. Lenin has drawn very important conclusions by generalizing the first experiments and experiences of the building of socialism, and these are solid foundation-stones of the political economy of socialism, but he could not see how later the already developed socialist system functioned. Therefore, the economics of socialism had to be created after Lenin's death, and so, the personality cult that has developed around Stalin and the dogmatic treatment of the Stalinist theses have caused a great deal of damage in this field. There were other obstacles too, to the development of the young science, the economics of socialism. Since in this case we are talking of a planned economy, in which the economic policy of the party and the state plays a decisive role, scientific research constantly comes across the economic policy, the economic facts and situations created by the economic policy, and it has to evaluate and possibly criticize them, in order to reveal the internal connections of the socialistic economic system. But the political economic criticism cannot develop in a place where the atmosphere is not favorable to criticism, and there was exactly such an atmosphere due to the personality cult around Stalin, and because of tendencies towards the suppression of democracy inside the party as well as of proletarian democracy. On the other hand, the socialist economic system has been built for a short time only, and so far only in a single country, the Soviet Union, and under extremely severe conditions. A generalizing analysis, therefore, can only rely upon the facts concerning the Soviet Union, and surely, in the Soviet Union's economy it is very difficult, and sometimes even impossible, to decide which are those characteristics, factors, and connections that really belong to the essence of the socialist economic system, and which are only special conditions, only consequences of concrete economic policy.

Consequently, the economics of socialism is still a new science, and there are still many problematical and unsolved issues, which require further research and analysis. However, this is not reflected in the textbook. It creates the impression that the economics of socialism has solved all problems and is a completed, problemless scientific system. Naturally, a textbook has to try to present crystallized basic knowledge, but it should not create the impression that 'all problems are solved', an impression which even sciences more developed than the economics of socialism should avoid. This is harmful because it discourages individual thinking, decreases the interest in this branch of science, and also renders it inflexible. Therefore the textbook should refer sometimes to the not yet properly elaborated issues of the economics of socialism, and mention the fact that certain theses are not sure and are problematic. Thus it would certainly further the development of economic thinking and of science. In connection with the situation and forms of the socialist economy developed in the Soviet Union, the textbook also creates the illusion of finality, although these continuously change and evolve. This deficiency is closely connected with the treatment of the contradictions appearing in the socialist economic system. Often, the textbook does not mention these contradictions or lessens their importance, and shows the functioning of the socialist system as being more harmonious than it is in reality. It makes sometimes critical remarks concerning existing faults, but these are usually superficial: it criticizes in these cases only certain political economic measures or certain human actions. The textbook does not pay due importance to that teaching of Marx, according to which socialism is a society which is just evolving out of capitalist society, and therefore in all respects '. . . bears the birth mark of that old society from whose womb it originated' (Marx–Engels: *Selected Works,* Vol. 2, p. 16, Szikra 1941). When private interest, group interest and common interest are made consistent with one another on the basis of the principle of material interest, contradictions necessarily arise in connection with the existence of collective farm production, the existence of commodities, trade, money, etc. And it certainly brings about further contradictions if the political economy does not deal properly with this feature of socialist society.

Perhaps the most difficult problem of the economics of socialism is economic policy and, generally, the correct description of the relations between human activity and economic laws. This difficulty arises because of the tremendous growth of the subjective element, in the form of increased consciousness (greater possibility of discovering the laws, essentially common interests, the party's power, the important economic role of the socialist state). The textbook does not adequately solve this problem and this is mainly due to the fact that the following of Stalin's last work has brought about the fetishization and mystification of the laws, as well as too rigid a separation of political economy and economic policy. The textbook creates the impression that the economic laws of socialism determine the development of socialist society in all details, and that procedure in accordance with the laws was ensured, because the laws could be discovered and known and also because the harmful consequences of not proceeding in accordance with those laws. Actually, the economic laws only determine the general lines of economic development (for example, the economic laws do not uniquely determine what percentage of the national income must be devoted to consumption and to accumulation, what the wage system must be, by what methods the socialist economy should be directed, etc.). The economic laws, in socialism too, describe only the general tendencies, and although it is very important to discover them, they must not be interpreted as exactly describing reality; also, their violation usually does not immediately bring about grave consequences. Besides, the textbook hardly examines at all how far the economic policy (including the methods of economy direction) fits the economic laws, whether it uses them successfully for the accomplishment of the tasks of socialist society. In the textbook one can feel the aspiration towards the justification of the existing relations (which does not manifest itself any more in the form of voluntarism, but in the form of 'whatever there is, and as it is, is in conformity with the laws') and therefore it does not contribute to the development of a healthy critical spirit.

Although the textbook, being based on Stalin's last work, treats in detail the commodity production and the economic categories related to it, still – as is seen from the discussion – it underestimates the significance of the roots of commodity production, the importance of commodity production and trade, the role of the theory of value and its relevance to socialism. Thus it gives, in a certain measure, theoretical justification to the over-centralized planned direction of the national economy. The textbook, following Stalin, justifies the necessity of the survival of commodity production and trade in socialism, only by the existence of collective farms. But this thesis is untenable, and also leads to incorrect conclusions. Could a socialist society, with its complicated division of labor, where abundance of products has not been reached yet, where work has not yet become a life necessity of first importance, that is, an economy in which every important branch has to be based on material interest – could such a socialist society exist without commodity production and trade in case it has no collective farms? It could not exist. For first of all, the consumer goods have a commodity character, and get to the worker with the many characteristics of commodities; the worker does not receive them allocated for his work, but buys them according to his free choice, for his 'wage', a wage that not only depends on the amount and difficulty of his accomplished work, and at a price that does not depend only on the amount of work put in the product. The workers buy their consumption articles for the wages, paid in money, there exists a market for the consumption articles, and on this market there is supply and demand. Secondly, the commodity character of the consumption articles, the material stimulation of certain workers or collectives in the enterprises, and the harmonization of the central planned direction with local independence, together make it objectively necessary to direct the work of socialist enterprises by the method of independent economic accounting. That is, they make it necessary that the fundamental links of the social division of labor, which are the socialist enterprises, be organized in a way as if they were independent commodity producers which sell and buy products, make profit, etc. And if we want to improve in this respect the functioning of the socialist economic system, and want to apply more efficiently the principle of material interest, and want to make more flexible the central planned direction of national economy – which is an objective necessity – then we have to strengthen the commodity producer character of the enterprises, for instance by raising the importance and stimulating effect of profit. Naturally, it would be incorrect to ignore the great differences between the commodity relations of the state sector and the collective farms, between the commodity relations of the state sector and its own workers, and between the commodity relations among the state enterprises themselves. It would also be a mistake to hide the fact that the relation between the state sector and its own workers has to a certain extent a commodity character, and so is in a certain measure the relation between the state enterprises which sell to each other means of production. Also mistaken is the statement according to which the means of production moving within the state sector are commodities only by their form and not essentially. True, in this case there are no separate owners. But there are (and there must be) separately producing collectives – separated on the basis of the objective economic category of independent economic accounting – whose separation, characteristic to socialism, will grow as a result of the objectively necessary decrease in the over-centralization of planned direction. To consider the special commodity producer character of the state enterprises that work with independent accounting as being merely the reflection of the existence of collective farms, has harmful consequences, because this view impedes the struggle for simplification of planned direction, for greater flexibility, for better utilization of the theory of value, for the development of local independence, for the increase of productivity.

The textbook treats unsatisfactorily, and sometimes unclearly, the mode of manifestation of the theory of value in socialism. It states that in socialism the theory of value cannot play the role of regulator of production, and that it influences socialist production. But it does not clarify what the influence of the theory of value on the production of state enterprises consists in. The economic categories related to the theory of value (price, production cost, profit, etc.) evidently have a certain impact on the production of the state enterprises in the present system of independent economic accounting. But are these impacts influences of the theory of value? For in many cases the state enterprises have tried to fulfill their production plans which supposed unchanged prices, by more profitable articles, in order to get the bonus for fulfilling the production plan. Is this too under the influence of the theory of value on production? According to the textbook, it seems that in the case of state enterprises, the influence of the theory of value on production consists in its stimulating effect towards the increasing of productivity and reduction of production cost. Today, this stimulation is done chiefly by giving bonuses, when the production plan is fulfilled. But why consider this as being the influence of the theory of value? Is this not a stimulation through the value categories, or the utilization of the value categories?

Even more unclear is the treatment of the regulating role of the theory of value in the field of trade. The textbook states that this regulating role 'manifests itself chiefly through price' (p. 506). But the intention of 'chiefly', and also the mode of regulation, are unclear. According to the textbook, the theory of value does not regulate prices; and prices regulate demand, but not supply. If so, what does the theory of value regulate?

How can the theory of value regulate trade, without regulating production (supply)? Why does not the theory of value regulate the trade of means of production? All these questions are constantly raised in teaching, and we cannot answer them satisfactorily. It seems that we shall be able to develop clearly the manifestation of the theory of value in socialism only if we thoroughly study the concrete facts, and do not consider as valid for all times the present methods of economic direction, and if we also reject a large part of the terminology created by Stalin's last work connected with the manifestation of the theory of value.

The textbook rightly states that the need for money in socialism arises from the existence of commodity production and the theory of value. But while earlier it underestimated the importance of commodity production and of the commodity character of products in socialist trade (or more exactly, of part of these products), it goes now to the other extreme and states that the general measure in socialism is, and can only be, gold (p. 511). The creed that in socialism the money is actually gold, and that the bills issued by the central bank are only representatives, substitutes, signs of gold, is unfortunately very popular in our Marxist political economic literature, although it has never been proved. In my opinion, the Marxian thesis saying that only the monetary product can fulfill the measuring function is not valid in the case of a planned socialist economy. In socialism, money is real money not because it represents gold, or because it is a sign of gold, but because it circulates, that is, because it functions as basis of trade (which of course, is planned). The payment for work 'is not money, it does not circulate' – said Marx (*Capital,* Vol. 2, pp. 363–4); and thus, in my opinion, he gave us a key for understanding the nature of money functioning in socialist countries. The correct theory of money functioning under socialist conditions must be sought by conscientiously studying, on the basis of Marx's words, the concrete facts, and also by rejecting any dogmatic construction.

The discussion of the planned direction of the national economy warns against the overcentralization of planning and stresses the importance of local independence and initiative. But in this case, the theoretical foundation of the textbook, the same as when discussing the problems of commodity production, does not follow definitely enough this correct political economic line. For instance, the textbook says (p. 465) that spontaneous and automatic procedure is incompatible with the development of socialist society. But unfortunately, it does not explain the meaning of this very important thought, nor the difference between spontaneous and planned development. The over-centralized planned direction of the national economy served as grounds for that generally accepted and harmful idea that everything that is not regulated by central (or at least coming from above) compulsory planning instructions, or departs from them in any way, belongs to the category of spontaneity. Not to point out the difference between spontaneity and national economic planned direction, and such unclear and unexplained statements that socialist production cannot develop 'without a plan determining uniform activity for the entire society' (p. 465), that the central plans 'are not forecasts but instruction-type plans' (p. 477), only strengthen this harmful belief, and give theoretical support to the existing practice. The textbook should also have mentioned that the process of development of our national economy is planned, instead of being spontaneous, only when it stands under the conscious direction and control of society (that is, the central organs representing the knowledge and will of society); it should also mention that in order to accomplish this, besides the plan instructions, we can and have to make use of many other means, and that the optimal harmonization of the central direction and local independence and the best utilization of the economic levers in the interest of planned direction are problems that are far from being solved.

Finally I shall discuss some problems concerning the treatment of the economy of transition from capitalism to socialism. The textbook develops the principal issues of the transition from capitalism to socialism in three chapters: the main characteristics of the period of transition, socialist industrialization, and the collectivization of agriculture. After the part dealing with socialism, it discusses in two separate chapters the economic systems of the European people's democracies and of the Chinese People's Republic. This procedure is not quite right.

Following the pioneering example of the Soviet Union and with its help, other countries today are also building socialism, and the diverse aspects of the building of socialism are beginning to crystallize. Therefore it would be more correct not to treat separately the particularities of the period of transition in the European people's democracies and in China, but to discuss them together in the general discussion about the problems of the transition leading to socialism. The experience of our teaching practice shows that we cannot teach the main characteristics of the transitional period as well as the socialist industrialization and the collectivization of agriculture, without treating special cases, experiences and problems occurring in Hungary. Even if this unification cannot be made, for different reasons, in the textbook, it should not treat the issues of the transition exclusively on the basis of the development of the Soviet Union, in the chapters 'The main characteristics of the transitional period between capitalism and socialism', 'The socialist industrialization' and 'The collectivization of agriculture'. In these chapters the specific characteristics of the development of the Soviet Union are inevitably mixed with characteris-

tics true of all, or many countries. The transition accomplished in the
Soviet Union was the first transition, and happened under very hard
conditions. But it is described as if all its details were general laws, and the
experience of the transitional economies of the people's democracies is not
developed and generalized. Also, the possibility of presenting a smoother,
more gradual, milder transition remains unexploited, while generalizing
the process of transition. By talking only about the Soviet Union's industrialization in the chapter 'The socialist industrialization', the description
of the methods and of the sources is one-sided, and such a fundamental
issue as the consideration of the problems of the international division of
labor in socialist industrialization, cannot even be considered. In the same
way, in the chapter 'The collectivization of agriculture', the explanation of
the collectivization, its essence and its generally true principles, should not
contain the details of its accomplishment in the Soviet Union. In its present
form, this chapter does not emphasize enough those aspects which are
particularly important in the case of the people's democracies: the task of
developing the agriculture, the volunteering, the moderation. The Soviet
way of liquidation of the kulak class is described as a general principle to
be followed, while in fact, in the people's democracies we can, and also
have to use different methods.

In the discussion of the transitional period it is very important to show
what is the basic program of the economic policy and what kind of
economic policy is implied by the economic conditions of this period, by
the economic laws functioning in this period, and by the cause of the
accomplishment of socialism. But this task is not fulfilled well by the
textbook. Theoretical principles and historical discussions are mixed
together, the fundamentals of economic policy are not deduced from the
objective conditions, and the much debated NEP concept is not clarified.
One of the sources of the obscurity is that the textbook does not clearly
distinguish between the NEP as a concrete historical concept, and the
whole economic policy of the transitional period. In my opinion, those
characteristics of the economic policy in the transitional period which are
generally valid – for every country, or almost every country – can be
summarized as follows: the gradual accomplishment of the transition,
using the forces of small commodity production and even the forces of
capitalism; the use of the market, trade and money for the building of
socialism, including the organization of the economic relations between
the state industry and the peasant farms; the extensive use of the principle
of material interest; the accomplishment of the planned direction of the
national economy; the socialist industrialization; the socialist reorganization of agriculture. Part of these main characteristics of the economic
policy in the transitional period have been elaborated in detail and pro-

claimed by Lenin in 1921, and exactly these guiding principles form the content of the concrete historical category of NEP. And this does not only consist in the fact that socialism has to be built by using the market, trade and circulation of money (this is how the textbook defines the NEP on page 372), but also private trade, free markets for the peasants, private small industry, state capitalism. Therefore the NEP contains certain concessions to small commodity production and to capitalism, in the interest of building socialism, and above all, in the interest of the economic alliance between the working class and peasantry . . .

PÉTER ERDÖS

Some theoretical issues of economic planning*

. . . Those who are acquainted with the universal history of economy and with the history of theories, will make a parallel between mercantilist state protectionism, e.g. 18th century Colbertism, and our economic management regulating everything by rules and prescriptions. Let us read the complaints of the Physiocrats against the host of paragraphs paralyzing all initiative in their age and intending to closely direct and influence the industrial life just beginning to develop. In spite of the old-fashioned articles and the comically primitive technical suggestions, they make us feel at home in many respects. It seems that not only socialist theory, but also its politico-economic practice have come of age, and it is high time to change this situation. This is affirmed at least by those who believe that socialism, as far as its possibilities are concerned, is superior in every respect to capitalism, and by those who are not ready to accept the idea that the existing faults are necessary. Of course, for the time being, this is only a matter of belief because we have not yet found a better way and in many important matters we do not even know in which direction to experiment. But the task is clear: we have to find the optimum between central management and local initiative. Everywhere we find that it is not freedom that is excessive but, on the contrary, there is excessive central control and insufficient possibility for local initiative . . .

What argument could in principle be raised against the claim that it is possible to plan by giving much less detailed central instructions than up to now, giving considerably more leeway to local initiative, and still assuring a high growth rate? No really important reasoning has ever been raised against it . . .

* Excerpted from 'A tervgazdálkodas néhány elméleti kérdéseröl', *Közgazdasági szemle*, III, No. 6 (June, 1956), pp. 676–94.

The 'cult' of laws

An important scientific merit of Stalin is that in his last work he set himself against the voluntaristic distortions and the enormous exaggeration of the state's role, all of which are alien to the true Marxist spirit. Giddiness over the success achieved is only one cause of these distortions; the personality cult, the belief in the unquestionable omnipotence of the leader is another. As long as the research worker had to recognize the state plan as being a basic economic law, it was completely impossible to discuss the correctness of realizing this 'law' in all its detail. In his last work Stalin reestablished the basic Marxist thesis about the objectivity of the laws of the society. (Reestablished, since as is known, Marx and Engels had considered the laws of society to be 'natural laws' of society, and considered the freedom of socialism to be freedom within the recognized necessity.)

But the personality cult backfired because, after the publication of Stalin's work, the 'cult' of laws spread everywhere. On reading some recent scientific books, the unsuspecting reader may find himself lost in an enchanted forest of economic laws. Here the laws have their own hierarchy, superiority and subordination, where they mutually determine and modify one another as well as every economic event. Once hurt, the laws immediately retaliate. Our clinging to these laws, turning them to our own use, seems analogous to the dead souls' clinging to the ship of Charon (that ship which sails relentlessly toward the inner gate of hell, never deviating, even slightly, from its precisely determined route). And even the fact that the destination in our case is not the pit of hell, but rather the marvellous socialist future to which there is a single route, precisely defined, does not change this inevitability of laws. This omnipotence of laws, their power to determine every detail of development, is in strange contrast to the fact that the majority of the actually formulated economic laws are too general and unfit to help solve any practical problem.

So what should one say when facing a fatalist outlook that makes a fetish of the laws?

Primarily, that the economic laws fix important economic correlations that become realized sooner or later, with or without the consent of the individual. But, whereas other branches of science, e.g. physics, or at least the physics of the macrocosmos, give a relatively exact description of the definite correlations of reality, the economic laws give only a general outline of economic development, are only realized as tendencies, and are only approximations of the true reality. I repeat: the economic laws are only tendencies. This is the case with the economic laws of socialism as well, which differ from those of capitalism only by the fact that socialist society as a whole has to promote the realization of the objective laws of the development of socialism by its conscious economic policy, otherwise there will be no socialism. (This is why only the proletariat can be the leading class of socialism, for this class must desire the development of socialism due to its objective class position. And, this is why socialism cannot be brought about until the proletariat has ceased to exist.)

Our second answer to the views that make a fetish of the laws is the following: 'the laws' means great, general and important correlations that are sooner or later necessarily realized. In a class-society the law is forcibly realized due to the fact that typical acts under typical circumstances, determined by the relations of production become necessary, and the general law will finally break through the many diverse accidental acts. In socialism, or in a socialism-building society, there is a theoretical, and always inexact, possibility of recognizing and foreseeing the laws, rules and necessities, and, on their basis, the planning of development is possible. If the plan is good and if harmony can be achieved between the direct interests and possibilities of the independently managed enterprises and state will, then the development will take the foreseen and desired direction without colliding with any law on the way. In such cases the requirements of the laws are realized without difficulty. But in practice the matter is not so simple. The interests of the state will never coincide completely with the direct local interests and it can never contend with all the possibilities and obstacles. Disagreements with, and deviations from, the plan will inevitably arise. But even in these cases, the laws themselves are not encountered by the planned economy, but only the necessities and regularities, and these latter cause the unforeseen deviations. The laws themselves show up only when the plan or its execution is completely wrong, or if there is a significant deviation in development. But even in such cases the law is not seen immediately, and only the subsequent accumulation of difficulties will call the attention of the entire society to the fact that the law itself had been violated. The actual hindering or helping possibilities and necessities encountered here and there follow from the prevailing, concrete potentialities.

Now we can formulate our third answer to those who believe in fatality and make a fetish of the laws. The past decisions and acts with all their consequences, as well as the efficient or inefficient economic institutions brought about through the leadership of inferior economic organs, also belong to the prevailing concrete potentialities, for the nature of their purposeful or wrong instructions greatly influence development. Development is always determined by causes and effects and by their dialectic correlation, but the so-called subjective factors, i.e. the will and acts of men as well as the institutions they have created, are also to be found among the determining factors. Although the latter are themselves determined, it is not only the economic factors or only the basic economic laws that determine them. Summarizing, the basic economic laws determine the basic tendencies of the economic development, but the development itself in all its details and concrete complications is left undetermined within certain limits. Therefore, making a fetish of the laws is scientifically untenable.

I will try to elaborate in greater detail this triple answer.

The 'great laws' and the concrete necessities that determine development

Let us begin with the great laws. If the laws are only tendencies then they can give but slight direction as far as concrete situations are concerned. The economic literature knows of two great laws that must be taken into consideration when making national economic plans. One is the so-called basic law, the other is the law of planned proportional development. Socialism cannot be built up without meeting the constantly increasing demands of the society and for that we must constantly raise the production rate with the aid of the latest technology. We must have reproduction on an increasing scale, based especially on the rapid expansion of sector I [producers' goods], but, at the same time, the output of sector II [consumers' goods] should also increase quickly providing its products to meet the needs of the working population. To this extent planning is directly affected by the basic law; but here we have already reached the domain of the law of planned proportional development. This latter law says that our economy must be centrally planned – which is a fundamental truth – but . . . it hardly says anything new from the point of view of practical planning. And the law of planned proportional development is by no means apt for showing, even approximately, what to plan centrally so that our entire economy would show a really proportional development, i.e. to foresee (and realize) every necessary detail. Secondly, the law says that economic expansion must be 'proportional'. But it is completely unfit also for deducing the most suitable concrete proportions of expansion at any given time. Of course, I do not refer here to what the popularizing literature exclusively points out: that in order to produce a certain number of machines a certain amount of steel is needed, for that again enough raw iron, further on ore and foundry coke is needed, etc. That which lies beyond these technical correlations would be of eminent economic importance (e.g. what should be the proportion of accumulation and consumption in a certain period). It cannot be deduced from the abstract notion of proportionality (neither can it be deduced from the 'basic law') . . .

Whereas the requirements of the laws themselves are very general, the development of the national economy is completely determined by many objective circumstances that are independent of our will. These circumstances themselves were partly created involuntarily, and partly somewhat voluntarily, but they are always objectively existing, i.e. facts to be taken into consideration and bearing determined necessities. Some of them originate from important national economic or even international economic and political circumstances. Everyone knows, for instance, that the demands and perspectives of the international and of the national class struggle extensively determine the particular aspects of certain developmental phases. Other circumstances have but a limited determining role, i.e. they determine only a partial area of the general development.

One of the most important components of the necessities determining both the general outlines of expansion as well as its details (local, of industrial branches, etc.) is the preliminary development itself and the potentialities it has created. Just these existing potentialities represent the starting points for further progress, and the later expansion will rely on them. However rapid the development in a socialist country may be and to whatever extent it may contain the elements of discontinuous development, in its entirety this development is still organic and continuous. Neither is expanded reproduction something new; it is a reproduction that contains as its basic element reproduction on a static scale: the old simple reproduction. (Among the existing potentialities also the elements of the new and emerging facts can be encountered, but in their majority they still look like what has to be reproduced without change, principally in the previous manner and without great alterations. The already achieved state, in this sense too, is one of the principal objective facts that necessarily determine the frames of further development.)

All this is relevant not only for the whole, or for the large sectors of the national economy, but for all its small components as well. For instance, the development of an enterprise can be sudden in certain periods, too. But, however sudden this development may be, it is always organic and continuous, originating from the developmental level of the enterprise; and it is based not on vacuum but on the interior and exterior potentialities of the enterprise, on the traditional and successful relations it has created during its production.

Among many other things this organic character of production, its relative stability and therefore the possibility of extending and generalizing previous experience, enables the recognition of the necessities. This recognition is not a purpose in itself for us, but serves for enabling the society – by its knowing the necessities – to plan and to realize on the basis of the plan, the correct and desired development. The dialectics of recognition are such that the process of planning itself leads to recognition. Part of the relevant objective correlations and the necessities arising from them are revealed by the national economic analysis already at the stage of drawing up the general national economic plan.

Long-range national economic planning must obviously begin by determining the decisive chains, the most important developmental trends. At that phase of planning the requirements take a quasi qualitative shape. The general form of reasoning is something like this: sector M must be expanded principally but the expansion of branch N is also very important, whereas the development of industrial branch R must be slowed down; on the other hand, the quantitative index of many sectors must be raised, etc. Afterwards the qualitative recognitions are matched with quantitative analyses. Here the balancing method will be decisive. Multiple correlations have to be compared and the possible numerical proportions have to be guessed that way. Meanwhile, the possible contradictions in the original aims are also elucidated and in such cases they have to be replaced by others. The end result is a closed system of indicators characterizing also numerically the main outline of the future development of the national economy. In this system not a single figure may be changed without simultaneously suitably changing the other data as well. Therefore, the system thus prepared has already taken into consideration many analyzed and also quantitatively measured necessities that are mutually dependent upon each other.

The national economic plan is necessarily general. It is good if it shapes correctly the principal tasks of expansion, that is: (a) if it establishes correct proportions, and (b) if it keeps to the correct proportions so that it chooses the decisive proportion out of the many desired proportions. No planning office can know exactly all the complicated correlations of the concrete economic life to the extent that it would be able to prepare a sensible national economic plan as detailed as is the production program of the single enterprises. That is why even the national economic plan prepared on the basis of the balancing method can be based only on average numbers. Thus its exactness too, can only be limited; its categories must be very general and be able to be filled out with diverse concrete contents. But the details of development even in their concreteness are determined by many further necessities.

The great and decisive necessities, the necessary comprehensive proportions of development can be recognized in the uppermost leading organs, whereas the scope that can be summed up from the enterprise is not suitable for their recognition. On 'lower levels' and finally, in the enterprises, further new necessities become valid and in correct planning these must be taken into consideration just as the correlations, but the top organs leading the entire economic life are unfit for recognizing these necessities.

The closer we are to the basic organ of economy, i.e. to the enterprise, the less is it possible to make a correct plan on the basis of general statistical considerations and the more concrete the starting points of planning must be. On the other hand, the enterprises have a greater possibility to make exact plans (possessing the knowledge of the concrete circumstances), all these of course within the frame of demands received from the central organs that reflect the higher correlations . . .

The limits of scientific cognition

After speaking so much in detail about the objective existence and the possibility of recognition, of rules and necessities determining the good plan, let me throw light on the other side of the question as well. Up to now the plan was shown as the expression of the objective necessities and the plan, in fact, is that. Now the question is, in what does it differ from that; what does it have in addition.

Let us begin with the well-known fact that the plans are only more or less reflections of the laws, of objective potentialities and of necessities, since the recognition of necessities is never exact and never complete . . .

But let us go further! Let us suppose the impossible: the plan is so good that it contains no error at all. This will be practically seen from the fact that the enterprises fulfill their plans exactly, though with difficulty, and consequently the national economy shows great expansion rates, and the plan can be harmoniously further developed at its termination period; meanwhile there has been a satisfactory rise in the welfare of the working population. More than this certainly cannot be expected from any plan. If everything actually was all right, then the demands of the objective laws of socialism had been observed during the planning and the balancing method had been applied well. But it does not mean by any means that this was the only correct way, or the best alternative way. The demands of the minor and major necessities are partly general and partly indeterminable from a quantitative point of view, and partly they can be satisfied variously. On the one hand, it is obvious that the same, or almost the same, end result can be obtained in different ways. On the other hand, in most cases it is obvious that usually we are practically unable to decide, on the basis of objective reasons, which end result is preferable if they are very similar. The political economist may well know, on the basis of several compulsive reasons, that the manifest rise in the living standard in a given period is one of the definitive central links of economic policy. But no objective compelling reason may justify the rise in the standard of living in that given period to be exactly 23 and not just 21 or 24%. And even if it is true that, on preparing the balance system, the change of one single figure must be followed by the change of all the other figures, it is not certain whether in reality it is not just that deviation from the prescribed number that would assure real balance . . .

The role of the subjective factors

The necessities are unavoidable necessities. But nobody is more obviously in the domain of iron necessities than the alpinist on the steep cliffs. A single incorrect step and he may break his neck. But he has also several methods to get further and it depends on him which one he chooses within the prevailing possibilities. He will not only take the objective conditions into consideration, i.e. the surface ruggedness of the cliff, its durability, the direction and strength of the wind, but also his own abilities, skillfulness and momentary physical condition. With my last sentence, however, I am referring to the third part of the former triple answer. It is about the so-called subjective factors.

Ever since our economists have dealt frequently and extensively with the objective laws in general, they have largely failed to elucidate the theoretical role of political economy. Yet, our classics have thrown enough light on the correlation of objective and subjective elements in the development of society for applying their teachings in this issue as well. One of the most important politico-economic organs is, of course, the plan itself. It is the reflector of economic necessities, but it is even more because: (a) it contains also incorrect 'recognitions', and (b) its planners had decided themselves concerning the details of the desired development (within the limits of the relative and practical uncertainty of the necessary development). In the plan they had fixed certain details, without exactly deciding on the basis of objective criteria whether the chosen variation is really the best one.

The practical significance is different in these two motifs. The consequences of the former one are well known. It may be that the plan contains unrealizable demands. In such cases, of course, the command of the objective possibilities, and not that of the plan, will be realized. It is also possible that the plan may be realized but finally it will have harmful consequences. If in such cases the plan is followed, sooner or later the violation of the objective necessities will be felt because different disproportions will arise. The departing of the plan from the necessities will finally have the consequence that the necessities will take the role of direction. They will take it by forcing their recognition and the consequent modification of the plan, or, if they do not come to light, they will cause an undesired deviation of development. Obviously, the latter possibility is the greater trouble because, if the necessities are not recognized, further contradictions and harms will result. In the case of great contradictions and mistakes, the rules, similar to the forces of nature, will of themselves finally come to demand respect by their destructive effects.

But now, instead of the possible errors of the plan, we are more interested in the essence and role of the plan that reflects the correct recognitions. The good plan is an intermediary between the necessities and between the social act, it is the result of the recognition of the necessities and of the subjective choice between alternatives, but it will itself become a material acting force if it mobilizes the will of the masses which is the subjective element of the social development. Under such conditions the real development will take place according to the directions and proportions fixed by the plan indicators. In this sense the plan will become the direct impulse of the development. But, I repeat, this takes place only if the plan interposes correctly between the will of the leading organs and the executors of the plan, i.e. of the entire working people.

. . . Let us summarize. It is not true that the laws determine the details of development. It is not true that the leading organs prescribe every detail of the activity of the economic organs and are in possession of general laws that regulate everything. And finally, it is not true that the end result of even the exact realization of the plan is the only possible, most advantageous development required by the objective laws. It is enough to think this over, and then the reasonings that intend to defend the present overcentralization of our economic direction by consequences allegedly originating from the objectiveness of the laws of socialism, will disappear.

This is clear and in principle it can be elucidated academically, even without special scientific research. We can already deduce from these abstract theoretical statements several practical instructions for economic science and for political economy. I am presenting here just a few examples.

Let us put an end to the fetishizing of economic laws! Let us not attribute to them a mystical role that determines every detail of economic development!

Let us cease to make a fetish of the target figures. Zero degree centigrade – the freezing point of water, or 100°C – the boiling point of water, are significant critical points. But the 100 % fulfillment of the production plan defines no real critical point. Thus we have no reason or right to make an artificial standard of it so that 0.1 % overfulfillment must deserve appreciation and a bonus, whereas 0.1 % below 100 % fulfillment deserves the following epithets: 'lagging behind', 'not fulfilling their duties', 'working badly', etc. In the latter case a poster was also distributed that showed the imperialists happily greeting the 'enemies' of the people who had a 0.1% minus in fulfilling the plan.

Let us not rely comfortably on the laws of socialism! Let us not suppose that they will be efficient without our collaboration. For example: it is true that rapid technical expansion is a law of socialism, but it is not surprising that we will be technically left behind if the material conditions of renewal are not created. Let us stop repeating simplifying statements such as: 'In our socialist industry the laws of socialism are completely effective and successful . . .', to which we sometimes add 'only the resistance of the class enemy and the other remnants of the capitalist past may somewhat hinder their predominance . . .', etc. The enemy's hand is one thing and our own awkwardness and lack of experience is another, and we should not confuse the two. If we see, for instance, that year after year we lag behind our technical developmental plans, then, before blaming the back-wardness or the enemy's activity, first of all we should examine which politico–economic institutions had set up the contradiction between the enterprise, the local economic leaders on the one hand, and the interests of the national economy on the other! That is: let us examine how we, ourselves, place obstacles, although with the best intentions, before the predominance of economic laws of socialism (it is known that the pathway to hell is also paved with good intentions) . . .

EDWARD LIPIŃSKI

On the subject of economics and economic laws*

Without overestimating the practical value of theory – there can be good economic theory and bad policy in practice – it must be recognized that precision and exactness in the field of science are of decisive importance for establishing correct theses on economic policy.

For years the creation of 'profound' economic works has been urged. But 'profound' works do not appear. The causes of this deficiency in economic science are manifold. For a long time the need for an 'apology' for the socialist economy replaced the need for analysis. Practical assis-tance was demanded of science, which it could not give (for example, revealing hidden idle capacities).

One of the causes of the weakness of our science was the lack of precision in the concept of the subject of economics itself.

The outstanding formulation by Marx that political economy is a

* 'O przedmiocie ekonomii i prawach ekonomicznych', *Ekonomista*, No. 5, 1956, pp. 17–42.

science of production relations, of social relations between people on the basis of a specific type of ownership of the means of production, became, in our conditions, rather an obstacle to the development of this science. It is true that social production has two aspects which are inseparably linked, although they reflect two sets of different relations, namely the production forces (relationship of man to nature) and production relations (relations between people in the production process).

Both these elements of the social production process form the object of investigation of political economy. But relations between men in the production process concern things – means of production and products. Man in his economic activity comes into contact with material production elements representing certain quantities, measurable in outlays and human requirements, costs and prices, and quantitatively and qualitatively definable. Between these quantitative elements of production and exchange (exchange in the Marxist sense *Verkehr,* which encompasses division of labor, social classes, production location, foreign trade, exchange, money, etc.) there exist certain relations and connections which have the character of 'economic laws'.

The growth of national economy, or what Marx calls expanded reproduction, is controlled by certain 'proportions' and regularities. Reducing this problem to the thesis that 'production of sector i is growing more quickly than production of sector ii' constitutes only the first, and very general approach to this problem. The same applies to the so-called theory of industrialization. What is popularly presented here as the 'theory of industrialization' is in fact no more than a few rudimentary and primitive theses of political economy that have little in common with any 'theory'.

A number of industrialization principles headed by the principle that heavy and engineering industry should be set up first, followed by 'light' industries, does not yet constitute a theory of industrialization. These are maxims of economic policy, based on the theory of economics and drawn from theory, but maxims that are not at all generally binding. The postulates of industrialization, established by the Communist party in the USSR, are quite correct for a large country possessing large resources of raw materials. However, the theoretically correct industrialization policy of a relatively small country, deprived of many raw materials, cannot be based on the principle that this country should begin with building all the heavy industries that are indispensable for establishing light industry. Quite the opposite is true. A scientifically correct policy of such a country should take into consideration the fact of international division of labor and the mutually complementary production of individual countries. Although small Switzerland partly possesses heavy engineering industry, this industry can exist and develop only on condition of supplying many other countries. On the other hand, the development of the precision industry is based on the import of raw materials, and even machines, and not on developing these branches locally.

The industrialization theory still awaits elaboration. This is also a theory of the selection of proper investment alternatives, the theory of investment types (capital intensive and capital saving), the theory of the correct relation of live labor to fixed assets, the problem of the relation of accumulation to consumption, etc.

Relations between things, between measurable magnitudes, are investigated by the economist when he analyzes, for example, the process of accelerated industrialization based on developing heavy industry. The economist then perceives and describes the decline in labor productivity in some production branches, as, for example, in agriculture, which does not obtain an adequate quantity of building materials, equipment and fertilizers. The economist notes that machines when not renewed become obsolete, for example, in the textile industry, and the decline in labor productivity and the low wages in that industry.

The economist builds a theory of industrialization which is not at all confined to the simple and banal theses that heavy industry should be developed first, followed by the processing industry producing consumer goods. This particularly in view of the fact that this order cannot constitute a law binding in all countries and under all conditions. The industrialization process itself encompasses many problems incomparably more complex, the analysis of which should be dealt with by political economy.

The investigation of quantitative relations and connections constitutes the subject of the economic theory of the socialist economy. In economics we inquire not only into the rules governing the transition from one social order to another, not only class relations, but also, e.g., inherent laws ruling the circulation of paper money,[1] or laws of production, or laws of equilibrium between investments and consumption.

Stalin justly criticized Yaroshenko,[2] who held that the science of economics is a science of the organization of production forces, but in spite of the progress due to his work, Stalin did not lay down the foundations for the development of the theory of socialist economy, since in Stalin's conception the dominating factors were sociological rather than economic. He takes particular interest in development phenomena related to the qualitative (i.e. connected with the type of ownership of the means

1 Marx, *Critique of Political Economy*, Książka i Wiedza, 1953, p. 116. [All quotations retranslated from Polish.]

2 An obscure participant in the discussion on economics (organized in 1951 in the USSR by the Central Committee of the Soviet Communist Party) summarily criticized by Stalin in the *Economic Problems of Socialism in the USSR* (New York: International Publishers, 1952, pp. 56ff.). [Ed.]

of production) transformation of economic formations and their historical evolution. The phenomena of equilibrium and growth are reduced by Stalin primarily to the law of 'planned and proportionate development', without a clear insight, however, into the problems involved in the laws of proportion governing the economy.

Whatever the socio-economic framework, we are concerned in economic processes with the basic elements of any 'production' and any 'exchange' of human activities and their social forms directly connected with the forms of ownership of the means of production, and hence with production relations. Nevertheless, the quantity of goods and the amount of available social labor are limited everywhere, there always exists sector I and sector II, certain proportions always operate in the process of social production, we are always concerned with necessary labor and surplus labor, consumption possibilities everywhere depend on social productivity. Only the social forms of production are different, but 'its foundations are common to all production modes'.[3]

For example, technical progress in capitalism is limited and dictated by the factor of capitalist profit. In socialist economy technical progress is realized for the purpose of output growth and increased satisfaction of needs. But in both cases the surplus values obtained are decisive though their social forms are different.

Capital is a social relationship and as such does not contain anything material. But capital can be expressed in terms of money, it is a measurable and tangible magnitude, it can be employed as any other material magnitude. The designer, calculating the strength of materials, deals with the same material, calculable elements, as the economist. The economist is right in ignoring production relations, relations between men, which lie at the base of the social phenomenon, category, capital, and treating them separately, independently, and dealing with relations existing between 'things', between economic magnitudes. He may inquire, say, into the regularities concerning the different modes of using capital. For example, capital investments are either capital saving or labor saving. In each case different measurable effects will result, which have to be analyzed.

Another example: price in capitalism is an instrument for realizing the surplus product, it thus reflects production relations. But within the existing production relations and on the basis thereof, on the changes of prices and price levels depend the direction of the flow of demand, on relations of prices of production factors depend the choice of certain combinations of these factors, the greater use of some of them, the smaller use of others, etc.

'Economic regularities' operate everywhere, and everywhere policy tries

3 Marx, *Capital*, Vol. III, p. 933.

to 'use' laws, though not always aptly. They are employed by the Price Office, which fixes high prices for industrial articles in the expectation that demand will thus fall for agricultural articles in short supply, as for example meat, not taking into consideration that demand elasticity of meat is relatively low and rarely will anybody give up meat for clothing made of 60 per cent wool or a television set priced at 6000 zlotys.[4] If we raise the price of a certain article, we arrive at a point when many buyers will cease to buy it, the law of elasticity of demand beginning to operate. These are also economic 'laws' functioning in any 'economy', i.e. a system of supplying human needs when no plentiful supply of goods exists and one produce has to be chosen at the expense of another, one factor of production instead of another.

These relations between economic magnitudes should, of course, be investigated on the basis of specific production relations. Herein lies the superiority of the Marxist economy over the bourgeois economy. But 'Marxism' does not contain or lay down any specified Marxist method of investigation for these quantitative relationships, it does not exclude any method or means of investigation, even if employed by bourgeois economists, the only important thing being that they should be effective.

The rehabilitation of the analysis of what is happening 'on the surface of the phenomena' becomes a postulate which must be fully realized by the Marxist economy.

The law of value governs prices – the market value constitutes the point of gravitation of prices[5] – but the price level itself or price changes automatically provoke changes in supply and demand, provoke reaction, which must be analyzed. Instances of such an analysis can be found in the works of Marx, and in particular in the chapter on competition in Vol. III.[6] The problem of different forms of capitalist monopoly, the changes in the forms of competition, the diminished role of competition owing to prices, the reaction of consumers' demand to price changes or changes in consumers' income – to name only a few of the problems – not only merit an analysis, but without such an analysis it is impossible to understand exactly the mechanism of contemporary capitalism, or to build an efficiently functioning planned economy.

The analysis of phenomena 'on the surface' is vulgar economics only in the case when it has apologetic and not investigative objectives, and when it confines itself solely to examining these phenomena.

---

4 The mentioned Price Office is well aware of the theory of monopoly prices in fixing a higher price for lemons than for oranges, knowing that demand elasticity for lemons is lower than that for oranges. Therefore the power of the monopoly is greater on the lemon market than on the orange market.

5 Marx, *Capital*, Vol. III, p. 203.   6 Marx, *Capital*, Vol. III, p. 217 and further.

Money emerges only under specific production relations, in a commodity economy, when the product changes its owner. This is true. But the mechanism of money circulation can be examined as though it were separated from production relations. Although the class sense of inflation is different in a capitalist economy from that in a socialist economy, the essence of inflation remains the same. Differential rent appears in different types of land ownership, but this does not alter the substance of rent. The scarcity of resources is an economic fact which exists in every economy.

Yaroshenko tried to limit political economy to a science 'on the rational organization of production forces' and the 'theory of economic planning'. The acceptance of Yaroshenko's assumptions – Stalin justly wrote – would signify 'the liquidation of the political economy of socialism', since 'economy investigates the law of the development of production relations between men' and does not treat the subject of rational organization of production forces, which is the task of economic policy.

But this formulation of the range of problems of political economy does not, as already pointed out, explain everything. For example, does the problem of economic growth (extended reproduction) and the laws of this growth, or the problem of the proportions of the growth, belong to 'relations between men'? Or the problem of the rate of interest, the laws of money circulation, the dependence of costs on the size of enterprise, the selection of the proper investment alternatives, the influence of prices on the proportions in the use of materials, reactions of demand to price changes, or relations between economic branches, etc., are all these 'relations between men'?

Production relations are economic relations between men, ensuing from a specific type of ownership of means of production. Assuming, however, that the form of ownership of means of production is given, then the task of economics becomes the investigation of the regularities governing the operation of this economy, an economy based on a specific ownership of means of production.

If we assume that the object of socialist economy is the incessant growth of production, which is attainable only by the employment of a technique that ensures the highest ratio of growth of production and the lowest costs, if we assume further that the object of that economy is the growing satisfaction of needs with simultaneous reduction of hard physical labor, then it will become clear that the theory of economy is also a science on the proper use of economic resources, intellectual and material, in line with the main objective. It is a science of the laws, regularities and relations between different elements of the economy. It is not a science on the growth of enterprise, on investments, on production incentives, on the location of plants, on the international division of labor, on proportions, on the impact of prices, on the regularities of demand, etc.

The above does not imply that the investigation of production relations in socialist economy is not a task of economics.

II

An important element of knowledge is incorporated in Stalin's conception that in each formation, changes occur in relations of production, i.e. in ownership relations concerning means of production and hence also in the 'exchange' of products of labor among men.

Such a change in production relations occurred in feudalism. The land could be utilized, or was utilized, by the peasants (the owner had no farm) or the owner himself used a notable part of the land as an estate. Land was not a commodity at first, later it became a commodity. Without affecting the principle of ownership, these changes in the form of ownership exercised an influence not only on the 'exchange' of products of labor, but also on class relations. After the laissez-faire capitalism, when means of production were owned by the individual capitalist, there followed the phase of monopoly capitalism. Principal means of production are owned by big 'monopolies' and therefore the forms of 'exchange' also change, the problems of market and prices develop differently, even political relations change, since the concentration of economic power in the hands of the monopolies is accompanied by the concentration of political influence.

The change in production relations in socialist economy is seen by Stalin in the existence of two types of ownership: the state or national ownership and the kolkhoz ownership. From the existence of these two forms of ownership arise specific forms of 'exchange' as well as specific forms of income of social groups. In 'exchange' the commodity form is retained to a certain extent, the kolkhozes obtain a share in the national income through a free buying and selling market.

But here Stalin commits an essential error in deducing commodity exchange from the existence of kolkhoz ownership of the produce of the kolkhoz.

Socialist economy, which is based on the exchange of equivalents, according to the principle 'to everybody according to his work', on the remuneration of the producer according to his production effort, after the deduction of an appropriate share for reserves, accumulation, etc., on the full freedom of choice of the consumer – cannot be but a commodity economy.

Socialist economy will cease to be a commodity economy when a state of full abundance of goods will prevail, when the exchange of equivalents will come to an end.

Assuming that the sole owner of means of production is the state, but consumer goods produced with these means of production are sold on the market according to the free choice of consumers, then means of production could be recognized as consumer goods in the making in varying degrees of maturity. We then picture the entire economy as one large enterprise directly managed by the state. In that case means of production would not be commodities.

But the above concept is a pure abstraction.

One national, wholly centralized enterprise cannot exist or function. Such an 'enterprise' can be imagined only as a single, gigantic, automatically functioning mechanism, one factory comprising many departments. May be something like that will be created in the distant future. But at the present level of production technique, considering the possibilities and exigencies of the development of this technique, the organization of the processes of production and exchange must be decentralized to a high degree. At the present level of technology, the role of man and his creativity is still decisive. Therefore, the individual enterprise will long continue to be the 'production unit', the center of disposition, decision, dynamics and adaptation.

The difference between 'national' and collective farm property does not lie in the fact that, in one case, means of production and products are national property and, in the other, kolkhoz property; since kolkhoz property is not private property, the difference lies only in the degree of the central element in the planning of production and investment and disposing of production. The development trend will lead to raising the decentralization element in national industrial enterprises and the element of centralization in collective farming. It is also not true that the distribution of goods and monetary economy will disappear when there will not be two types of ownership. The distribution of goods and monetary economy might disappear only when the mighty development of technology will make possible the creation of such a large surplus of products with so small an input of labor, that the problem of proportional, rational allocation of labor to separate production sections will cease to be an economic problem . . .

. . . The difficulties in the development of production forces (I refer, of course, only to Poland and not to the USSR) are connected rather with the excessive centralization of planning, coupled with the too weak functioning of incentives for progress and growth of production. Not centralization, as conceived by Stalin, but decentralization of planning becomes a condition necessary for the removal of contradictions that hamper the development of production forces.

The difficulties stem from the existence of a bureaucratized, mechanical, centralized system of managing the economy. This system of management acts as an impediment to the functioning of the entire economic system. Centralized planning proved its undisputed dominance in respect of production expansion, the quantitative growth of production forces. Without centralization the accelerated industrialization could not have been performed. Here, however, errors appeared quite early, as far as the mobilization of the efforts of local or small producers is concerned, which could develop only in conditions of decentralized initiative. However, as the newly built enterprises began to yield production, the system of centralized planning, of assigning tasks and resources to plants from above, began to show serious deficiences, so that the problem of reform became historically ripe for a solution.

III

In a socialist economy, though it is not an economy of private producers, the socially necessary labor used in the production of a given commodity cannot be expressed 'directly', in absolute terms of working hours, or working days, but always only in a 'roundabout way' through exchange, i.e. in relative terms. Only by selling the product to a producer or consumer can I assess if the amount of labor used in the turning out of the product was socially necessary, corresponding to social requirements. If I allotted too much labor to the production of machines which manufacture certain consumer goods, the demand for these goods would show whether the amount of labor was or was not compatible with social requirement. Let us assume, e.g., that due to the growth in the productivity of social labor, the amount of labor necessary for the production of one quintal of wheat fell by half, but economic authorities maintain the former price. In this case the profit from the production of wheat will go up and this will begin to act as a stimulant for the growth of its production. The supply of wheat will rise, but, due to the too high price, demand will not increase accordingly and part of the wheat will remain unsold.

In a socialist economy the principle obtains of the exchange of equivalents. For the work performed by them 'producers' receive from society in exchange an equal part of social labor, after allowing for appropriate deductions for social funds.[7] The product of labor assumes here the form of 'value', meaning that for a certain product of labor other products of labor are obtained in exchange. Products of labor of other people are obtained, and these products have to be compared as to the amount of

7 Marx, *Critique of the Gotha Programme, Selected Works*, Vol. II, Książka i Wiedza, 1949, p. 14.

social labor incorporated in them, so that there can be an exchange of equivalents. If, however, the product appears as a value, has a price expressed in money, then the law of value operates and equates price with value. This equation can take place only if the allocation of labor to separate production branches was proportionate to social requirement. Thus the law of value operates as a regulator of production, i.e. as a law of equilibrium. 'After the abolition of the capitalist mode of production, with social production retained, the determination of value (*die Wertbestimmung*) will remain a dominant factor in the sense that the regulation of working time and the division of social labor between production groups, and also the relevant accountancy, will become more essential than ever.'[8]

The assumption that means of production are not commodities and thus are not values, since they are not sold to any buyer, but are 'allocated by the state to its enterprises' (Stalin) and the state does not lose its title to its means of production, stems from a misunderstanding. Though the state allocates means of production, it cannot do it arbitrarily, in disagreement with economic laws, in disagreement with the law of value. The fact that the state does not lose its right to the ownership of means of production, has no fundamental economic significance. The statement that directors of enterprises, receiving means of production, are merely 'plenipotentiaries' of the state, who employ these means in accordance with plans fixed in advance, relies on a mechanistic, bureaucratic conception of the enterprise as an office. The socialist enterprise should become the center of decision, disposition and adaptation; its role cannot be purely passive.

Society controls resources of past and live labor and allocates them to separate production uses, depending on the social requirement of products of labor or commodities. The value of a commodity is the amount of labor allocated for its production out of the aggregate labor resources, provided that the amount of labor is socially necessary and that in exchange for the amount of labor used in one production branch, the latter obtains out of the aggregate social product a quantity of goods equivalent as to the amount of labor. The market prices of products (commodities) can be higher, lower or equal to value, depending on whether the given branch of production has been allocated an amount of labor equal to that socially necessary, lower or higher.

In this meaning the law of value is a law of economic equilibrium, or the law of 'proportionate' distribution between production branches of the amount of past and live labor available in society. This is an inherent law and all deviations of prices from the equilibrium price must produce certain disturbances of equilibrium.

8 Marx: *Capital*, Vol. III, p. 907.

In the absence of an 'equilibrium' price queues will form outside the shops, there will be speculation by buyers or sellers and unsold stocks will accumulate. Similarly, in the case of capital goods, too low a price will provoke the use of certain capital goods in excess of production capacity and too high a price will reduce the use of production factors priced higher than indicated by production possibilities, etc.

Market disturbances and switches of demand which produce economic difficulties are signs that either the allocation of labor to individual uses was not in accordance with the law of value, or prices were fixed at a 'false' level, not compatible with social requirement.

This type of law of value operates in any commodity economy, be it a capitalist or a socialist economy. The difference is that in a planned socialist economy it is incomparably easier to adapt prices to 'values' than in a capitalist economy. The difference lies also in the fact that in a capitalist economy the changes in value, and thus the changes in prices, caused by the growth of productivity of social labor, may lead to the outbreak of a crisis, since due to the general fall of prices the capitalist is unable to reproduce the depreciated capital and obtain a profit, while in socialist economy, the reduction of prices caused by the growth of labor productivity does not, in general, produce any disturbances. But in substance there is no difference in the operation of the law itself. The fact that in a socialist economy, in certain conditions, we do not raise the production of commodities that enjoy an exceptionally high demand and we do not even increase their prices to equate demand with supply, does not concern the essence of the law, but is associated most closely with planning and economic policy, with certain social and political objectives, etc.

Is there any difference in the operation of the law in relation to consumer and capital goods? There is, of course, no essential difference.

We would point out that we are concerned with theoretical concepts and entirely disregard economic policy and its goals. As can easily be seen, this postulate has nothing in common with the political or nonpolitical character of science. But there is a difference between an inquiry into inherent laws of reality and deliberations on practical action for the realization of certain socio-political objectives.

If the problem is thus posed, it will become obvious that in a socialist economy, with collectivized means of production, the latter do not cease to be 'commodities'. The socialist enterprise, as already mentioned, is a component of general economic accountancy. It uses social means of production, which are subject to depreciation, and it is governed by the law of value and the law of proportions. The enterprise 'buys', that is, selects, the most useful and rational means of production, it does not get them 'gratuitously', since these means of production require an outlay of social labor (this outlay of labor being their price). They do not fall from the skies like manna from heaven, and the outlay of social resources must be retrieved from products turned out with these means of production. The price of capital goods is not an arbitrarily fixed and irrelevant magnitude. The price must tend to correspond to value and must be fixed at a level more or less equating supply with demand, if the economy is to avoid disturbances and waste. The prices of lime and cement cannot be fixed arbitrarily and their price relation cannot be fixed arbitrarily, as on these prices depends their use and their demand relation. Too low a price of timber and iron causes a highly harmful waste in the use of these materials.

It is evident from the above that the law of value operates in the same way in relation to consumer goods and capital goods. The law of value is inherent. It does not operate from outside, it is a law inherent in the economy. One would not refer to the impact of the law of value on production, but rather to the employment of a policy incompatible with, opposed to the operation of the law of value, which results in disturbances and waste.

The socialist economy is a commodity economy. Will the communist economy be a commodity economy? We do not know and we cannot know how the communist economy will operate in the future. We only know that all production is associated with costs and outlays, that the same outlays may produce different production growth, and that only the existence of specified proportions ensures the highest production growth. If that is so, then certain laws operate in every economy, and primarily the law of allocating available resources of labor to individual production uses. Let us remember the words of Marx: 'It is self-evident that this necessity of division of social labor in certain proportions can in no way be abolished by a certain form of social production; only the form, in which it manifests itself may change. Laws of nature cannot be abrogated.'[9] Differences exist only in the form in which this law manifests itself. In a capitalist economy the entrepreneur, watching the price movement, estimating the expected profits, decides more or less blindly, on investments or on the expansion or contraction of production. In a socialist economy decision lies with the planning agencies of the state, the socialist enterprises. The difference concerns not the essence of the matter, but the degree of planned conduct. In both cases we are concerned with the same law, only differently manifesting itself. 'And the vulgar economist – says Marx – thinks that he embarks upon a great discovery when he boastfully juxtaposes the inner connection of things to their surface manifestation. In fact, he boasts

9 Marx, *Letters to Kugelmann*, Książka i Wiedza, 1950, p. 63.

while taking appearances for the essence of things. What is science needed for then?'[10]

Marx called the function of the production 'regulator' an equilibrium function in relation to the division of social labor. 'The exchange or sale according to value is the rational *(ist das Rationell)* natural relationship, and constitutes a natural law of equilibrium of exchange; deviations should be explained, proceeding from this equilibrium, and not vice-versa deriving the law from deviations' (Marx). If the division of labor corresponds to social demand, the market price equals value, if it does not correspond – price deviates from value, depending on the extent of supply determined by the amount of allocated labor and on the demand expressing the level of social demand (of course, effective demand). Where production is subject to the real, predetermining control of society – Marx says – society creates the link between the amount of social working time expended in the production of certain goods and the extent of social need to be satisfied by these goods.

Stalin's remarks on the 'influence' of the law of value on production, on the educational role of this law, have little in common with economic theory. They marked, however, a certain progress as compared with the view that in socialist production no laws and regularities operate.

The vestiges of that period are not yet completely liquidated. In the Soviet textbook of political economy we find a formulation clearly testifying to it: 'However, the law of value does not control state prices, but is only one of the factors influencing these prices. In state and cooperative trade a "free play" of prices does not exist . . . The state utilizes the price mechanism for determining such proportions in the distribution of resources between separate branches as are required by the needs of the planned development of the national economy';[11] and the manual enumerates the factors, apart from prices, which influence the level of development of production branches. This would indicate that the law of value involves consideration of the level of prices in the allocation of social labor. In fact this concerns only the modes of manifestation of the law of value, and not at all the law of value itself.

IV

The assumption that in a socialist economy the law of planned proportionate development operates instead of the law of value which functions in a capitalist economy, is highly dubious and unclear. Stalin under-

10 Marx, *Ibid*, p. 69.
11 *Political Economy. A Manual,* translated from the Russian, Książka i Wiedza, Warsaw, 1955, p. 792.

stood the law of value, which is the regulator of production, as the law of deviation from value, i.e. he took into consideration the mode of manifestation of the law of value. Therefore, Stalin could ask if the principle of planned development of the economy abolishes the principle of profitability of production. The issue at stake was that in socialist economy certain branches of production are not being developed although in view of their limited scope high prices could be fixed and great profits obtained. On the other hand, branches temporarily not profitable and even deficit-causing are being developed. But this has nothing in common with the operation or nonoperation of the law of value or with the substitution of the law of value by the law of planned development, it solely results from the fact that in planned economy we are able in a planned way – and always within the economic laws – to regulate, for example, the relations of accumulation to consumption.

The fact, for example, that we do not produce commodities which fetch or might fetch high prices, and could, therefore, ensure high profit, is not derived from the superiority of our economy over the capitalist economy, but either from a certain shortage or from a planned curtailment of consumption for the purpose of increasing accumulation. These are temporary phenomena. In principle socialism signifies the satisfaction of needs, and thus the production of such commodities as are demanded by society. High prices are signals that society experiences an insufficient supply of certain commodities.

There certainly is a great difference between the manifestation of the law of value in socialist economy and capitalist economy and it is true that in socialist economy the law of value cannot produce crises, i.e. a fall in the value of goods caused by a general rise in the productivity of social labor, and it does not produce a crisis, as it does in the capitalist system.

From the confusion of the law of value with the form of its manifestation ensue, for example, such formulations as the 'influence' of the law of value on the production of capital goods. Stalin says that the law of value as the regulator of production would have influenced, for example, the production of agricultural raw materials, should there have operated the law of competition and anarchy of production. But – says Stalin – this is not so, because prices of agricultural raw materials are rigid, determined by the plan, and not free. Stalin refers here not to the law of value, but to the manifestation of the law of value. The fact that the extent of the production of agricultural raw materials is determined by the plan and not created spontaneously, or that the tools needed for the production of these raw materials belong to the state, does not at all imply that the law of value does not operate here, the law of allocating to the production of agricultural raw materials such amounts of labor which will make the prices of raw materials tend to equate value. The state may allocate for the production of agricultural raw materials less labor than is required by social demand, but then the price fixed by the state will tend to equate supply with demand, otherwise disturbances or signs of waste will appear.

Stalin's statement that in a socialist economy the law of value is not a regulator of the production of capital goods, but that it is itself 'controlled by facts peculiar to socialist production', or that the law of value 'influences prices of agricultural raw materials, but does not regulate them' is based on a misunderstanding, the confusion of the law with the forms of its manifestation.

It is interesting that in a capitalist economy, which is based on oligopoly or 'price leadership', the movement of prices as a system of signals for investment and production operates in quite a complicated manner. Competition by means of prices produces such great risks that oligopoly avoids this form of struggle. It is not the movement of prices of goods already produced, but the expected high profits from production new to the market, that is the 'regulator of production' . . .

. . . The law of value incessantly tends to equate prices with value. The law of value governs the price movement, be it in laissez-faire, monopoly capitalism, or in socialism. If the amount of labor incorporated in commodities falls, prices fall and vice versa. Monopoly may hamper or slow down the operation of this law, but it cannot abolish it. In the last resort the tendency prevails for price changes to be in accordance with changes in value.

If, for instance, there is a fall in the production costs of cars, prices must eventually decline, in spite of the existence of a monopoly. The monopoly price equals marginal costs multiplied by the ratio of elasticity of supply (or sale) to elasticity of demand, which is less than 1. As a result of reduced costs the monopoly owner will obtain a higher maximum profit through lowering the profit margin and increasing turnover than by retaining the existing price and turnover. In both cases, the monopoly owner obtains a maximum profit, but in the second case, at a lower price and greater turnover. The monopoly price, however, is higher than would have been the competitive price, and the turnover is lower.

In a socialist economy, where there is no competition between enterprises, prices are controlled from above. In the economic sense, the commodity market has the form of a monopoly, a social monopoly, which by its price policy aims at exercising a certain influence on accumulation, consumption and production.

But the limits of the influence exercised on prices are determined by, say, economic laws. The structure of the price relation cannot be arbitrary, since there always exist certain given production and marketing possibilities. If 'too' low a price increases demand for a given commodity, the limited supply possibilities will create an appropriate limit to the policy of low prices.

Specific relations, let us call them proportions (they are, of course, variable) exist between all the factors of the economy. They can be listed in detail, but examples will suffice: the increase in industrial production requires greater productive capacity and a greater number of workers. The necessary additional number of workers can be obtained through natural increase, from agriculture, or by raising labor productivity in other production sectors. The transfer of workers from agriculture has certain limits which cannot be exceeded without endangering the extent of agricultural output. The increase in labor productivity depends on the workers being equipped with more efficient machines, and the rise in the intensity of work – on the possibility of a wage increase, which in turn is determined by the extent of the production of prime necessities. An 'excessively' high ratio of accumulation, preventing the growth of wages or lowering the wages, decreases labor productivity and intensity, creates sources of waste, etc.

A development free of disruptions, economic growth free of 'crises' is possible only on condition that certain 'proportions' are preserved. This does not at all mean that in certain conditions, heavy industry, for example, could not and should not be developed more quickly, 'proportionately' more intensely than industry producing consumer goods. Nevertheless, even then there are certain relations between economic phenomena, which have to be observed if we desire to prevent obstructions, bottlenecks, waste, fruitless investments, prolonged standstills, defective production, etc.

This is called the law of proportionate development. There is no law of planned proportionate development (since planning is a policy, not a law).

Does such a law operate also in capitalism? Of course, it does. Wherein does the difference lie? In a socialist economy, which is a centrally planned economy, the possibilities of a planned development policy, a policy of economic growth, can reduce to a minimum disruption, waste, and bottlenecks, so that in socialism development proceeds without crises.

But does the very fact of central planning eliminate the occurrence of real disturbances in economic life, does it on the strength of its principle eliminate wastefulness, bottlenecks, etc.? Of course not. All depends on the way of planning, the way of taking decisions on productive investments, wages, etc.

A socialist economy, a centrally planned economy, does not lead to crises, since in that economy even the worst enterprises cannot go bankrupt, and do not stop production, even if nobody buys their products.

Crises are also impossible, because even some unprofitable enterprises do not reduce investments, since they obtain the means for investment free-of-charge, and investment decisions are taken outside the enterprise, in the central planning bureau. But it is clear that considerable waste of resources can result from bad, inept planning. A socialist economy – bad socialist economy – though not confronted with periodical crises, may nevertheless experience lasting damage.

The superiority of a socialist economy over a capitalist one does not at all emerge as the mechanical product of collectivization of the means of production and central planning. This economic superiority is created by men, is the outcome of organization, effort, initiative, work, creativeness. Planning is a difficult and complicated art.

The path leading through a certain terrain may be formed spontaneously, but it may also be planned. If it is formed spontaneously, it is a short cut through the terrain, though it is certainly convenient. If it is planned by a planner, for example, in a park, the direction of the path may be contrary to the logic of space, the law of proportion. In this case people will begin to walk on the lawn, and not along the path. But a clever planner may plan the path better, more rationally, more in accordance with the logic of things, than is done by spontaneous development. This is correct planning, compatible with planned, proportionate development.

V

The development of modern technology inevitably leads to the centralization of investment decisions. The construction of furnaces or power plants cannot be the outcome of the decentralized local decision. Even in the capitalist system such a decision may be taken only on the basis of an analysis of the entire economy of the country and its growth prospects. Therefore, there can be no planned economy without far-reaching centralization of decisions. But at the same time it is difficult to imagine an integrally centralized economy functioning efficiently. Even as regards investment initiative, there is room for wide local initiative, not only in respect of the mobilization of the local production forces, but also in respect of production of a general character, which may develop in small, artisanal forms. Modern technology often enables small enterprises to achieve a level of costs and a quality of product which are not inferior to those of large-scale ventures.

Economic decisions may concern investments, innovations and adaptations. In the first case, the building of new plants or the extension of existing ones is involved, in the second, new plants or the extension of existing ones, in the third, the process of adaptation to changing conditions with regard, for example, to price policy, publicity, extent of production, etc.

Central decisions should concern projects and plants of a country-wide economic character. Decisions on local enterprises and installations may be more or less decentralized. Innovation and adaptation decisions should be left to the enterprises themselves.

The mechanistic conception of the principal law of socialism prevents the building of a properly functioning expansive model of the socialist economy. Determining an objective does not yet imply the mobilization of forces for its realization.

In the capitalist system the law of competition causes the failure of enterprises which are not equal or superior to others in matters of technique, progress or changes. But in our socialist economy do enterprises fail if they do not raise production, employ most advanced technique or turn out products best suitable for the satisfaction of social needs, but, on the contrary, waste the resources allocated to them, produce commodities unfit for use and desperately defend themselves against any attempt to improve their technique or product? Not only are they not eliminated, but they have an assured existence. The mechanized, centralized, bureaucraticized economy offers maximum protection to technical backwardness, wastefulness and defective production.

In order to build a developing, expansive model of socialist economy employing the most advanced technique, the driving force behind such a model and, above all, the role and functions of a socialist enterprise should be analyzed.

The basic law of socialist economy is not confined to the statement that the aim of the economy is the growth of production on the basis of the most advanced technique in order to meet growing needs, for when speaking about the law we refer to tendencies, exigencies, inevitabilities. In formulating the basic law of capitalism, Stalin pointed to the factors which impose the objectives themselves as well as indicate the mechanism for their realization. The capitalist entrepreneur as the personification of capital strives and must strive for the highest possible profits, or risk going out of business. In striving for profit, he stimulates production to a varying degree, achieves certain technical progress and expanded reproduction, activates processes entailed in the 'equilibrium' tendency of the entire system, i.e. the tendency to observe proportions to a maximum degree.

In the formulation of the basic law of socialism precisely those elements are missing which, owing to the essence of socialist economy and its organization, render inevitable the growth of production on the basis of the most advanced technique and growing satisfaction of needs.

One can easily visualize the central planning bureau as the initiator of production growth, technical progress and the lowering of production costs. But it is difficult to understand how central planning could ensure the rational operation of independent production units, separated for technical, social and organizational reasons, and also because of location, transport, etc.

The organization of the production process should ensure not only the determination of objectives for the realization of the fundamental law, but also and above all the mobilization of appropriate resources and driving forces.

Production progress is expressed in the growth of production at decreasing expenditure of social labor, that is in the steadily improving technique and organization of work. It is also expressed in the increasing range of products, their quality and ability to satisfy existing needs, as well as needs arising from technology and production.

The motives for development, the pressure on the degree of progress realizable in socialist economy, in which the profit motive does not operate, may emanate from various sources, as, for example, the action of the masses of consumers themselves who strive to raise their living standard. The law of the struggle for raising living standards constitutes not only one of the fundamental political laws in socialist society, but also the principal motive of economic progress.

Another motive for progress lies in international competition, and even a certain competition in our socialist market, though the Yugoslav examples are rather deterrent.

But of the greatest importance is the organization of enterprise itself as the center of technical and market knowledge, of initiative and creative activity.

The economic system is the combination of the operations of macroeconomic and microeconomic elements. Economic theory must take into consideration not only the proportions between section I and section II, but also the motives for the decisions of the fundamental cell of economy, the enterprise . . .

III   Scope and methods of planning

Introductory note

A Soviet-type economic plan is an instrument of economic policy and management. First it is a detailed program of action which sets specific targets for the economy as a whole and for its sectors and branches. Secondly, it is a system of binding plan indices and detailed operational instructions (in physical and value terms), covering all the activities of the individual firm including investment and capacity expansion, techniques of production, quantity of inputs used, and the types of output which are produced. (See Mikhail Bor's text.)

In the early 1950s – after the completion of the first round of East European Five Year Plans – it had become clear that planning on the Soviet model was leading to overcentralization and economic dislocations throughout Eastern Europe. Discrepancies between targets and results developed out of inflexibly set input-norms and excessively detailed specification of output and deliveries. Planners were faced with increasing cost, technological lags and the presence of perverse incentives. This type of planning, as the Hungarian economist György Peter pointed out was predicated on the assumption that the party's leadership was omnipotent and capable of making the entire economy move like a 'gigantic clock in which cogwheels must be very precisely and closely connected with each other'. But if this assumption was increasingly appearing to be fallacious and obsolete few dared as yet to challenge the closely related notion of the primacy of the plan as a management and policy instrument. This primacy was indeed still considered the hallmark of socialism: the market could be called into use only as an auxiliary to the plan – never the other way round.

Perhaps the most painstaking discussion as to how exactly the market could serve the plan took place in 1957 in Poland. Lange, Lipiński, Brus, Bobrowski – the outstanding economists of that country – while stressing the necessity of abandoning certain war-economy features embodied in the Soviet-type system, nevertheless emphasized the need to maintain the compulsory character of plan indices. Lange, for instance, stressed that simplification and decentralization should be encouraged 'without touching the directive character of planning'. Lipiński, after asserting that the socialist economy is centrally planned but not necessarily centrally administered, specified that this implied for him 'the planned determination of the relationship between accumulation and consumption' along with centralized decisions on most investments. At the time, Włodzimierz Brus, who was to become a proponent of the market mechanism, affirmed that the overwhelming majority of Polish economists opposed 'any attempts whatsoever' to give up the advantages of central planning, namely, 'the ability to define the main development trends not from the point of view of the interests or possibilities of one enterprise or branch, but from that of the national economy as a whole'. Finally, another economist, Bobrowski, noted that 'planning does not interest us' as an economic forecast but as an instrument for 'directing the entire economic development in an efficient manner'. The key attempt to combine the plan and the market within these frameworks is then attempted by the Polish Economic Council. (See the essays by Lipiński, the Polish Economic Council and Brus.)

The *Theses* of the Council were not implemented. They represented, however, a crucial effort to change the very nature of Soviet directive planning and the challenge remains unanswered until today.

A decade or so after the publication of the *Theses*, a study by the Hungarian economist Janossy underlined the inescapable, and highly distortive effects left in the structure of an economy by the methods of directive planning. Janossy contrasts the development of Hungary to that of the Soviet Union under a regime of forced industrialization. But what he says applies not only to Hungary, but also to any other socialist country – including the Soviet Union itself. Janossy points out that the result of forced industrialization is the creation of what he calls a quasi-developed state, a state in which the economic structure is in appearance developed but which in substance remains backward and inefficient. The liquidation of this state is for him the very precondition to development. What Janossy also carefully points out is that even when a centralized directive administration is largely dismantled, the maintenance in the center's hands of the responsibility for investment, and the commitment of this center to its previous priorities, may also be conducive to dysfunctional results.

MIKHAIL BOR

National economic plans*

How a plan is formulated

... A national economic plan is a very intricate structure. To erect it, one must choose the architecture and the bricks or blocks from which it will be built. In the case of a plan these are first of all its indices, the combining of these indices into interconnected groups, tables (forms of the plan) and sections of the plan.

Let us continue the comparison of plan formulation with the erection of a big building. For the building not to collapse in the process of construction there must be uniform rules for performing separate jobs which are obligatory for all builders, and reciprocal co-ordination between the construction elements. For [Soviet] planners such uniform and binding rules are the system of plan indices and methodological instructions for the formulation of a national economic plan.

The range of the indices, forms of tables and structure of the plan by sections and the methodological instructions are drawn up for each new long-term plan.

In the case of current plans this work is usually limited to correcting the existing forms, indices and methodological rules. These modifications can be more or less essential, depending on what changes in the economy or forms and methods of management must be taken into account.

It is the duty of the USSR Gosplan to elaborate the forms of the tables, plan indices and methodological rules for them.

The binding nature of the forms, plan indices and methodology of calculation for all planning links makes it possible to ensure their comparability in drawing up plans by sectors of the economy both for the country as a whole and for Republics, economic areas, territories, regions, cities, etc.

The system of plan indices includes indices of different kinds: indices in physical terms and value terms, quantitative and qualitative indices, approved indices and accounting indices.

Indices in physical terms are given in definite physical units of measurement (tons, pieces, meters, and so on). They cover assignments for the production of industrial goods in physical terms (types, assortment, etc.),

---

* Excerpts from *Aims and Methods of Soviet Planning*, by Mikhail Bor (translated from the Russian by Maxim Korobochkin, Lev Lempert and Lev Nazarov), London, Lawrence and Wishart, 1967.

the volume of goods carriage and average daily loadings, the commissioning of capacity, labor productivity in physical terms and purchases of agricultural produce. These indices are of great importance for dovetailing the development of separate sectors and categories of production. For example, material balances are based on indices of industrial output in physical terms. Planning of the carriage of various goods combines the development of industry and transport; planning of productive capacity ensures conformity in the development of production and construction.

The system of indices in physical terms, however, does not offer the possibility of establishing the total expenditure of social labor, of determining and comparing the general results of activity in separate sectors, economic areas, enterprises and their associations. That is why planning the volume of production and construction, the commissioning of fixed assets, trade, production costs and profitability is done in value terms, in terms of money.

Value indices (volume of industrial output, size of capital investments, volume of trade, national income, etc.) are measured in monetary units (roubles) and are determined by evaluating indices, given in physical terms, in operative prices. This is necessary for co-ordinating the planning of production with the planning of manpower, of production costs with finances, and of supply both with financing of trade and with the population's incomes.

These indices must ensure the possibility of analyzing the plan in three major aspects – sectoral, territorial and departmental.

The *sectoral* aspect reflects the grouping of targets by sectors of the economy: industry as a whole (including the steel, fuel and engineering industries), agriculture, transport, etc. These targets fully cover the given sector, irrespective of the location of production on the territory of different republics and regions and also the jurisdiction of separate enterprises. The sectoral structure of the plan enables economists to build into it the production ties and proportions for the balanced dovetailing of separate sectors both in the country as a whole and in republics and economic areas.

The *teritorial* aspect of the indices reflects above all the grouping of the state plan targets by Union Republics which bear responsibility for fulfilling their shares. The territorial aspect of the plan also includes the breakdown of assignments by economic areas. This section is elaborated by Republican Gosplans and approved by the Councils of Ministers of the Union Republics. In the long-term plan of the USSR targets are broken down not only by Union Republics but also by territories and regions (for example, targets for the purchase of agricultural produce, the lists of the biggest construction projects).

Moreover, in formulating the national economic plan for the USSR as a whole some indices are also calculated for big economic and geographical areas. These calculations are needed to ensure the comprehensive development of the main economic areas.

The *departmental* aspect reflects the grouping of indices by ministries and departments.

Another important grouping of indices is by sections of the national economic plan.

. . . Let us stress one highly important aspect in developing and improving the system of indices of the industrial plan which was true up to the present economic reform [1965].

The changes affected mainly the quantitative side of the indices. Indices of the industrial plan were formed mainly during the first and second five-year plans and were preserved essentially without serious qualitative changes until recently. The changes were mainly of a quantitative order, the number of indices was cut or increased, the indices were differentiated or aggregated, but their system was not essentially altered.

The main, characteristic feature of this system was that it concentrated efforts only on the quantitative side of production. In conditions of dynamic development and high economic growth rates, when the prodigious, intricate tasks of converting a backward land into a highly developed industrial country were being accomplished, chief attention was paid to the quantitative side, to indices of the volume of production and to a system of indices for industry in line with these demands.

But a new stage in the development of the USSR has set in, new economic conditions have arisen, making obvious the inadequacy of the existing system of industrial planning and the need to go over to other criteria in assessing the operation of enterprises, to indices which would promote the optimum development of the country's economy as a whole and of industry as its major and decisive part.

. . . The new system of indices now being introduced in Soviet industry is based on the close interconnection of the following three groups of indices:

(1) Value index of the scale of production (volume of goods sold).

(2) Target for the production of goods in physical terms.

(3) Profit index.

As pointed out earlier, value indices alone are insufficient for co-ordinating demand and production. Production which is at the same time productive consumption objectively demands concrete, qualitatively definite goods for satisfying the demand. Of course, the demand made on various industrial goods differs. Output satisfying personal non-productive needs is one thing and goods satisfying the needs of production is another. In the case of goods which satisfy personal non-productive needs, present-day conditions dictate abandonment of the policy of setting a detailed nomenclature and assortment by way of a directive. The detailed assortment must be determined on the basis of direct contacts with trading organizations representing the interests of the consumer. The Statute of Socialist Enterprises (approved by the USSR Council of Ministers on October 4, 1965) says that enterprises should alter the nomenclature and assortment of consumer goods in conformity with the demand and change of orders by trading organizations, and that such alterations need not be sanctioned by higher agencies.

The situation is different in the case of means of production. The high growth rates of the Soviet economy and its intricate tasks make it essential to preserve for a certain time a more detailed nomenclature and assortment as obligatory assignments for industrial enterprises. For this reason, the nomenclature of output for consumer goods will, as a rule, be of an aggregated nature, with a more detailed breakdown of the assortment in the plan of enterprises themselves, while in the case of means of production the same obligatory nomenclature of output as existed until now is preserved in the main.

A combination of an aggregated value index of the volume of production and a more or less detailed nomenclature of major kinds of goods in physical terms ensures the necessary co-ordination of production and demand . . .

Planning and programming

In the last two decades most West European countries as well as Japan and many developing countries have begun systematically to use long-range economic programs. The programming of capitalist production started in France (the Monnet Plan, 1947 to 1952/53), and was then applied in the Netherlands ('The First Memorandum on the Industrialisation of the Netherlands', 1948 to 1952), in Norway (the 'Economic Development Programme', 1949 to 1952) and in Sweden. Programming was later used in Belgium (the plan for 1962 to 1965) and Great Britain (the plan for 1962 to 1966). In Italy programming agencies have been set up and a new national program has been worked out (much greater attention is being paid to it than to the recently ended Vanoni program).

Some Western experts call the practice of economic programming 'indicative planning' and contend that this is the only rational method of running the national economy. It is certainly not ineffectual; but at the same time it differs in principle from socialist planning both in the problems it sets and the means it chooses to solve them. To outline the gap which exists between programming and planning, it is worth while comparing present-day methods of programming with previous forms of state interference in capitalist production.

The difference between programming and planning

Present-day programming is by no means the first attempt to introduce an element of planning into the capitalist economy. At the close of the last century Lenin wrote: 'The socialisation of labour by capitalism has advanced so far that even bourgeois literature loudly proclaims the necessity of the "planned organisation" of the national economy.' A little more than sixty years have since passed and today the capitalist world is full of plans for 'planning'. Something similar was in evidence following the economic crisis of 1929–33: the idea of planning acquired numerous advocates in the capitalist world even at that time. This was reflected in the establishment of various organizations for studying planning, various congresses on planning, etc. Some of these organizations which sprang up in the 'thirties are still functioning, in particular, the National Planning Association in the USA, PEP in Great Britain, etc.

However, the end of the world economic crisis and the outbreak of the Second World War left planning in the 'thirties at the level of theoretical discussion.

The Second World War witnessed a gigantic acceleration of the development of monopoly capitalism into state-monopoly capitalism. State interferences in economic activity became more intense and varied. The state and monopoly sector grew considerably. This process continued after the war and was reflected in particular in a wide wave of nationalization of industries and services which swept most countries of Western Europe. The emergence of numerous state enterprises and even sectors led the West European countries to the problem of long-term planning.

... In contrast to the policy of current Keynesian measures aimed at eliminating those contradictions of capitalism which are evident on the surface, economic programming involves going deeper and, in particular, dealing with such an essential aspect of production as long-term investment policy. Programming creates a certain framework within which all other forms of state interference function, i.e. it plays a co-ordinating role as well. Thus, economic programming combines long-term forecasts with a system of co-ordinated state interference effected mainly in the form of financing selected industries to solve the most essential problems facing the monopoly bourgeoisie as a whole. This means that, first, functioning economic programs comprise not one aspect of the national economy or two (e.g. war production or the generation of power) nor even the development of a whole area, but the total complex of the most important aspects of the process of production; functioning economic programs aim, moreover, not at short-term but at long-term results. Second, and this is the main peculiarity of programming, it lays emphasis not so much on the interests of individual monopolies as on the solution of general problems of capitalism as a whole confronted with the need for competing with the world system of socialism . . .

. . . It is no discovery to say that the problem of planning confronts today the programming countries of the West as well as the socialist countries. What are the ways for solving this crucial problem opened by the system of socialist planning, on the one hand, and the Western practice of programming, on the other? Where do they touch, affording possibilities for business co-operation, and where do they differ in principle?

Let us begin with the principle of centralization, one of the first principles of socialist planning. The development of the national economic plans begins 'at the top'. Not only are the main reference points of economic development projected in a centralized way (which is characteristic of the Western practice of programming as well); the means for meeting the scheduled targets are specified for all enterprises in a centralized way too. Some Western economists interpret the principle of centralization as meaning overdetailed instructions for the activity of each enterprise. This interpretation does not correspond to a scientific approach to planning (incorporating the principle of operational independence or self-enterprise, which follows from the objective requirement that every enterprise must be self-supporting) or with the Soviet system of cost accounting in general.

Contemporary rates of scientific and technical progress make it necessary to aggregate national plans for production and resources and impel enterprises to increase not so much the volume of production as its efficiency. At present it is generally recognized that central planning agencies (the USSR Gosplan and the national and Republican ministries) should specify the key targets of contemplated production at a sufficiently aggregated level – national and sectoral – and intrude into the sphere of activity of enterprises themselves only as far as there is a reasonable need for it. Now, where does the limit of this 'reasonable need' lie? This is perhaps one of the crucial problems of the theory of socialist planning.

The range of problems that the Central planning agencies must deal with at the macro-level is delineated quite definitely. It includes the entire complex of problems involved in determining plan targets for nation-wide quantitites like consumption, saving, national output and national income. Formally, the problems of planning in this sphere of activity are similar to those of programming. They are to determine, on the basis of constructing an aggregated optimum inter-sectoral structure (of several dozen sectors), the optimum relation between consumption and investment in terms of a given criterion (which differs, of course, in different social systems). However, in contrast to capitalist programming, dependent on 'final demand' and therefore unable to go beyond the development and stimulation of general trends of sectoral production, socialist planning, taking advantage of state-run production, can be based on a scientific analysis of economic inter-relations inside each sector. Without this it would be impossible to solve sufficiently accurately the problem of determining the coefficients of industrial consumption of the inter-sectoral input–output tables.

The possibilities for raising the effectiveness of national production grow accordingly. A road opens towards a thorough and versatile control of the national economy depending on a deliberately selected criterion, which is expressed by the choice of the best input–output variant. This criterion may be a maximum of consumption per capita (national scale) or a maximum of the productivity of labor (sectoral scale) or a full load of productive capacity or finally a maximum rate of profit (enterprise level), etc.

It is in the latter case that we run into the problem of the limit of penetration of directive planning into the sphere of activity of an enterprise. The development of the productive forces makes it imperative to furnish a material basis for economic initiative. This is ensured by decreasing the centralized part of the national income and increasing that part which remains at the disposal of enterprises as their individual funds.

Now, what is the limit of the extension of the independence of enterprises inevitably involved in this approach? Should this limit be the same for all enterprises, or should it be differentiated according to the range of products and economic capacity of each enterprise?

This question has still to be answered. However, it is already clear that most of the planning of the range of goods, especially for the sectors producing goods not in excess demand, is to be shifted to the system of contracts between enterprises, so that the corresponding item in the plan is an estimate, not a directive.

For example, it appears inexpedient to include in the competence of high-level planning the determination of the total range of products (down to grades and sizes), the rules of organization of production inside the enterprises, or the concrete forms of inter-enterprise relations. These aspects of production can be best determined by enterprises themselves, aided by the stimuli furnished for them by the central planning agencies.

Such is one of the aspects of the problem of centralized planning in the Soviet Union. Inquiry in this direction is in progress in the programming countries of the West as well, but the impossibility of a centralized controlling influence on private enterprise bars the road to the effective organizing activity of the state (let alone private organizations) aimed at the most productive structures and proportions in national production. It is true that an extensive system of state stimulants (tax relief, privileged loan terms, preferential rates for state services, etc.) act in capitalist countries as very active catalysts. However, these 'flexible' controls are very rigid in other respects: having given an impetus to the development of some sectors, they cannot later check the inertia of unpredictable processes, the 'braking distance' proves to be too prolonged, and losses from resulting accidents known as 'recessions' are still considerable. Hence the tactics of 'intermediate plans' to which some programming countries (France, Japan) resort during depressions, and hence the failures of the economic 'stop–go' policy (in Britain), etc.

The spontaneity of technical development and the alternation of favorable and unfavorable market situations impel the managers of private enterprises to be guided as a rule by nothing except a local optimum of production based on the rate of profit, which rules out any plan in a strictly assigned direction. Indeed, is any effective planning of production possible without specific targets? Without any sanctions which would secure the attainment of these targets? Without any obligation on the part of enterprises to meet these targets? And finally without any real possibility for enterprises to co-ordinate their operations? Such is the situation in the West European countries. Neither the General Secretariat of the Equipment and Production Plan (France), nor the Central Planning Office (the Netherlands), nor the Department of the Plan (Norway) can enforce an economic program.

In contrast to socialist planning, the Western programs do not take the form of specific economic assignments for specific enterprises. Finally, the over-all projections of programs cannot be identified with the targets of socialist plans, the correlation of which depends mainly on the aims set and not on the market situation, and which have the validity of production assignments for definite enterprises. On the other hand, it would be wrong to equate the programs of capitalist production with mere passive forecasts. The projections of West European programs combine forecasts and expert estimates (the passive element) with indices computed as indicative prescripts of the monopoly bourgeoisie (the active element). For example, the programming of the growth of exports represents a passive forecast based on abstract analysis and expert estimates. On the other hand, the programming of an annual 10 per cent growth of machine-building (France, 1954 to 1957) is an active projection. This does not mean that capitalist programming was able actually to secure this 10 per cent rate of growth; but without the orientation on this rate, it would have

been unrealistic even to pose the problem of French industrial modernization.

Let us see what is being done in the capitalist countries to secure
compliance with economic programs.

Programming is purely advisory, and this is its basic characteristic. In
the West European countries there are no special agencies which could
secure the fulfillment of adopted economic programs. Characteristically, in
no country except France are the programming agencies incorporated into
the state machinery: elsewhere they remain semi-official advisory agencies. This status can probably be traced to the desire of ruling circles to
have a larger leeway for maneuver in their domestic policies. It is true that
in some capitalist countries (for example, France, Great Britain, Italy)
there exist administrative forms of influencing private enterprises through
legislation (licences for industrial construction in some areas, or supervision over the issue of securities). Nationalized enterprises, with respect to
which state programs are obligatory, also constitute an exception in a
sense. However, the mainspring of the programming mechanism is the use
of the economic law of capitalist profit, and not of the objective conditions
of planned and proportional economic development . . .

The state's selection of the most important directions for private enterprise has created new relations between the capitalist state, defending the
common interests of the capitalist class, and individual monopolies guided
by their own separate interests. Formally, these relations appear as a
working agreement between the state and the monopolies, and essentially,
they express the struggle among monopolies for an additional rate of
profit. This struggle is waged in the framework of special agencies concerned in the development of investment programs and constituting an
important element in the programming mechanism . . .

To sum up, the principal means for ensuring the operation of a program
is a system of purposive state benefits. If a capitalist refuses to follow the
recommendations of a program (which correspond to his general class
interests but do not always suit his particular line of business), he is
deprived partially or completely of substantial financial aid. Therefore,
when the entrepreneur finds he cannot invest more profitably than in the
direction recommended by the state, he complies with the state program;
and conversely, he is completely indifferent to state recommendations in
the contrary case . . .

EDWARD LIPIŃSKI

A 'model' of the socialist economy*

I

The socialist economy is based on social ownership of the means of production and social control of the production process. However, social ownership of the means of production does not imply centralized management of the production process, conducted by the state. The principal unit in that process is the independent enterprise, which faces and solves tasks in the areas of technical progress, production ranges, production technology, organization and control of production processes, changes in techniques, costing and marketing, and adjustments to changing techniques and markets.

The socialist economy is centrally planned, but not necessarily centrally administered, since the highly negative aspects of central administration justify its application only in exceptional cases, as during war when manpower and resources have to be concentrated on a single principal task to the exclusion of other, hitherto realized projects.

The 'model' of the socialist economy is expected to solve the following problems: (1) the most efficient method of initiating and deciding on investments and their appropriate placement; (2) the best conditions and incentives for the improvement of production techniques; (3) the introduction of new or improved products; (4) the most efficient method of managing the production process; (5) a price and wage system ensuring the best possible satisfaction of needs, the best distribution of resources and means among separate branches, and the mobilization of the most rational stimuli to augment labor productivity; and (6) the best method of foreseeing and adapting to changing market conditions.

Also at issue are such problems as the correct transmission of initiatives so that they will be realized, the appropriate flexibility of the system, and the reduction to a minimum of red tape and inertia. We omit here the problem of educating and instructing workers, scientists, technicians, and managers capable of directing, of carrying through initiatives, and of efficiently performing all the specialized tasks in the production process.

The problem of constructing a model is one of systematizing forces, means and incentives necessary for reaching the maximum and optimum aims of production – its continuous growth, its achievement of the highest

* '"Model" gospodarki socjalistycznej', *Nowe Drogi*, No. 11–12, 1956.

level of technique, and its expansion of the possibilities of satisfying society's requirements. The whole system of forces, means and incentives could be presented in quasi-mathematical formulas, and thus the exact shape of the 'model' could be outlined – this is the task of economic theory. Perhaps our science will complete this task.

Most important at present is the discussion of the principal elements of a practical model of the economy, a model that will ensure the smallest possible waste and often the greatest possible effectiveness of applied and mobilized forces and means. The main elements of a practical model involve making decisions on the following: (1) the direction and pace of general economic development; (2) the development and its direction of the enterprise; (3) production techniques, assortment, and technology of products; (4) price and wage policy; (5) changes of already undertaken resolutions and projects. Here interact the principles of authority and subordination, democracy and authority, centralization and decentralization, and decisions from above and the operation of the law of markets.

It seems that there is no way of basing the model on entirely uniform principles as, for example, in the utopian model of 'perfect' competition, where decisions on production and exchange are dispersed among a large number of independent enterprises and where the law of markets leads through competition to the attainment of lowest cost and prices, the best location of production, the most effective use of available resources, and the greatest satisfaction of needs conforming to individual preferences.

The initiative on construction of new enterprises and launching new production branches cannot be left to enterprises or local bodies alone; if the scope of the proposed establishment exceeds the limits of the local market, the decision should be centralized, since it would require the consideration of overall conditions in their actual as well as anticipated state.

Planning economic development in the sense of coordinating and balancing the entire economy must naturally be centralized; on the other hand, in planning the development of existing enterprises local decisions are possible in many cases. Decisions as to technical progress in enterprises may also be decentralized. As to the assortment of products, it is impossible to introduce a uniform principle: the number and types of locomotives to be produced per annum by local factories can only be centrally decided, but in the light, consumer goods industry a far-reaching decentralization of decision making is possible.

The same distinction must be made regarding prices. The prices of coal, iron, or cement cannot be fixed otherwise than centrally, but those of textile articles should be determined on the basis of agreements between suppliers and users. The payment problem, within the limits of existing funds, could also be largely left to collective agreements.

The administration of enterprises requires a mixture of the elements of democracy and skill, authority and self-management, freedom and subordination, and hierarchy and equality. There is no doubt, however, that there are functions in the enterprise which cannot be carried out simultaneously on the basis of two opposing principles of conduct. The functions of directing the production process, of selecting production techniques, the assortment of goods, and the future development of the enterprise, belong to the domain of authority and skill and cannot be executed on the basis of democracy, just as decisions on doctors' functions in hospitals cannot be adopted by a majority of votes of the hospital staff. However, it is not for me as an economist to assign the proper function to the principle of democracy.

In a socialist economy the owner of the means of production is the entire society, but the socialist enterprise managers administer and develop these means. The operator of the socialist production enterprise is its staff, that 'collective worker' of Marx. Does this mean that the staff manages the enterprise, just as the capitalist manages it in capitalist society? The problem is complicated and involves many real dangers.

Even in capitalist countries the management of enterprises has been depersonalized, bureaucratized, and 'collectivized'. Not only the function of controlling complex work, but also the function of adopting decisions, has been transferred to professionals and experts. The manager or management of the enterprise makes decisions on the basis of a comprehensive preparation of materials by specialists – analysts on problems of markets and sales, specialists on credit problems, experts on labor relations, technicians, specialists on transportation and communications, accountants, statisticians, engineers working on the production process and engineers specializing on the product itself, psychologists, economists, etc.[1] Thus management decisions are filtered through a whole army of experts, each of them a specialist in his field.[2]

The idea of workers' 'associations' managing an enterprise is a conceptual transformation of the substance of private ownership. Private ownership of the means of production has good and bad aspects. It is assumed that a workers' association will eliminate the bad aspects of private ownership and implement all the positive aspects, the will of the owner being manifested by a majority vote of the workers.

In a big modern enterprise, numbering tens of thousands of employees,

1 Forest D. Siefkin, 'Executive Decisions at the Top Level', Papers and Proceedings of the 63rd Annual Meeting of the American Economic Association, 1950, *American Economic Review*, May, 1951, p. 91.
2 Ralph E. Flanders, 'How Are Top Executive Decisions Made', *American Economic Review*, loc. cit., p. 93.

the individual workers' consciousness of coownership of the enterprise cannot become a factor stimulating functioning to a great degree. If its ownership is represented by chosen workers' representatives, a workers' council, then it becomes a collective of unskilled administrators representing the interests of the whole. This type of representation has the peculiar properties and characteristics of any set of parliamentary representatives. However, since the enterprise cannot be administered in a parliamentary fashion, the council members can perform their function – other than in matters of pay, distribution of profits, and living conditions – only as real or apparent professionals and specialists. It does not contradict the postulates of socialist democracy and the character of social ownership of the means of production if the staff of the enterprise or its representatives cooperate in preparing decisions on the selection of production techniques as well as on the assortment of products to be manufactured.

The two principal functions of the enterprise are: to organize the process of production, and to plan and coordinate technical progress. The first function does not require analysis in the current discussions on the reorganization of the enterprise, but the second constitutes the main point of these discussions, and is most closely connected with the demand for decentralization.

The field of discussion should be clear on this subject. Stalin's contention that capitalism retards technical progress and drives the horse backwards, and his formulation that in socialism the most modern and best technology can be applied everywhere, irrespective of costs, solely for the alleviation of workers' labor, are untrue. Although the type of technology selected in socialism does not depend on the calculation of direct profits on capital, it must also be the outcome of a cost calculation, that of comparing increments of social costs with social advantages.

In socialist economy too there is resistance to technical progress and the introduction of innovations. But by operating day-to-day with defective planning and faultily determined incentives, which led to an economy in which progress is avoided like fire since it interferes with premium payments for the fulfillment of scheduled production, the path of progress would not have been free of obstacles even had we removed this resistance.

The basis of any progress in technology – in the technique of the production process, in the organization of production, in fabricating a new product or establishing a new service, or in improving a product – is the progress of science, and in fact, of pure science, whether we develop this science ourselves or take it over from others.

The second stage is a readiness for the possible introduction of progress. This readiness, as well as the possibility of taking advantage of it depends on a whole complex of objective and subjective conditions. In the whole world the technology of production has made great progress. But in our places of work, models dating from many decades ago are calmly launched. Every smallest everyday item produced in the West provokes a sensation by its usefulness as well as by its appearance. Some objects, in spite of their simplicity, are extremely useful and desirable, but they cannot be produced locally. The thorny path of, for example, the Institute of Industrial Design, and its boycott by our representatives of commerce and production are only too well known.

Overcoming routine and inertia cannot depend only on economic 'stimuli', it requires a sociological analysis.

II

The more the process of mechanization and specialization progresses, the greater is the necessity for the decentralization of decisions.

The great advantages of giant concerns still exist, but there is no doubt that big size also creates difficulties and losses. Decentralization tendencies spring from striving to link the advantages of bigness with the positive elements inherent in the decentralization of decision making and responsibility.[3] Therefore, big concerns try to join elements of centralization and decentralization in various combinations of geographic and functional establishments. (In General Motors, financial and legal matters are centrally organized; in the firm 'Koppers', the buying function and, of course, general planning and control are always centralized.)

The necessity of combining technique and science always creates the need to build large establishments. Before the television industry had matured enough to produce TV sets, 20 years of immensely costly studies were required. It is doubtful if laboratories and research institutes outside the production establishments can fulfill the same tasks as factory laboratories.

III

The superiority of socialism over capitalism springs only partially from socialist planning. The substitution of the motive of social advantage for the profit motive creates an additional measure of superiority of planned socialism over 'unplanned' capitalism, for many obstacles to technical progress then disappear, and the size of enterprises is determined not by casual factors or by strivings for market domination, but by considerations of greatest efficiency and similar social goals.

3 Raymond Villers, 'Control and Freedom in a Decentralized Company', *Business Review*, March–April, 1954, p. 89.

Mainly, however, the superiority of socialism stems from the planned determination of the relationship between accumulation and consumption. It is clear that only to the degree that we reduce the share of consumption for the benefit of production are we able to accelerate the growth process. The limits of this acceleration are restricted and this assumption does not require proofs. However, the problem of speeding up development should be analyzed from the point of view of the economy as a whole, and not only from the viewpoint of accelerating the development of its separate parts.

Acceleration of development can be real or apparent. Besides the growth of production factors, we must take into account the process of diminishing capital stock, the loss of unrepaired or unreplaced production plant, and the delay in making new installations operable, due to the shortage of complementary components or so-called bottlenecks, which prevent for a time the mobilization of entire production complexes (as lack of baths prevents the completion of dwellings, etc.). Therefore, a distinction must be made between the net growth of production installations and their gross increment – to arrive at new growth (decreases) in capital stock.

Apparent acceleration also takes place when we concentrate available resources on producing a given object, as, for example, when we develop onesidedly the heavy or armaments industry and neglect many other production branches. In this case, though a great number of steel works, cement works, armament factories, etc. were built, agriculture, the processing industry, and residential building declined, roads were not constructed, railway tracks were not repaired, and so on.

Such a one-sided growth of production installations does not permanently augment the productive forces of the country; it does not increase them in proportion to the social costs expended. All production branches and all elements of the economy are closely connected to each other and complement each other. The retarded development of transport, insufficient residential building, inadequate medical care for the population, the stagnation of agriculture and sectors producing consumer goods – all these prevent the full operation of those factories and establishments which came into being as a result of the one-sided industrialization. It is generally ignored that in the industrialization process a decisive role is played by infrastructure – communications, roads, dwellings, etc.

The principle of the priority of heavy industry in industrialization, though it contains elements of truth, emanated mainly from the demand to create our own armaments industry. Every country must possess branches producing consumer goods as well as capital goods. Thus we have the problem of the limits and scope of local heavy industry, especially in a country relatively small, not self-sufficient, and dependent on international exchange as one of the bases for its development and expansion of its welfare.

Should not agriculture have rather been developed, instead of being sacrificed to the building of heavy industry, and the bacon, butter, eggs, etc. exchanged for some machines, raw materials, wireless sets etc. from, for example, the USA? It seems that social costs would then have been lower.

It should be added that a one-sided development of heavy industry, where machines replace the worker, leads to the growth of national income, but reduces the income level of the working people. In addition, the concentration of huge masses of economic resources in heavy industry hinders the possibility of advances in the processing industries and agriculture, which results in hampering economic progress in the entire economy. The country becomes richer in steel, cement works and machine factories, and poorer in means to satisfy the requirements of the population. The announcement that the capital goods produced will at some time in the future make possible the production of consumer goods carries only partial truth.

The natural growth of the population and the exodus of masses of rural population to towns caused a huge demand for apartments. Yet the construction of residential apartments was recognized as being of infinitely less importance not only than the building of factory buildings, but also than the erection of costly palaces for red tape. This was a great error. One of the great sources of the growth of productivity and efficiency of human labor was destroyed.

Labor productivity decreased, the drawing into the cultural process of masses of people cut off from rural centers was prevented, and they were pushed into the humiliating, degrading and brutalizing environment of workers' hotels. In contrast, in the USA 30 per cent of investment outlays are being assigned to residential buildings.[4]

Another error of our investment policy lay in according priority to the construction of new factories often built for advance growth, such as Nowa Huta, and neglecting infrastructure installations, such as roads, railways (Polish railways are worse today than in prewar years), streetcars and other municipal transportation (the additional social advantage from new transportation facilities is greater than that from building a central department store), and the building industry. (Due to the inadequate development of the building industry, the construction of new industrial projects is unusually expensive and takes far too long – often completed sections cannot be put into operation because complementary parts are unfinished, etc.)

4 W. Arthur Lewis, *The Theory of Economic Growth*, London, 1956, p. 211.

Too little means were assigned to inventories and reserves (normally over 10 per cent of the country's investment goes into stock), and hence we had discontinuities in the production process, interruptions and breakdowns, all leading to prolonged pauses in which neither technical installations nor manpower reserves could be employed productively.

All this does not imply that during the past period we did not obtain a large net increment of production capacity. It merely indicates that this increment could have been incomparably higher, had it been more evenly developed.

The economic shortcomings existing today do not arise only from the defects of the present model, which is based on the principle of administering from above the incorrect proportions of resources and means assigned for various objectives, which considerably reduced the social effectiveness of these resources and means.

In a socialist economy there is no state ownership, but a social ownership of the means of production. Society controls the production process through determining production aims, prices, wages and incentives in such a way that socialist enterprises, which represent the principal form of administering socially owned means of production, may harmoniously cooperate in implementing output targets. The enterprise works in line with the aims of socialism, on the basis of the plan; but it constitutes an independent center of decisions on innovations, production methods and range of products (as far as the range of products is not specified in the plan).

Socialist enterprise cannot be separated from the social ownership of production means, since it constitutes an instrument of this ownership, an instrument which, however, is independent, decentralized, and entrusted perhaps with autonomous decisions, the freedom of maneuver, and the right to take risks.

[POLISH] ECONOMIC COUNCIL

Theses concerning certain modifications of the economic model*

1. The following theses of the Council on the Economic Model concern nationalized socialist industry. They constitute an attempt to determine trends in the economic model, and to delineate phases of concrete economic and organizational changes.

* 'Tezy Rady Ekonomicznej w sprawie niektórych kierunków zmian modelu gospodarczego', in *Dyskusja o polskim modelu gospodarczym*, by O. Lange, *et al.*, Warsaw, Książka i Wiedza, 1957.

2. Modifications are necessary because the methods of management and planning must develop hand in hand with the production forces. The production methods suitable for one phase restrict the growth of production forces at another. Hence the need for continuous improvement.

The following are the general assumptions of the Council on the question of planning:

1. The deepening and improvement of central planning comprise one of the most important conditions for our proper economic development. The crucial factors in the process of improving planning are not the number of indices, the degree of detail, or the use of formal balancing, but are rather a thorough economic analysis and a carefully formulated prognosis of economic development when exact economic calculations are not possible.

The following factors are the crucial components of the central plan:

(a) a general analysis of the reproduction process, of the division of national income into the part going toward accumulation and that going toward consumption; an analysis of the distribution of income among the different branches of the economy, and among the different regions of the country; and an analysis of the connections between these divisions;

(b) an analysis of consumption demand and an analysis of trends in consumption development;

(c) an analysis of the economic effectiveness of investments both from the point of view of the most effective technical–economic solution for each investment problem, and from the point of view of trends in investment;

(d) an analysis of import and export profitability;

(e) an analysis of the distribution of national income among various strata and groups;

(f) an analysis of the conditions in and capabilities of various regions;

(g) an analysis of the demographic process, and an analysis of the developing employment rate;

(h) an analysis of problems in the international division of labor;

(i) an analysis of the main currents of technological development, and a determination both of the resulting economic change, and of the correlation between the technological development and this economic change.

The growth of the national income should be considered the basic index of economic development.

2. Long-term planning based on the principle of regular reconsideration of the fundamental premises of economic development is of special importance. Short-term planning should be continuous. The shortcomings of the system of one-year planning should be overcome by setting up investment programs with a time horizon of several years, for example, a program of

two-year planning for the engineering industry (which has a longer production cycle and supplies individual customers), etc.

3. The long-term and one-year economic plans are in the nature of directives, and are binding on all managerial economic institutions. This characteristic of the plans, however, does not necessarily imply that the firms must accept the plans as specific orders.

The effectiveness of central planning (i.e. its instructive character) requires:

(a) an integrated system of incentives, economic instruments, and (in the concrete cases where such orders are indispensable and effective) detailed orders. A harmonious system of economic instruments and orders should be used. The system should be optimal in any specific case, and the use of orders should be seriously reduced. The use of incentives should be systematically extended, while the use of orders should become less specific and detailed;

(b) broad application of the above-mentioned system of instruments to ensure fulfillment of the plan;

(c) organizational forms which take into consideration the specific features of the branch and the character of the firm. These forms should take advantage of the central plan, and of the firm's relative independence.

4. The development of central planning methods and the economic conditions of the firms should enable each firm to do its own planning. This planning can be limited to the actual planning of specific tasks, within the concrete demands derived from the central plan. The extent and forms of this planning should result from the needs of the firms, and not from any compulsory scheme. The process of this planning cannot be analogous to the central planning in those cases where it would not suit the production process.

The directives of the central plan should not conflict with the economic calculations of the firm.

5. In order to fulfill the economic plan, the responsible institutions should employ effective and flexible means. The present practice of universal and routine administrative means should be abandoned. In order to build an industry which can develop and function in a guided, planned manner, the responsible institutions should employ:

– economic instruments first,

– administrative means when absolutely necessary, and

– direct contact rather than administrative–instructive relations.

The means mentioned above should be employed until both the desired direction of industrial development and its effectiveness are guaranteed.

6. Democratization of economic management requires active participation in the process of planning by the workers, the workers' councils, the

people's councils and the Sejm [parliament]. Such a participation is possible only when information on economic life is declassified, and when the plan is formulated in terms which enable a rational approach to genuine economic alternatives.

I. The central planning of industry

1. The sphere of centralized decisions concerning industrial investment should be different from the sphere concerning production. The sphere of decisions concerning investment should be greater, but the degree of independence on the part of the firms with regard to their investments should be greatly increased over the present norm.

2. The majority of important industrial investments should be determined at the central level, on the basis of a study of their effectiveness. These decisions should take into account the trend of development deriving from the options included in the long-term plan. Such investments should be financed by a non-returnable credit on which the firms would pay interest. The firms should be granted:

(a) complete liberty to use the designated financial means for renovations and repairs, while securing proper maintenance of fixed capital;

(b) liberty to use the money earmarked for depreciation, with the option of withdrawing the money or freezing it. The options should be dictated by the general investment policy for that period, or by the intention of permitting the liquidation of the firm after a specified time;

(c) the ability to use credits in order to modernize and complete their equipment. These decisions should be made independently by the firms, which will have to pay back the credits.

3. The plans for branches of industry or for groups of industrial firms should include:

(a) The value of output at market prices and

(b) the value of output at factor cost.

In addition, central plans should include quantitative instructions on the production of raw materials and intermediate goods. Prices used in the plans should be valid for the planning period.

4. The determination of output at market prices and at factor prices for a certain branch should be carried out for individual firms as well.

5. Specification of assortments should take place only when necessary, especially when the distribution of materials is strictly controlled and the main raw material is regulated. Depending on the particular conditions, the specification of assortments should:

– determine the assortment of the products completely,

– determine the basic components of the products,

– or determine how much of the value of the total production is to consist of the value of certain groups.

6. With regard to material distribution, which should be constantly limited, the following instructions should be accepted:

(a) the distribution should concern only those basic materials – raw or semi-processed – which are in short supply;

(b) there should be a tendency to achieve balances with as few potential sources of disproportion as possible. This principle should be applied especially to materials subject to further production processes;

(c) high and differential fines and other sanctions (prescribed in the contract) should be applied when a breach of contract occurs.

7. The enterprises' wage fund should be determined at the central level. If other methods are used, the income and expenditures of the population should be balanced.

II. The firms and superior organizations

A. Firms

1. Firms operate, under conditions of profit and loss accounting, on the basis of their own plans, which are connected to the national economic plan. Their main target is defined as the satisfaction of society's needs with minimal input. The goal of the superior organizations is to create economic conditions which will ensure harmony between the interest of society and that of the firm on the one hand, and between the interest of the firm and that of its employees on the other hand.

The firms should function on the basis of profitability, conditioned by any instructions which may be issued. Planning instructions should not replace economic instruments functionally, but rather should support them when the economic instruments are imprecise or insufficient. Conflict between commands and incentives should be made impossible.

The director of the firm is officially responsible for the execution of the planning instructions.

The main criterion for the evaluation of a firm's operation should not be an index of aggregate production.

2. The relations between superior units and firms should be strictly defined. The scope of necessary control over the firms should be specified. With respect to other areas, the firms should be treated as separate, autonomous economic units.

3. The areas within which the firms are to be independent should include the following:

(a) management of fixed capital with the guarantee that it will be properly maintained, and manipulation of the firm's financial assets (from profit and amortization) and of the credits for investments;

(b) planning of production based on an evaluation of the market and of available supplies, while taking into consideration any commands which may exist;

(c) management of supply and marketing in the following ways:
(1) directly,
(2) by entrusting, on their own initiative, part of their supply and marketing tasks to central organizations;
(3) by asking a central organization, subject to a superior organ, to deal with supply and marketing, preserving the general binding rules concerning the circulation of goods;

(d) redistribution of the wage fund according to collective agreements;
(e) redistribution of that part of the profit which is due to the firms;
(f) those affairs which concern the internal organization of the firms.

4. The following are the authorities of a firm:
– the workers' council, which constitutes an organ of workers' autonomy and acts under authority of the law;
– the director, who manages the firm, is responsible to the State and the workers, and represents the firm outside.

5. A firm is responsible for the economic results of its operation.

Notoriously bad management of a firm leads to the dismissal of the administration and workers' council, and introduction of a compulsory administration.

B. *The superior organs and cooperation of firms*

The existence of superior levels of industrial organization is indispensable. The functions of such organizations, fulfilled until now by central offices, require serious reforms. From this derives a need to create a new type of organization. The following are instructions for the formation of the new superior units:

1. Every firm works under a superior unit, which is determined by a minister. This does not exclude the possibility of independent firms being directly subordinated to a ministry.

2. Affiliation of firms to superior organizations cannot be based on criteria uniform for an entire industry. Along with the principle of affiliation by branch, a firm should apply the principle of affiliation according to cooperative connections.

3. The degree of organizational cohesiveness should vary, in accordance with the needs and character of the given branch of industry, from that of an organization responsible for certain common activities of firms to that of cooperation based on joint accounting. A firm subject to one

organization is entitled to cooperate with another organization, if it is so interested.

4. Firms, subordinated to superior organs or directly to ministries, are entitled to form associations for definite economic targets (export targets for example), for technological development, training, etc.

Scientific institutions, central laboratories, project and design bureaus, and units specializing in technical and organizational consultation are indispensable institutions appointed to help firms operate.

5. The superior organizations should function on the basis of economic accounting, or on principles which take the results of the firms' activities into consideration.

6. The superior units should be created on the basis of the following instructions:

(a) the scope of functioning and degree of centralization of these units should vary. The scope should be determined by the specific needs of a branch or of a group of firms included in a unit;

(b) in addition to the director, who manages the current activities of the unit, a supervisory control and advisory body may be needed. Additional functions of this body should be determined by statute;

(c) this body should be composed of persons appointed by authorities (director of the superior unit and representatives of the firms included!), and of others if necessary.

Detailed principles defining the functions and structure of the superior units, and the mode of appointment by the authorities should be stated in the statute issued by the organs of the State.

7. Firms producing for local consumption should be subject to local people's councils. The possibility of affiliating small-sized firms with key industry firms should be foreseen.

III. The instruments of planned management of industry

A. Material incentives for employees in industry
1. The formation of an appropriate system of incentives should be founded on the following main premises:

(a) departure from the practice of relating economic incentives in a general way to the accomplishment of set goals;

(b) connection of incentives to the dynamics of the firm's economic results, disregarding those factors which are independent of the firm's activity;

(c) principles determining the formation of incentives which are stable for several years, so that these incentives may work over a long period;

(d) simple and explicit principles for stipulating incentives;

(e) avoidance of uniform solutions by allowing the superior organizations and firms to adapt the general principles to their specific conditions and needs.

2. When the limit of the wage fund is determined, and firms are allowed to dispose of it, this fund should be formed according to specific rather than general production. Overdraft of the wage fund should be compensated for from that part of the firm's profit to be paid to the employees.

3. The main source of the material incentives (other than wages) should be a fund created from the firm's profits. The formation of the fund should be based on the following principles:

(a) there should be explicit and predetermined ways for distributing the profits between the firm and the state. This distribution should take into consideration the real economic conditions of the branch and firm, and the needs of economic policy. An upper limit on share in profits should not be defined except for short transitory periods;

(b) the principles of profit distribution should be corrected only on the basis of conditions independent of the firm;

(c) a firm should be entitled to use its money share of the profits. Also, it should be free to form principles for the allocation of this money among its departments and employees.

4. Special forms of material incentives (those other than wages and share in profits) can be applied only in extraordinary cases and for strictly defined targets.

B. Prices and their role as economic instruments

1. Because of the right of firms to decide on important economic processes, and because of the role profit plays in the system of incentives, prices have a special role in the system of economic instruments used by the State. A correct economic account of the firms and superior organizations is impossible without a correct determination of prices.

2. This determination should be based on the following premises:

(a) casual determination of the level of prices and of their mutual relations should be terminated. The determination of prices should take into account the real economic conditions which exist in production and exchange. The practice of using two entirely different methods for determining prices, one for production and the other for consumption, must be terminated. This practice has caused an artificial discrepancy in prices, prevented the use of money as a uniform measure of value, distorted the proportions of distribution of national income, etc.;

(b) the concept of a spontaneous formation of prices, without any control or influence by the State, must be rejected. The influence of the State on prices can be expressed:

– in a form of direct determination of prices by the appropriate organ of the State, or by determination of the principles of price calculations;

– in a form of indirect influence on production and on the market.

Any option should depend on several circumstances, but one of the most important criteria should be the elimination of every form of a firm's monopolistic status;

(c) the system of prices should be flexible, independently of the influence of the State. The flexibility of the system should not be conceived as a reaction of prices to short, accidental phenomena. It should be conceived as an adaptation of prices to permanent changes in the economic system.

3. An immediate general reform of the prices of means of production is indispensable. This reform should take into consideration the following factors:

(a) a real calculation of the total costs of production;

(b) the level of and relations among international market prices, and the prices of basic raw materials;

(c) the terms of profitability of those firms which are the main producers of any given item. In cases where for objective reasons a uniform price does not yield a profit for a producer who nonetheless is instructed to produce a special price should be established for him. At any rate, the new determination of prices should put an end to planned losses;

(d) the role of prices in production–consumption equilibrium.

4. Determination of the directions for changes in the prices of consumption goods and elaboration of a correct system of prices of the means of production should occur simultaneously.

Retail price reform requires conditions which ensure a general economic equilibrium and attention to the interest of the customer.

C. Additional economic instruments

1. In addition to, and in close connection with, its price policy, the State should use to a greater degree such additional economic instruments as the rate of interest and other forms of credit policy, taxes, a system of tariffs and of import–export coefficients.

2. The rate of interest and a differentiation of credit terms should be applied in order to influence the amount, direction, and modes of manipulation of banking credits devoted to investments. In order to prevent investments with limited effectiveness, firms should receive interest on their own bank accounts.

3. From the point of view of a whole rational use of means of production and of the principles for a correct calculation of costs and prices, the

question of whether a firm should pay interest on its means of production must be reconsidered. This problem should be solved in connection with the establishment of a method for financing industry from a central fund, a method which would exclude multiple payment of interest. An amortization and investment fund created independently by firms should be regarded as an important economic instrument.

4. In order to reconcile conflicts between the immediate interests of the firms and the long-term requirements of the national economy (introduction of new production and technological development do not bring rapid profits), special funds must be created at a superior level. The money should be used when the usual economic instruments are not sufficient.

5. The most essential factor for the proper functioning of the economic instruments is the proper attitude of the superior organizations, especially their interest in the general result of the management of firms . . .

WŁODZIMIERZ BRUS

Controversy on the role of the central plan*

The major part of the matters related to the 'model' discussed in passionate polemics will certainly not find a solution in general discussions, but – all things considered – in deliberation about the concrete elements constituting the notion, already slightly worn out by excessive use, of the economic model. I am, however, not of the opinion that, therefore, general conceptional discussions are purposeless, especially if they are related to the thorough analyses and observations taking place right now in the Economic Council . . .

If we have to consider as correct the assertion that the main subject of the discussion up to now has been the problem of relating the central plan to the economic instruments based on the whole set of commodity and monetary forms, and that in general all the participants in the discussion agreed that it is necessary to have a symbiosis of both elements – then it appears that the main differences of opinion are related to the two following groups of problems:

1. the role of the central plan, i.e. of the relation between priorities at the central level and priorities at other levels;
2. the methods of connecting and harmonizing the central plan with the plans of the enterprises and the structure of needs.

In the first matter, the overwhelming majority of the participants in the

* Excerpted from 'Spór o role planu centralnego', *Życie gospodarcze*, No. 12, 1957.

discussion (both those in favor of the law of value – among whom I belong – and those against this law) pronounced themselves unanimously against any attempts whatsoever of giving up the advantages given by the possibility of central planning, and thus the ability to define the main development trends not from the point of the interests or possibilities of one enterprise or branch, but from that of the national economy as a whole. Judging from papers I know, it seems to me that in this matter only S. Kurowski and J. Popkiewicz[1] have a different opinion.

Both Kurowski and Popkiewicz clearly assert the necessity of central planning. But at the same time they deny (although not always consistently) any independence whatsoever to the priorities of the central planner, telling him that he has to adjust himself to the signals and incentives coming from the market through the independent enterprises or at the best to fulfill the role of coordinator of these signals and incentives. This is how I understood the thesis of Kurowski on the role of the central plan as 'coordinator at the second level', a notion under which one has to understand – as he wrote in the paper 'Democratization and the law of value' – 'that the plan should assure that the processes of adjustment in the national economy, occurring according to the law of value, develop without disturbances and restraints', possibly with the correction of certain economic processes but not through 'putting his own priorities (those of the central planner) in place of the priorities of all the consumers'. In his last paper, too ('The model and aims . . .'), S. J. Kurowski sees one of the evil phenomena of the past period as being the elevating of the priorities of the central planner to the rank of an objective necessity, which, as I understand, is a reproach not raised against the petrification of determined priorities, but against the thesis of an objective necessity for directing economic processes by the central plan. I believe that this is an opinion almost entirely in agreement with the view held by J. Popkiewicz, who wrote that 'only from the market can enterprises and economic management bodies at all levels receive the signals determining the actual state of social needs and the rate of their satisfaction, as well as the correct and economically most effective orientation, nature, structure, rate and location of production and production investments'. Popkiewicz writes clearly on the decisive role of the law of value as the regulator of commodities' turnover and of production, while rejecting (this time very consistently) in

---

1 S. Kurowski, 'Demokracja i prawo wartości' (Democratization and the Law of Value) in the collection *Ekonomiści dyskutują o prawie wartości* (Economists are Discussing the Law of Value), Warsaw, 1956; 'Rynek i plan' (The Market and the Plan) in the collection *Diskusji o prawie wartości ciąg dalszy* (Discussions on the Law of Value, Continued), Warsaw, 1957; 'Model a cele gospodarki narodowej' (The Model and Aims of National Economy), *Życie gospodarcze*, No. 7, 1957. J. Popkiewicz, 'Prawdżiwa rentowność' (Real Profitability) in the collection *Diskusji o prawie wartości ciąg dalszy*.

a resolute and general manner the criterion of 'profitability on the scale of the whole national economy'.

I think that this is the core of the matter. Is there at all a notion of the interest of the national economy as a whole, which does not cover only the interest of the individual enterprise or the direct interest of the citizen as a consumer? To answer this question, the argument that in the past the notion of profitability on the scale of the national economy had been misused and used more than once in a manner having nothing in common with the actual interest of the economy, by no means will suffice. A behavior often camouflaged by the false signboard of the interest of the national economy does not mean, as yet, that the notion itself is nonsense. If the interest of the national economy always agrees with the interest of the individual enterprises – acting according to autonomous market signals and incentives – then there actually is no priority of the central planner and the whole wisdom of the economic policy of the state is reduced to securing the optimal free play of market forces; and the general interest is the resultant of the activity of the enterprises which react elastically to changes in market conditions due to demand by the consumers. It is not difficult to observe that such an understanding of the matter is to a great extent analogous to the thesis that the state of equilibrium of the individual enterprises is equivalent to the optimum scale of the national economy. This thesis never found its confirmation in the practice of the capitalist economy, and since the publishing of the work of Keynes, *The General Theory of Employment, Interest, and Money,* it has been refuted by the bourgeois economic theory also. I do not see any basis for reactivating it in the socialist economy in which the general interest can and should be expressed far more widely and directly than in a capitalist regime, even one with a highly developed state interventionism.

Let us try to explore the problem more closely. S. J. Kurowski divides investments into two groups in the paper 'The market and the plan': the first, in which the enterprises will have the initiative (rebuilding and enlargement); the second, in which the initiative will depend on the central planner. I consider this division as correct but I raise against the author the objection of lack of consistency. Indeed, why put the means of investment into the hands of the central planner? If we hold the view that the market is the decisive factor for all matters, then the volume of investments should depend on the possibilities of the various enterprises of a sector, i.e. on the rate of their profitability. Each redistribution of means from a more profitable to a less profitable sector would be in contradiction to the thesis of the lack of a specific scale of priorities of the central planner. And perhaps the central planner should fulfill only the function of a money-box accumulating means and giving them automatically to those who are ready to offer the highest rate of interest and the quickest repayment of the credits? It seems that this sort of thesis could be applied only with regard to the choice of variants of realization of an investment trend, but not to the definition of the trend itself, especially for longer periods. The decision as to whether or not, and to what extent, to develop mining, the chemical industry, or shipbuilding cannot and should not be made on the basis of the calculation of net return resulting from the immediate profitability of the various branches at the moment concerned. Even not taking into account reasons outside the economy, such a decision has to take into consideration several factors passing beyond the field of vision of the enterprises or branches: dynamism of employment, general possibilities of materials, influence on other production branches and on the balance of payments, etc. The correct view that economic decisions not based on the calculation of net return definitely have to be eliminated is not identical with the view that the calculation of net return can only be carried out at the level of enterprises or branches. Optimal consideration of big investment problems can only be secured as a result of the calculation of net return at the level of the national economy, i.e. on the basis of the scale of priorities of the central planner. It is the task of the whole social, economic, and political system to secure such conditions that this scale of priorities not be based on arbitrary tenets, but on objective and economic justifications.

And if so, if the choice in the range of the greatest part of the investment program should be carried out on the basis of the scale of priorities of the central planner, it means that the production program of investment goods as well as export and import policy have to be properly adjusted to these priorities.

More than that: the decisions related to investments that are left to the management of the enterprises can also not always be free from the influence of priorities at the central level, especially when national accounting is conducted as it should be from the point of view of profitability. For the enterprises, for instance, it makes no difference whether the means destined for rebuilding are used for saving of material or for the saving of live labor, if the financial effect will be the same. But from the point of view of the national economy, this can make an essential difference, if there is, for instance, lack of raw materials or an excess of the labor force, or vice versa. It is not at all beyond the realm of possibility that, for instance, unprofitable export production will be in fact profitable, if account is taken of the necessity of keeping workers who would be dismissed in the case of a production standstill.

One could say that in such circumstances incentives have to be created, so that the enterprises will reach decisions compatible with the interest of the national economy. This is correct, most correct. But it already means that alternative options do not follow from the action of market forces, but that they are formed by the priorities of the central planner.

Even the production of consumer articles, a sector in which the priorities of the central level occur particularly and naturally in a relatively low degree (I have in mind the structure of production), and in which incentives and signals emitted from the market should play the greatest part, even this sector, under certain conditions, cannot be left to itself, either. I have the impression that S. Kurowski, who wrote most on this subject, makes in a certain sense a fetish of the very notion of consumers' priorities, that he makes something absolute of them. It is most desirable that the production structure should be adjusted to the structure of effective demand, but is the demand structure alone a notion so definite that there are already no more problems? Let us consider a most simple example.

If, for a certain price level, demand for commodity A exceeds supply, whereas demand for commodity B is lower than supply – then restoration of the state of equilibrium (assuming the appropriate elasticity of demand) is possible either through changing the supply structure and not changing the prices, or through changing the price structure and preserving the dimensions of supply.

Insofar as it will not clash with the social interest or with the interest of the national economy as a whole, one can rely on the market and let the economy adjust to the resultant it will form. But under certain circumstances, one has to proceed differently: to subject market conditions and together with them the decisions of the consumer to a higher priority. For instance, if the increase in supply of commodity A is not favorable or would be impossible for general economic or social reasons, there should be a rise in prices together with collection of an appropriate tax, in order to eliminate undesirable incentives for the producer. And the contrary: if the market processes start bringing about tendencies towards a rise in prices and a restriction of demand in a manner threatening the interests of social consumption, it would be purposeful and necessary to apply measures of counteraction.

At what time does this passive adjustment to spontaneous market phenomena represent the best form of securing the interests of the consumer and at the same time the best way towards the appropriate, waste-eliminating, structure of social production? Can the active policy of market formation and the structuring of demand and supply be given up? And what is such a policy, if not a reaction to market processes from the point of view of priorities of a higher order?

I do not think that we have to dwell for long on this subject. For the sake of order, I want to state once more that orientation according to the 'regulating role of the market' does not supply the basis for so essential a decision as the division of the national income into consumption and accumulation. I agree entirely with the view that the 'decision' on economic decisions cannot be reached in an arbitrary way, as was the case up till now, but that it has to be the object of particularly careful social control, which has to be guaranteed in the best possible way by the institutions. But this already has not got much to do with the regulating role of the market and with the denial of the priorities of the central level.

I am in advance prepared for the answer that all these matters are fundamental, and perfectly and long understood in the whole world and more obviously in relation to the socialist economy. S. Kurowski will even be able to refer to some formulations of the paper 'The market and the plan' and declare that the whole matter consists of a misunderstanding, since he had not in mind the importance of the central plan, but only the way of mutually connecting the priorities of various levels.

Well – I am ready to admit a battle against a shadow, especially insofar as the role of economic instruments in the planned economy is concerned. I see in the articles of S. Kurowski and J. Popkiewicz many views I do agree with. But I must say that the central idea of the two authors mentioned was understood quite generally in the way I tried to present them. Should that not be the case – all the better for the idea of changing the economic model.

The correct definition of the role of the central plan has an essential significance for the improvement of our economy. Holding the view that general priorities expressed in the central plan should define the main lines of development of the national economy and should in this sense hold a superior position, we have to admit at the same time that the program of changes in the economic model should contain as one of its main points the task of deepening central planning and of basing it on really scientific foundations. It would be a great misunderstanding to oppose to this thesis the thesis of the necessity of decentralization, independence of the enterprises, application of economic instruments, etc. It is already high time that we should cease to identify central planning as such with bureaucratic administrative forms of planning with which we were and are still dealing up till today. Central planning of employment – the laying down of the general lines of economic policy in this field on the basis of a thorough analysis of demographical data, migrating tendencies, dimensions and structure of production and investments in the territorial and trade-branches cross section, etc. – is, of course, necessary, and has nothing in common with a bureaucratic division of directive limits for ministries, central management bodies, and enterprises still sub-divided in sub-groups and sub-sub-groups. The same is true for other problems.

FERENC JÁNOSSY

The origins of the present contradictions in our economy and how to eliminate them*

A long-term economic plan is capable of favorably influencing future economic development if it represents the concrete application of a carefully considered concept of economic policy. If no such clear concept is available at the time of planning – for either subjective or objective reasons – then the long-term plan is necessarily reduced to the more or less successful extrapolation of the current process of development. The plan thereby loses its ability to fulfill its proper purpose, which is to serve as a directive in deciding among economic alternatives as they emerge during the planning period. The long-term plan serves its purpose if it indicates correctly – from the viewpoint of future development – the timing and direction of the necessary divergence from currently perceived daily requirements. If no such economic–political concept on which to base decisions bearing on the future is available, the detailed elaboration of a long-term plan is at best only a strenuous and successful self-deception.

... In the following, an attempt will be made to develop a concept, starting from the general laws of economic development, which could serve as the basis for a long-term economic plan for Hungary for the next decade or two.

In order to clarify the starting point of our thinking, the following should be said in advance.

Far be it from us to derive the present economic structure of Hungary, and the well-known difficulties of development following therefrom, directly from the forced industrialization policy of the Rakosi period. Nevertheless, we have to begin with this period, because the structural changes then instituted gave rise to those contradictions which, characteristically, have reproduced themselves ever since.

This starting point is also correct, in my view, because we did not substitute some other concept, different in principle, for that, so clearly defined in the first five-year plan, of industrialization at a forced pace. The concept of forced industrialization lives on like a dying love affair, maintained only from habit and dissolving finally and irrevocably when a new love takes its place.

It is true that in our economic practice we took account of reality, that is, we did not force the extensive growth of industry. Nonetheless, we con-

* 'Gazdaságunk mai ellentmondásainak eredete és felszámolásuk útja', *Közgazdasági szemle*, July–August, 1969.

tinued to believe implicitly that along this road development could really be accelerated. The concessions we made were those of practice, not of principle, for we did not realize that the old concept was problematic not because of transient difficulties, but rather because it diverged fundamentally from an objectively feasible direction for our economic development.

We acted as does the impatient inexperienced mountain climber who, instead of walking along comfortably on a slowly rising road in the narrow valley between two mountain ranges, turns off and pushes painfully forward on the precipitous mountainside: he does not rise more rapidly than he would along the road in the valley, but he hopes that he will find a road that rises more steeply. As a starting point for the discovery of a really promising way for the future we have to find a satisfactory explanation of why this much sought-after steeper path, that is, the path of continued forced industrialization along which we have started, has not been found, and why, in my view, it will not be found in the future either.

Conditions and limitations of forced industrialization

Let us start by comparing the planned economy with the market economy, leaving aside the question of the specific forms these two systems may take and concentrating instead on the two extremes, that is, unfettered free competition and its obverse, centrally directed planning embracing all enterprises and products.

In a pure market economy, the law of value really becomes operative only through the risk of bankruptcy: that is to say, the law of value can be broken only – to use Marx's expression – at the 'cost of extinction' (*bei Strafe des Untergangs*). This obligatory profitability imposed on every entrepreneur is completely absent in the planned economy – and in this sense it completely eliminates market effects. Whether this absence benefits or harms economic development depends entirely on the degree to which this additional freedom is properly utilized, for this new degree of freedom creates a risk in that it makes it possible for us to choose the wrong solution. Despite this danger, it is undeniable that the elimination of obligatory profitability expands the range of our possibilities. Thus we must not forget that this new degree of freedom constitutes a real potential advantage.

This increased degree of freedom is similar to the additional freedom of buses over trams. The route of buses can be determined freely, independently of that prescribed by the rails. Whether the additional possibilities prove to be an advantage depends in this case, too, on whether the freely selected route is more or less favorable than the one to which the trams are constrained by the rails. By socializing the means of production, we liberated ourselves from the rails on which the market economy must travel; nevertheless, we must not think that the new direction is fixed by the absence of rails.

I think that the most important new option gained from the additional freedom within a planned economy – and this too can be turned to advantage only under certain conditions – is the possibility of a more rapid change of the economic structure. In other words, there is the new possibility of moving more rapidly from a structure consistent with a lower level of development to another, consistent with a much higher level. This more rapid structural change (which, below a certain degree of industrial development, is possible in every country), can be achieved mainly by forcing the pace of industrialization.

Characteristics of forced industrialization

What is the difference between forced industrialization and industrialization in general? What are the characteristics of the forced pace?

In the process of industrialization in every country it is necessary to bring about a mass transfer of labor (mainly from agriculture) into industry. As long as this inflow of labor does not exceed that which industry can normally absorb without endangering the functioning of newly established enterprises or the quality and modernity of the products and thereby their profitability, we can speak of normal – that is, not forced – industrialization. Forced industrialization, on the other hand, entails an expansion of industry greater than this limit, so that there arises such a tension between the employment structure and the labor-skills structure that the newly established or expanded enterprises must temporarily produce unprofitably. One of the conditions of forced industrialization is that one pays the price of temporary unprofitability in order to achieve the necessary rapid rate of change in the labor-skills structure.

Under conditions of forced industrialization, therefore, the transition from a lower to a higher stage of development (from the point of view of productivity) does not follow an unbroken upward line, but shows at the beginning – before the acquisition of new techniques and the accumulation of experience – a downward trend. The renewed upswing comes about – i.e. the planned forced pace begins to be achieved – only when the skills and experience of the labor force reach equilibrium with the expanded industrial structure. (Why the fall in productivity here outlined does not appear in statistics is a question which could be satisfactorily answered only after a thorough analysis, taking us far from our present concern.)

Plan, market, and forced industrialization

It is evident that a pure market economy – that is, the unfettered operation of the profitability requirement – is in principle inconsistent with even the possibility of forced industrialization. The capitalist entrepreneur cannot take this route. The capitalist cannot afford uneconomic investment. He cannot take upon himself such a sacrifice even though this way he would, in the final reckoning, increase the pace of development. This route is blocked by the risk of bankruptcy, for competition forces him to stick to an uninterrupted upward course. He cannot, therefore, set out on a road which – as is characteristic for the process of forced industrialization – necessarily leads downward (at least from the point of view of productivity).

A planned economy eliminates the limitations arising from obligatory profitability and enables us to take the route of forced industrialization. However, it does not even remotely follow that simply because we are able to take this road it will under all conditions lead to the expected results.

It is the undoubted advantage of a planned economy that it opens routes of development which are completely excluded in a pure market economy, as, for instance, the route of forced industrialization. But this advantage involves the danger that this course can also be taken when – under certain specific conditions – it will lead not to the expected result, but rather to a dead end.

Thus, in the following we will have to find the conditions under which one can successfully take the route of forced industrialization.

General conditions for the success of forced industrialization

The following are the conditions – in addition to the elimination of profitability restrictions – necessary for successful forced industrialization.

It is indispensable that a given country possess some – loosely defined – extra-industrial economic resource, with which the 'tuition fee' imposed by the forced pace of industrial expansion can be continuously paid. This resource must be relatively abundant so that it can on the one hand cover the costs of the initial period of accumulation and, on the other, yield exportable surpluses, since forced industrialization can be successfully achieved only with the help of techniques imported from economically more developed countries.

It should be emphasized that such an extra-industrial resource is required only under conditions of forced industrialization. This is because the financing of the 'tuition fee' imposed by forced industrialization becomes a substantial burden only because of the forced pace; what is more, it is precisely this forced pace which deprives industry of its ability to finance it from its own means. It is of decisive importance, especially to countries poor in raw materials, that this extra-industrial resource be exportable, since forced industrialization generally brings about a deterioration in the ratio between a country's ability to export and its import requirements . . .

Forced industrialization in the Soviet Union and Hungary

In the Soviet Union the fundamental conditions for forced industrialization were, as a result of the following circumstances, basically satisfied:

(a) in the period following the war and civil war, the population was extremely undemanding and ready for sacrifices;

(b) despite considerable transfers of manpower to industry, the agriculture sector was able to provide the population with food (even though the level of supplies fell temporarily);

(c) the natural resources of the country were abundant enough to meet industrial requirements for raw materials and energy;

(d) the abundance of natural resources made it possible to export enough raw materials to pay for imported machines and equipment.

Because of these four conditions, economic equilibrium could be maintained in the Soviet Union despite grave transitional difficulties, even though the pace of industrialization was so forced that for years industrial output was used almost entirely to meet the needs of the industrial sector itself (and only to a minimal extent to meet the needs of the population).

. . . If we compare the conditions of forced industrialization in Hungary and the Soviet Union on the basis of the four points above, the following picture emerges.

(a) The living standard in Hungary before World War II was higher than that of the Soviet Union prior to World War I. Because of this, the requirements of the population were greater and grew much faster . . .

(b) Agriculture could supply the population with food, so in this respect conditions in Hungary were similar to those in the Soviet Union.

(c) The natural resources available in Hungary were far from enough to satisfy industrial needs for raw materials. As a result, the expansion of industry led to greater importation of raw materials.

(d) It was possible for a while to use the export of agricultural products to finance a certain percentage of the imports needed for the installation of modern techniques, but this was far from sufficient and in time became even less so.

To sum up, the Soviet Union needed imports only in connection with the establishment of new plants, and could satisfy this demand for imports relatively easily by exporting raw materials, while in Hungary even current production required a steady import of raw materials.

Thus, in Hungary, the general precondition for forced industrialization, that is, an abundant extra-industrial resource, was missing. It follows that our industry itself had to pay for an overwhelming share of its imports of raw materials and machinery, by exporting industrial products. This restriction limited the feasible pace of forcible industrialization. Because it was so closely bound up with foreign trade, the pace of industrialization could not, under any circumstances, exceed the limit beyond which the rapid inflow of new and inexperienced manpower would frustrate the export of manufactured products, by lowering the quality of the products to an unsatisfactory level.

Beginnings of forced industrialization in Hungary

In the forced extensive development of industry during the Rakosi period [1946–53], the Soviet Union undoubtedly served as our prototype. We attempted to follow the Soviet industrialization model without realizing the basic differences in conditions. With the launching of the first Five-Year Plan, we set out on the road of forced industrialization.

From the point of view of the problems here analyzed, it is irrelevant whether the forced structural change

– was carried out consciously and consistently, with the intention of accelerating the transformation of the manpower skills structure, or whether its rate resulted spontaneously from the removal of the limitations imposed by profitability;

– was crucially affected by the Western embargo, or was determined exclusively by the decision to adopt the Soviet model of industrialization;

– was suggested by the real or apparent danger of war, or was merely an attempt to maintain without interruption the pace achieved during the period of [post-War] reconstruction.

What is really important here is not so much the uncovering of motives and historical reasons as the fact itself – namely, that the rapid structural change had started and the concept of forced industrialization had taken root and become the basic principle of an effective economic policy.

In spite of the unfavorable preconditions, forced industrialization did not immediately encounter insurmountable difficulties, and in the beginning the maintenance of the forced pace was not even limited by foreign trade (as it now is). That the contradictions between the planned course and the objective possibilities were only revealed later was due to the following initial extenuating circumstances:

– at the outset of the period of forced industrialization a trade balance was more or less maintained with the help of agricultural exports;
– after the war the demand for manufactured products was so great – primarily in the Soviet Union, but also in the West – that even obsolete goods could be sold;
– the Soviet Union could easily supply Hungary with the necessary raw materials in exchange for the above-mentioned exports.

This extenuating circumstance – that in the years following the war the Soviet Union became an insatiable customer for all kinds of finished products and in exchange for them supplied us with raw materials – proved to be of decisive importance. Had Hungary depended exclusively on its trade with the West during the fifties, the policy of forced industrialization would have led very quickly to a grave catastrophe.

For the reasons enumerated, this sobering catastrophe was avoided, but the hidden contradictions did not disappear, and in fact *grew* (as was inevitable under the specific circumstances).

Rising levels of development and forced industrialization

At a very low level of economic development, almost every country – even the smallest – is self-sufficient. Simple reproduction can be maintained without any connections with the outer world. Long ago – and to imagine this initial level of development one does not have to go quite as far back as the first settlement of the country – Hungary was almost certainly self-sufficient, or at least could have been so in principle. With the progress of industrial development, this 'idyllic' state naturally came to a gradual end.

Because of the scarcity or complete lack of some industrial raw materials in Hungary, nearly every industrial product contains some proportion of imports – in the form of raw materials, energy, or amortization of machinery. This dependence on imports did not arise in leaps and bounds, however, but evolved in the course of development as the result of a gradually intensifying process. The higher the level of development attained, the higher the import quotient – even, and this has to be particularly stressed, in goods for personal consumption. This increase of the import quotient originates not only in the shift of personal consumption from agriculture to industrial products, but also in a similar shift in production imports (for instance, in agriculture there is a change from dung to chemical fertilizers, from draught animals to tractors).

It should be stressed in this connection that the import quotient resulting from the structure of consumption depends exclusively on the level of development already attained and not on the rate of development. In addition, the process of development itself requires imports – here, the greater the rate of development, the greater the import needs – in order to modernize the means of production, either directly through imports of machines and tools, or indirectly through the purchase of patents and know-how.

. . . As a consequence of this process, a situation may arise in which the import requirements of simple reproduction absorb the entire capacity to export so that no balance is left to cover the import needs of further development. To avoid this dead end we may choose only a course of development which ensures that the export capacity will always be greater than that needed to acquire the necessary imports for the simple reproduction of the level of development already attained. The higher the level of development, the more dangerous is the reduction of the export capacity inevitably resulting from forced expansion.

Consequences of forced industrialization

During the period of forced industrialization . . . a considerable but evenly distributed tension exists between the employment structure and the skills structure . . . The tension arises not only because the rapid change of branch structure forces labor to change employment and acquire new skills, but also because a continuous modernization takes place in every enterprise. This tension makes reeducation and learning necessary, and makes it possible to gain the experience needed for the new branches and new techniques.

Even though it is possible to recognize in the present economic structure of Hungary a few general characteristics of the structure which evolves under the classical conditions of forced industrialization, our country's structure hardly satisfies the above requirements for an even tension. In Hungary, the conditions unfavorable for forced industrialization created a specific structural situation characterized by powerful tensions in the industrial branch structure and, simultaneously, by a total absence – at least in some places – of an accelerating tension in the individual enterprises. We shall call this specific economic structure 'quasi-developed'.

Let it be said that we never consciously strove to create this quasi-developed structure. It arose spontaneously both during the first rush of forced industrialization and later, in the following way. The extensive expansion of industry, involving the building of new factories as well as the expansion of the old (this expansion was misleadingly called 'reconstruction'), absorbed almost all investment capacities from the very beginning; this meant that no investment capacity was left over for the modernization of existing industrial plants. This type of expansion of industry led to continuously growing import requirements, without a corresponding growth in our export-capacity vis-à-vis the more developed countries. To ensure the export cover for our import requirements despite all this, we attempted an even more forced development of our industrial production, again entirely by expansion of the existing industry.

This negative spiral – that is, the continuous expansion of industry in an attempt to cover the increasing import requirements even at low efficiency – was ill-suited to the task of closing the initial gap between the import requirements of industry and its export capacity. On the contrary, this gap kept growing. Because of this – seemingly inevitable – spiral, the modernization of the continually increasing stocks of machinery and equipment was pushed into the background. In particular, there was a decrease – at least relative to the chronically neglected and therefore cumulative needs of industrial modernization – in our ability to develop our industry with machinery imported from the West.

Thus, at present, there prevails the powerful macrostructural tension generated by rapid migration of manpower from agriculture into industry. This tension is of advantage because it enables thousands to acquire industrial skill and experience. At the same time, however, even today there are a large number of industrial firms with equipment which has scarcely been modernized for decades, and which therefore lack even that minimum of tension needed for the acquisition of knowledge.

In the formation of the quasi-developed structure, a large part was due not only to the extreme limitations on imports of machinery from developed countries (and to the inadequate acquisition of up-to-date production techniques) but also to the forced expansion of our own heavy industry, notably machine-building.

. . . Another characteristic of the quasi-developed structure which should be mentioned here briefly is the very high degree of concentration relative to the general industrial development. There is a preponderance of large-scale enterprises and a lack of small and medium-size plants. These large enterprises are in many cases merely an administrative combination of several small industrial units, and are therefore – considering their mode of production – only 'quasi-large' firms.

. . . We may also characterize the quasi-developed structure as a discrepancy between form and substance. In this connection, everything that is economically measurable and can be grasped with economic statistics is related to 'form' alone. The substance, which by its nature is qualitative, can thus be easily ignored. The 'how much' which we measure is mostly only a form of the 'what' of the quantitatively unmeasurable quality, that is of the substance. Here and there, so and so many workers are employed, so and so much is produced, invested, etc. – this is form. But what the quality of manpower is, what the products are like, what it is that we invest

– this is the hidden substance. It seems to me superfluous to illustrate the discrepancy between form and substance – that is, the existence of quasi-developed structure – with a long series of examples . . .

The quasi-developed state remains hidden not only in statistics, but often also with the direct inspection of production, since the present-day production process is in general a most impressive spectacle even in the extreme case where a huge factory produces nothing but rejects. The difference between a well-mastered, smoothly running production process and another which works only approximately is apparently insignificant but really fundamental, and may be recognized only by the experienced specialist – and even he will be able to uncover the real difference only after a thorough inquiry.

Only the user experiences the quasi-developed state directly; by 'user' we mean not only the individual consumer, but also the enterprise, as a user of inputs. It is the practice for every enterprise to explain the unsatisfactory quality of its own products by the poor quality of the raw materials, semi-finished products, tools, etc., which it receives. For the most part, this is no false excuse. The liquidation of the quasi-developed state is such a difficult undertaking because it can be achieved only stepwise and yet must simultaneously embrace the entire range of production.

We are thus back at our starting point. Economic planning creates greater freedom of action, which makes possible movement along both advantageous and retrograde routes. The existence of the quasi-developed structure is the result of a retrograde movement since it can exist only if those who experience its disadvantages – both consumers and users of inputs – are unable to influence production. (This happens if the market is not effective or if it is controlled by producers instead of users.)

The road to 'quasi-self-sufficiency' depends upon foreign trade

Dependence on foreign trade arises sooner or later in the course of industrialization – even at a normal pace – in every small country with scarce raw materials, and then increases with the rising level of development. As an outcome of forced industrialization – which, as explained above, leads to an increasing gap between export capacity and import requirements – this dependence on foreign trade becomes the most important bottleneck to further development . . . The two opposing tendencies – on the one hand, a shift of the economic structure towards autarky and, on the other, the worsening of foreign trade limitations – are thus seen to be neither mutually exclusive nor offsetting.

The well-known dilemma of whether to strive for balanced foreign trade by increasing exports or by import substitution does not go to the root of the problem, for unless the quasi-developed state is liquidated, neither of these two courses will eliminate the foreign trade limitations which hinder further development. For instance, it is quite hopeless to try to eliminate the foreign trade bottleneck by a further expansion of our quasi-developed machine-building industry, regardless of whether we use its obsolescent, low-quality products locally as import substitutes, or instead export them at the forint rate of 100 to a dollar.

The only solution to this problem is to find a way out of this foreign trade dilemma which threatens to throttle our development. The throttling effect emerges from forced industrialization, which gives rise to ever-increasing difficulties in balancing our foreign trade; the effort to maintain the balance leads to an attempt to invent and produce everything, as a means of saving foreign exchange; this autarky leads, in turn, to a quasi-developed structure, with a low export capacity, high dependence on foreign trade, and essentially autarkic nature; this results in a further decrease of our export capacity, and so on.

The quasi-developed state and further development

Not only the foreign trade difficulties described above follow from the quasi-developed state; so too do still further obstacles to development. Productivity increases most rapidly in series production, and especially in mass production. Relative to this rate of growth, the increased productivity in repair and maintenance work is negligible, so that maintenance work becomes increasingly expensive, especially since, in addition, it requires highly skilled manpower. If the quality and reliability of capital and durable consumers' goods in a quasi-developed state are low, if they do not conform to the level required by development, then 'cheap' mass production will be accompanied by disproportionately high and rising costs of repair and maintenance. The inadequate quality of machines, instruments, raw materials, etc., frustrates completely the achievement of certain levels of technology, especially that of complete automation of the processes of production . . .

Discontinuity in economic management and its consequences

At the time of the takeover of political power, the leadership was changed – to some extent, necessarily – in almost every controlling position in the economy and the administration. The simultaneous widespread discontinuity posed a difficult problem for the new leading economic functionaries (often themselves surprised at being appointed) – namely, how to become, in the face of their lack of experience, instant 'leaders', those who will decide difficult questions. Thus, even those who possessed the professional training necessary to fulfill their tasks were forced to teach themselves how to be leaders, since in their environment there was no one from whom they could learn the managerial experience required in their role as leaders. They had to carry out their tasks, for better or for worse, guided solely by common sense, unaided by their own or someone else's experience.

Nevertheless, the two circumstances mentioned below created the illusion that, despite their unavoidable amateurism, these self-taught men succeeded in mastering the task of economic management.

. . . This apparent success of amateurism undoubtedly strengthened the view that 'knowledge and experience are secondary to political reliability' and at the same time helped to spread the voluntarist view which doubts the very existence of objective difficulties.

The approval of self-taught management on the one hand and the belittling of experience on the other quickly spread to the field of technology . . . The well-known and understandable wish of technicians to invent, design, and construct everything by themselves was happily paired with the prevailing foreign currency scarcity. The managers were glad to save currency and the engineers enthusiastic in their interesting and creative work. The researchers happily worked on innovations which had long been discovered by others, instead of looking for ways to apply the technical achievements of the developed countries. Naturally, one can only in the rarest of cases expect researchers or planners to initiate a plan to buy know-how or a license from abroad, unless they are themselves responsible for profitability or have more interest in it than in the realization of their own pet ideas. I think the weakness of economic management – relative to the definite conceptions of the technicians – contributed a great deal to our developing in a way which resulted in a 'quasi-self-sufficiency' in relation to foreign trade.

As a result of the discontinuity in time (the rupture in the flow of past experience into the present), quasi-autarky caused a 'spatial discontinuity' (by way of a rupture in our acquisition of the experiences of economically more developed countries). He who has not sufficient experience himself often underestimates the necessity of learning from the experience of others, even though it is in exactly these cases that it is particularly necessary to rely on the experience of others.

This fatal interaction of objective and subjective factors led to economic isolation, a situation in which everything we did, we did on our own.

The fetish of measurability: its origins and effects

Overemphasis on anything that could be measured by quantitative parameters – at the expense of the nonmeasurable or the difficult to measure – was the result of numerous circumstances. The primary factor was surely the effort to find a substitute for market control. Although market control, too, seems to be purely quantitative, since it measures solely in money terms, there is hidden behind this quantity a highly differentiated evaluation of the qualitative characteristics of goods.

It became evident very quickly that a detailed plan, designating the production of goods in quantitative terms, is far less meaningful than one dealing with the monetary amounts to be obtained from the sale of those goods. The control of plan fulfillment released a veritable avalanche of prescribed and to-be-measured parameters. Nevertheless, there inevitably remained a mass of characteristics of production and of products which could not be measured in practice. Therefore, the plan could be fulfilled precisely at the cost of the latter, since it was those features of production and products which were nonquantitative, unmeasured, or unmeasurable which did not exist from the point of view of the plan . . .

Economic mechanisms and the economic policy concept

. . . To repeat, while the unlimited operation of the market excludes forced industrialization in principle, the planned economy – if it eliminates the free operation of the market – creates the theoretical possibility for it. The planned economy thus widens the range of possibilities open to us, but it does not determine which course will be taken. Whether we ought to proceed along the route of forced industrialization, or along some other path, depends on a consciously conceived economic policy.

This self-evident fact needs to be stressed, since there is a tendency nowadays to attribute the entire shape of our economic development, and especially the difficulties resulting from it, exclusively to overcentralized planning, i.e. to the 'old' economic mechanisms. If this view were right, we would need only to make appropriate reforms in the economic mechanism; the validity of the economic policy concept would scarcely be relevant.

The opposite of this incorrect view is even more misleading. This opposite extreme opinion may be defined as follows: The model of the centralized planned economy provides maximum freedom and thus the widest room for maneuvering to select any desirable course. Accordingly, *everything* depends on the right economic–political concept. If this concept is found, there is no need whatsoever either for a new economic mechanism or for the restriction imposed by the market. If we consciously proceed in the right direction, it is not necessary to do so through the market mechanism, that is, through the risk of bankruptcy.

This view, as it appears above, is really correct; the trouble is that the line of reasoning – as is all too often forgotten – is based on the word 'if'. *If* we could decide upon and accomplish, in all its details, that solution which is right, given the framework of directive planning, everything would be in order. However, the market does not merely reduce the number of attainable possibilities; it is also an indicator which provides *a priori* orientation for innumerable individual decisions or, at the least, provides an *a posteriori* check and thus helps in finding the right solution. The extent to which we fail to use the market as an indicator depends in the last analysis on the specific economic policy concept we select.

If we look at the connection between the economic mechanism and the policy concept from this angle, the following can be said. Under conditions of forced industrialization, with industrial expansion as the main aim, the restrictive role of the market is more important than its function as an indicator, since in this case the goal – to attain the structure of some more highly developed country – is quite clear, and therefore may be aimed at and achieved (although not easily) without the checks of the market. It is different in the case of a concept – and for Hungary the evolution of such a concept is an absolute must – the purpose of which is to transform the distorted quasi-developed structure into an effectively and harmoniously developed structure. The purpose of such a concept coincides essentially with the achievement of intensive development. In this case, the market is an indispensable indicator, and its restrictive role is less important. The old economic mechanism became an obstacle to development not because of its own functioning but rather precisely because it created the framework for the no longer practicable forced industrialization.

To find the path for a practicable economic development, we must break not only with the old mechanism, but with the old policy concept as well.

The liquidation or surpassing of the quasi-developed state

. . . The overriding goal is to liquidate the present quasi-developed state, by the general acquisition of the skills and experience which conform to the presently existing technology and by the modernization of those branches of production which, as a result of forced expansion, are now obsolescent. In the future, therefore, we must emphasize (as we have not so far) not the 'more' but the 'better' – in order to achieve the 'more' in the future. If, as a result of attaining the 'better', the efficiency of the entire process of production increases, we shall in the end have better quantitative results than we would if we were to continue the effort of quantitative expansion, since the continuation of this effort would merely reduce its effectiveness even more.

. . . Because the quasi-developed state is partly the outcome of an excessively rapid structural shift, and because this distortion may be largely ascribed to the lack of experience and tradition, it is obvious that – at a minimum – the practice of a decade will have to be accumulated . . . Perhaps impatience is the most important feature of the period of forced industrialization. In the future, we shall be able to achieve even less by impatience . . .

If the concept of liquidating the quasi-developed state were really accepted – something I do not think is probable, since we would have to overcome the tremendous forces of inertia – we would have to undertake the (probably very lengthy) task – similar to the elaboration of the new economic mechanisms – of finding ways to achieve this concept while at the same time evolving a long-term plan based on it. I do not exclude the possibility that this concept may not be explicitly integrable into the long-term plan, that is, that the long-term plan might contain the concept only implicitly, by not contradicting it . . .

IV   Interests, incentives, goals

Introductory note

A central tenet of Soviet planning is that individual material interests do not conflict. The interests of individual members of such diverse groups as factory workers, laborers on collective farms, university professors and government bureaucrats are assumed to be held together by an overriding preoccupation with the common good and a concern for the overall development of the economy. The Soviet writer G. Glezerman maintains that 'the abolition of private property relegates to the past the interests it engenders . . . Here [under socialism] the interests of those who own the means of production and those who work are no longer diametrically opposed. They are one and the same people.' Glezerman recognizes that the socialist society is fragmented just as was its predecessors by divisions of social labor among and within production units, organizations and administrations. But he contends that these divisions are qualitatively different from those which prevailed under capitalism; these, as well as the individual interests are assumed to be harmonized within the framework of a socialized economy.

The main challenge against this fundamental Marxian tenet was raised in Czechoslovakia by the economist Ota Šik and by his followers, who ultimately brought about that unique phenomenon, the 'Prague Spring' of 1968. According to Šik, *the main driving forces* of the socialist economy and society are, as under capitalism, personal and collective (group) interests, rather than the highly abstract social needs. It is not the alleged *identity* but the *divergence* of interests which must be seized upon if the economy is to progress. From this crucial shift in emphasis a number of decisive consequences follow concerning goals, the structure of production, incentives, the workers' rights in the enterprise and in the society at large, and the general policies of the state toward individual interests. The Czechoslovak economic writers of the 1960s – Šik, Lantay, Komenda and Kožušník, Kýn, Kouba, and many others – carefully and cogently pointed out the distorting influences which, they claimed, the theory of the identity of interests had with respect to the welfare of the society in general.

Consider first the questions of goals and of the structure of production. For the planner of a Soviet-type economy, the policy makers' top priorities and targets must be fulfilled at the cost of the lower priorities if necessary. These goals are apportioned among all firms, viewed as integral parts of the national enterprise. But, as Šik, and Komenda and Kožušník point out below, not all the details of the firms' activities can be centrally determined. The specific interests of the plants' managers and workers will necessarily express themselves through the resulting loopholes. In opposition to the injunctions of the directive center, each firm will assert these interests by its choice of the information it furnishes to the center, by its selection of inputs, and by the quality and mix of the goods it produces. Only by recognizing the *specific* interests of the enterprises can the perverse incentives of the directive system be avoided and the economy set on an efficient course.

For the socialist planner, it is always the changes on the supply side which determine the patterns of demand within the prevailing social relations. It is the changes in production which are supposed to fashion the patterns of demand – and not the other way round. Furthermore, given the assumed identity of interests, everybody within the socialist society is presumed to welcome the expansion of heavy industry which in turn will eventually help develop light industries, agriculture, and consumer goods in general. It is this emphasis on production, and its combination with the theory of the identity of interests, that the Czechoslovak reformers of the 1960s rejected. Instead, they stressed the necessity of relying on consumer demand in order to guide production toward the output of goods which are really needed and wanted, outputs which alone could properly motivate the workers as producers and as consumers.

Indeed, in the Soviet-type directive system, incentives are keyed to some technical plan indicator, e.g. norms of piece-work, input utilization, gross output, overall deliveries, etc. The quality of production is rather secondary in a perennial sellers' market. The material rewards obtained in the fulfillment and overfulfillment of this low quality output (of which consumer-goods form the most neglected part) also give access only to these same goods: this ultimately discourages the consumer, dampens the stimulus for work and increases the gulf between what the planner aims at and what the worker would like to obtain.

In the reformers' conception, the production of unwanted goods, the play of distorting incentives, the neglect of individual interests could all be ended if the concept of the identity of interests would be discarded, if consumers' demands would be taken into account, and if the plan would be viewed as a probabilistically-oriented projection supplementing the operation of markets. This is the message of the 'Prague Spring', eloquently presented below by some of its main voices.

In the final piece of the selection Karel Kouba points out that Oskar Lange, in his well-known model of a socialist economy, also assumed that the interests of the enterprises' managers and of the Central Planning Board (CPB) would not clash. Kouba stresses, however, that the East European experience shows precisely the opposite. Since the diverging interests of planners and managers would necessarily affect the information provided by the latter to the former, the prices set by the CPB would not fulfill the parametric function assigned to them by Lange and would not be able to provide a substitute for market determined prices. Incidentally, the tendency of the firms to misinform the CPB is present even in the framework of indicative planning. It is enormously strengthened within a directive planning framework, within which the CPB's targets serve also as criteria of evaluation of the firms' performance.

G. GLEZERMAN

Sources and role of interests in socialist society*

Sources of interests

... The abolition of private property relegates to the past the interests it engenders. Dominance of social ownership of the means of production subordinates the economy to the interest of the working people. Here the interests of those who own the means of production and those who work are no longer diametrically opposed. They are one and the same people: the direct producers are also the owners of the means of production.

Social property is the basis for shaping a fundamentally new interest, as compared with class societies, namely, the social material interest of people in the development of production. This interest is new above all because it unites all the members of society. If we examine material interest as the force which, to use Marx's expression, holds together the members of society, under socialism this force is produced by the very domination of social ownership of the means of production. The social interest here is really common for all social groups in society – the working class, peasantry, intelligentsia – and also for all members of society.

* Excerpted from G. Glezerman, *Socialist-Society: Scientific Principles of Development*, Moscow, Progress Publishers, 1971, pp. 84–104.

The source of this material interest is above all that the well-being of every member of society depends on the general level of development of social production. Under socialism, the expansion of social production, the rise in the productivity of social labor and the general growth of the national income also signify an improvement in the living standard of all the people. The welfare of all and, consequently, of every individual, depends on the development and improvement of production.

This is the basis for the development of new ideological, moral stimuli to work. Such stimuli are quite diverse and, just as in the case of material interest, can be divided into social and personal. For example, among the personal spiritual stimuli can be the interest of a man in his work where he can develop his abilities to the full; the interest in exploratory endeavor which is especially displayed in the mass movement for rationalization and inventions; the desire to win the respect of fellow workers, and so on. But social stimuli are undoubtedly the main ones among moral stimuli. The desire to contribute their labor to the building of the new society, patriotic motives, awareness of civic duty – such social stimuli to work are an expression of appreciated social interests, i.e., the interests of the entire socialist society. They are engendered by social ownership of the means of production.

Social material interest which underlies moral stimuli to work, links together both phases of communism. It naturally will remain at the higher phase of communism when labor turns into man's prime vital requirement. At the higher phase of communism, just as under socialism, every member will be interested in the social results of his labor, inasmuch as the general and, consequently, his own well-being depends on them. But, as distinct from socialism, at the higher phase of communism social interest will prompt man to work directly and not through the mechanism of remuneration for his personal labor.

The disappearance, under communism, of the personal material interest of each workingman in the results of his labor, therefore, does not signify the disappearance of material interests in general. People have never developed, and never will develop, production only for moral reasons – they will always be prompted by material interests. Thus, the social material interest constantly accompanies social property in the means of production and develops together with the latter.

The existence of two forms of property under socialism – state and co-operative – creates, as will be shown subsequently, the specific interests of the working class and the collective-farm peasantry. The collective farmer's personal property in subsidiary farming also gives rise to certain specific interests. Eventually, the disappearance of differences between the two forms of socialist property and the transition to one communist property will lead to the further development of social interests and to the absorption of all specific interests by them.

The interests of people are shaped not only by the distribution of the means of production among the members of society, but also by all the other aspects of production relations. The forms of exchange of labor activity and the produced goods also greatly influence people's interests. Exchange of labor activity is based on the forms of the division of labor, which in conditions of commodity production also determine the exchange of the products of labor. The division of labor between economic sectors gives rise to specific interests of these sectors (for example, of industry and agriculture and also of separate types of production within them), which may not coincide. The vocational division of labor, in its turn, produces interests of separate trades. In this connection Marx spoke of the endless fragmentation of interests created by the division of social labor among the workers and also among the capitalists and the land-owners; the latter, for example, are divided into owners of vineyards, arable land, forests, mines, and fisheries (see *Capital,* Volume III, Chapter LII). Private ownership of the means of production counterposes such interests and introduces competition, while social ownership, on the contrary, makes for co-operation and mutual assistance between people connected with different kinds of social production and sectors of labor.

Consolidating the entire economy of socialist society into a single whole, social property exists in the form of a system of state enterprises which possess certain economic independence and of co-operatives which are the property of separate collectives. That is why at the first phase of communism commodity exchange is a necessary form of the economic ties between them. Socialism excludes from commodity exchange the land, enterprises and also labor power, but does not eliminate commodity relations in general; the economic independence of enterprises makes the commodity form of ties between them an objective necessity.

The economic independence of separate production units engenders certain specific interests. This is obvious in the case of collective farms, which have a common form of property (co-operative), but each of which is operated independently because this property is not united on a nation-wide scale. Each collective farm, consequently, has also its own interests.

Specific interests also exist in enterprises which fall into the category of state property. As distinct from the collective farms, these enterprises belong to one owner, the state, which represents the entire people. They are economically united into a single whole. A socialist enterprise represents a part of the single national economic organism. Therefore, its interests cannot differ radically from those of the entire economy. But at the same time an enterprise is a relatively independent economic unit; the satisfaction of the collective needs of its personnel depends on the results of its operation and, consequently, it also has its own interests. The Regulations Governing the Socialist State Enterprise lay down that every enterprise carries on its activity 'in the interests of the entire national economy and the collective of its workers'.

The interests of people are also shaped by the methods of distribution. First of all they determine the group or personal interests of producers, the degree of their interest in the development of production. Capitalists employ numerous wage systems designed to make the worker interested in producing more, to weaken somewhat the paralysing influence exerted on his labor activity by the basic fact that he is separated from ownership of the means of production and is doomed to a proletarian existence, to exploitation. By applying different wage systems the capitalists, moreover, seek to divide the interests of various groups of workers, to weaken their class solidarity.

Under socialism, a prime source of labor activity is the transfer of the means of production into the hands of the entire people, the emancipation of labor from exploitation and its conversion into labor for one's own society, for oneself. The socialist principle of distribution according to work done makes the worker personally interested in developing social production, in raising the productivity of his labor and advancing his skill. An increase in output, and a rise in labor productivity meet the interests of all of society and at the same time the personal interests of the individual producer, inasmuch as this brings him a higher income. In socialist society every workingman is interested in results of his labor both as a member of socialist society and as an individual worker. He is interested in the most rapid development of social production because this increases the consumption fund as a whole, raises the welfare of the entire society and, consequently, his personal welfare; as an individual worker he is interested in raising the productivity of his labor, inasmuch as his share of the consumption fund depends on the quantity and the quality of his work. Thus, the socialist principle of distribution firmly links together the personal and social interests of the worker.

The personal material interest under socialism differs qualitatively from such interest in preceding societies. This follows from the nature of socialist relations of production and above all from socialist distribution according to work done. Remuneration according to work for all able-bodied members of society abolishes the injustices of capitalism where distribution is made not according to work done but according to capital and there is no equal pay for equal work: for example, women receive less than men, a colored worker is paid less than a white worker, and so on. The socialist method of distribution expresses the substance of the new, socialist relations under which there is no exploitation of man by man and labor is the duty of all able-bodied people. It makes the worker materially interested in conscientious labor for society to the full of his ability, in raising the productivity of labor and advancing his skill.

Under socialism, economic interests are engendered not only by direct production relations but also by forms of economic organization, of planning and so on, which are an expression of production relations. For example, various forms of uniting enterprises into firms which operate on a cost-accounting basis make the personnel of these firms interested in their activity. Similarly, the setting of some indicators for planning and evaluating the operation of enterprises may make them interested either in increasing total output (this happens when gross output is regarded as the main indicator) or also in raising the quality of goods, improving technology and more thrifty management. This enables society to stimulate the activity of enterprises in the required direction by elaborating the most effective indicators.

Community of the basic interests of people in socialist society by no means excludes the great diversity of their specific interests. Moreover, any man, inasmuch as he is connected by diverse social ties with other people, collectives and society as a whole, has many interests. A collective farmer, for example, has personal interests linked with his subsidiary farming; he has interests as a member of the given collective farm and at the same time of the entire class of the collective-farm peasantry; he has interests as an inhabitant of a given republic, region, district and village and as a citizen of the Union of Soviet Socialist Republics, and so on. These interests are interlocked and do not always coincide. This may open up the possibility for contradictions, which society must consider and solve if it is to advance.

Specific interests of various communities and associations of people can play both a stimulating or a retarding role in society's development. This depends on how these interests are combined and utilized. For example, specific interests of enterprises in general play a stimulating role in the socialist economy. They promote the better use of the resources of enterprises and raise the efficiency of their operation, which meets the interests of the entire society.

But these interests might also play an adverse part if they run counter to the interests of the entire national economy. At times an enterprise (for example, a clothing, furniture, or similar factory) might be interested in producing expensive goods which are not in great demand and, on the contrary, neglect the production of goods the consumer needs only because they are cheap and therefore 'disadvantageous' for the fulfillment of the gross output plan.

Consequently, the interests of an enterprise must be combined with the interests of the entire economy which, just as the general interests of the people, are supreme as regards a separate enterprise. Such a combination is achieved by elaborating optimal planning targets and a system of bonuses to enterprises and their workers, by improving the wages system, and so on.

Personal interest, too, can play a similar dual role. Generally speaking, it can be a powerful driving force of production. Under socialism, personal material interest strengthens the ties of the worker with his enterprise. Given the proper organization of payment for work and appropriate educational activity, personal interests, far from running counter to social [interests], are placed at the service of the latter. Payment according to the actual labor contribution of each worker to the common cause accustoms to social discipline persons of inadequate civic consciousness, and fosters in them the habit to work for society; in the case of highly conscious workers it acquires the significance not only of a material incentive, but also of a certain moral appraisal of their labor effort. High wages, for example, make the worker feel that society really appreciates his labor.

But if production and payment for work are improperly organized, the personal material interest may lead to the counterposing of the interest of an individual worker to society's interests, promote money-grubbing tendencies and thus act as a negative factor.

The possibility of rationally combining interests is determined by the objective conditions of socialist society's development, by its economic and political system. But this possibility is translated into reality only by removing contradictions engendered by life.

At one time the opinion was current that socialism allegedly precludes contradictions between personal, collective and social interests. Such an opinion is wrong because it gives rise to the illusion that a rational combination of interests is established automatically and there is no need to achieve it by conscious effort.

In reality, the socialist system, removing the ground for irreconcilable conflicts between the interests of people, does not eliminate the possibility of contradiction between them – contradictions between basic and non-basic, general and specific interests. These contradictions are resolved by the proper policy of the Party, by its organizational and educational work.

Driving forces of socialist production

A study of the diverse interests produced by economic relations enables us to reveal the mechanism through which relations of production affect the development of the productive forces. It demonstrates the economic relations in action and shows how and in what direction they impel people to act. That is why, as Engels put it, 'the economic relations of a given society present themselves in the first place as interests'.[1]

Proper understanding of the role of interests makes it possible to solve an important theoretical problem: what are the driving forces of the development of production? At the same time, it is the point of departure for settling a major practical question, that is, how to utilize in socialist conditions these driving forces for the most rapid expansion and improvement of production.

. . . One of the important economic advantages of socialism is that it creates new stimuli for the development of production. The emancipation of labor from exploitation, its conversion into labor for oneself, for the entire society, creates, as pointed out earlier, the social interest of the working people in the results of their labor; the collective and personal interests of workers in raising the productivity and efficiency of their labor are thus combined. This is the basis for the rise and extensive spread of socialist emulation.

The socialist economic system converts the worker from being an appendage of the machine to being its master. Technology is developed with an eye to easing labor and extending the opportunities for displaying the creative abilities of the worker.

Lastly, socialism opens up favorable opportunities for the application of science in production. It has no such obstacles to the introduction of technology as unemployment and cheap labor power which frequently makes comprehensive mechanization and automation of production unprofitable for the capitalist. The close co-operation of workers by hand and by brain accelerates scientific and technological progress.

The advantages of the socialist economic system create objective prerequisites for the accelerated development of production. But the growth rates of production also depend on the utilization of these advantages, the efficiency of economic guidance. In contrast to the spontaneously developing capitalist economy, the socialist economy cannot function without purposeful guidance on the scale of the entire society. One of the important aspects of this guidance is the ability to consider properly and combine reasonably the diverse interests of people, because on this depends the full use of the possibilities for developing production created by the socialist economy and, consequently, in the long run the scope of the stimulating role played by socialist relations of production.

A correct economic policy must rationally combine the diverse interests both on a nationwide scale (and even of the entire community of socialist

1 K. Marx, F. Engels, *Selected Works*, Vol. I, p. 622.

countries), and also on the scale of production units. Society faces the task of properly combining diverse interests when determining the main economic proportions. Let us take, for example, the allocation of the national income to the accumulation fund and the consumption fund. The growth rates of the productive forces largely depend on the volume of the accumulation fund and the way it is used. Economic progress is possible only if society expends its labor, not only for satisfying current requirements but also for further expanding and improving production. This gives rise to the need for properly combining the people's long-term, basic interests with current interests. The former are embodied in the policy of priority production of the means of production; the very possibility of extended socialist reproduction ultimately depends on the implementation of this policy. One must not neglect the long-term interests; priority growth in the production of the means of production is needed for ensuring a stable advance of the socialist economy. But at the same time, the Communist Party of the Soviet Union is against ignoring the current interests, for this may lead to neglecting the daily needs of the people.

. . . It goes without saying that the measure of combination and consequently the degree of subordination of current to long-term interests, of personal to social interests, cannot be the same at different stages in the development of socialist society. In the first years of socialist construction the need for satisfying the basic social interests dictated restricting for a time the satisfaction of the growing personal needs of the people. To build up heavy industry rapidly the Soviet people had to make certain sacrifices, to restrict personal consumption temporarily. But the policy of the Party has always been aimed at ultimately satisfying more fully the requirements of the people.

. . . Combination of the personal, collective and social interests directly affects the growth of production. For production to develop swiftly and uninterruptedly the interests of a separate enterprise must be dovetailed with the interests of the national economy, and, within an enterprise, the interests of the individual worker with those of the enterprise and the state.

Life shows that the unwise setting of plan targets counterposes the interests of an enterprise to the interests of society, and personal interests to the general interests. Indicators for assessing the operation of an enterprise, divorced from the interests of the economy as a whole, inflict great harm on the state and frequently lead to economic paradoxes.

. . . Contradictions between the interests of an enterprise and the interests of the country most frequently arose where gross output was the only indicator for assessing operation. Fulfilment of the plan for gross output often concealed disregard for the assortment and quality of the goods. Evaluation of an enterprise's operation according to gross output also ran counter to the requirements of technological progress. In some branches of the engineering industry output was calculated in tons, with the result that enterprises sought to produce heavy machine tools, and this increased the expenditure of raw materials and hampered the development of technically more improved machines.

The elimination of such contradictions necessitated the elaboration of economic criteria for evaluating the operation of enterprises in which the interests of an enterprise would coincide with the interests of the entire economy. In this connection the question arose of the role of the profit factor in assessing the economic efficiency of an enterprise. Profitability as one of the prime economic indicators is of tremendous significance for the socialist economy. The use of this indicator necessitated granting enterprises more initiative and independence in operating on the basis of the state plan.

The relation between the economy and separate enterprises is the relation between a whole organism and its parts. The interests of society are embodied in the general state plan which determines the bounds of an enterprise's activity. But within these bounds an enterprise must have definite independence. Under the old system of planning and management, when the independence of an enterprise was exceedingly restricted, concern for the interests of the whole frequently infringed the interests of its parts, and this ultimately harmed both. But the independence of an enterprise must not be unlimited. A definite measure is needed here. To grant unrestricted independence to an enterprise, generally abandoning state assignments to factories, would mean giving free rein to spontaneous development with all its adverse consequences and creating the possibility of counterposing, from another angle, the interests of an enterprise to the interests of the entire society. Such a fallacy is inherent in the concept of the 'self-regulating economy', which in effect leads to renouncing the advantages of a planned economy.

Proper combination of the planning principle and local initiative can be attained only by introducing the most efficient indicators for assessing the operation of an enterprise, which make it possible closely to link the interests of society and of a separate enterprise. A flexible mechanism for managing production can be created in this way.

Development of the socialist economy is not determined by the spontaneous 'play of interests' which comprises the mechanism of the capitalist economy. Socialist planning excludes anarchy and spontaneity, but it does not at all rule out the use of the interests of people, which helps to achieve more rapidly the necessary economic results than bureaucratic super-centralization. Not to regiment each step of people – this in general is impossible – but to place them in conditions in which their work prompted by their immediate interests would not act contrary to their basic interests, to the interests of the entire society – here is the crux of the matter . . .

ANDREJ LANTAY

Problems of the identity of interests in socialist society*

The identity of interests in a socialist society appears to be, at the present moment, one of the most important problems. This problem, as yet, has not been explained in detail, although our society today is faced with the very urgent task of solving the contradictions between social interests in general and those of groups and individuals.

The period of the personality cult left very serious marks on this sector; during that period man stopped being the measure for the aims of the socialist society and his justified human interests were often sacrificed for other aims based on a-prioristic dogmatic ideas. The elimination of the results of this approach to the interests of man is a particularly pressing problem with us today, as difficulties in our economy often emphasize the contradictions between the interests of society and the interest of its individual members.

In this article we want to contribute to an explanation of these matters. We shall deal with the dogmatically falsified picture of an identity of interests in socialist society, with the consequences of this picture and with the problem of their elimination.

Basic identity and contradiction of interests in socialist society

For the Marxist political economy it was obvious from the beginning that economic development takes place on the basis of certain internally determined relations in society. The main propelling force, the regulation of human activity, is material interests which in the consciousness of people reflect the material conditions of their lives. The interests of people and their activities as motivated by them – even though they are subjectively independent – are objectively determined mainly by existing production relationships which are fixed by the economic structure of society.

In socio-economic bodies based on exploitation, the activity of people is motivated by contradictory interests reflecting antagonistic class contradictions. As a consequence, the laws of economic development are realized in a struggle of contradictory interests as elementary forces, not regulated

* Excerpted from 'Problémy jednoty záumov v socialistickej spoločnosti', *Ekonomický časopis*, XI, No. 6, 1963, pp. 573–89.

by society. Under these conditions society is incapable of consciously operating the economy.

The socialist order abolishes class contradictions and puts all working people in an equal position in relation to the means of production. Objective conditions are created so that all working people are, in principle, united by one identical and basic interest. Instead of antagonistic class contradictions there are the unified interests of the society as a whole which enable a conscious direction of productive social activity according to a plan. The possibility is created of stopping the conflicts of contradictory interests and/or orientating the activities of all members of society towards a common aim.

Under socialism the interest of society as a whole represents a generalization of the basic, permanent, common interests of its members which is created by the introduction of socialist production relationships. In theory, we can define with comparative ease the content of the interests of society as a whole – it ultimately is the basic, common interest of all working people in building socialism which will satisfy their needs at a growing pace, and communism which will be able to satisfy their needs completely. But in reality the interest of society as a whole does not exist except but as as the common interest of its members, that is to say, only inasmuch as people combine it with their own interests. The interest of society as a whole (and similarly, group interests) exists only in the identification with the direct personal interests of members of the society.[1] This is a unity of contradictions: between direct personal interests and between the interests of society there exists a contradiction which stems from the different character of these interests.

The main feature of this contradiction – which is a nonantagonistic contradiction, a contradiction within people – is the interest of society. The basis of successfully building a socialist and communist society is the satisfaction of the interests and needs of society as a whole; without this it is impossible to satisfy harmoniously either personal or group interests and needs. But the direct personal interest remains even under socialism the main motive of human economic activity and this will continue as long as the development of the forces of production does not make it possible to satisfy people in a communist society in accordance with their needs.

It follows from this that even under socialism it is necessary objectively

---

1 This naturally concerns mainly material interests, because the satisfaction of material needs is the basis of people's existence. But it does not concern only material interests. A great role in the life of a human being is played by creative work, self-assertion, family, children, health, culture, sports, recreation, rest, entertainment and other non-material values which are the objects of the many-sided human interests. These are connected with motives of a moral nature. Ultimately, all human interests converge in an image of a happy life and this image itself varies greatly.

to respect personal interests, to make allowances for them, to succeed in combining them with the interests of society. The theoretically defined interest of society as a whole is not in itself a propelling motive for the masses to attain the aims of society, not even when propagandistic efforts try to make these aims clear to the people.

It becomes a motive only when society consciously solves the contradictions between social and personal interests. Such a solution can be arrived at mainly by the application of the principle of material incentives, i.e. the creation of such conditions that in satisfying their direct personal interests, people will simultaneously perform activities in the interest of society as a whole. A combination of social and personal interests is mainly served by a distribution of remuneration according to results achieved, whereby the principle of material incentives is realized. But it is impossible to stop only at this form of a solution of the contradictions between society and its members; this is one of the basic contradictions in socialist social relationships and society has to solve it while managing the whole process of its development.

One of the basic tasks of planned management is the necessity permanently to solve the contradictions in society in such a way that the interests of individuals (or groups) are directed towards achieving the aims of society.[2] This necessity will become apparent in spite of all administrative, political and legal measures that may stand in the way. If the contradiction of interests is not solved, education and propaganda are not efficacious, because people become convinced by their own daily experience that to satisfy the interests of society is in contradiction with their own direct interests. This ultimately leads to people satisfying their direct personal interests, regardless of the interests of society as a whole, or even against these interests. Contradictions of interest are thus further sharpened and the conflicts are increased instead of all activities of working people being directed towards the common aims of society.

During the period of the personality cult these unquestionable conclusions of the political economy of socialism were seriously and dogmatically misinterpreted and in practice these misinterpretations have not yet been eliminated. 'Dogmatism in the political economy of socialism and in socialist economic practice showed itself mainly by presenting as absolute the unity and harmony within the socialist economy as an expression of a conscious application of the laws of economics. Contradictions were admitted only as a sign of insufficient knowledge of these laws or as a sign of contradiction between objective reality and the people's consciousness

2 Compare Rudolf Kocanda, 'K obsahu zákona plánovitého rozvoje národního hospodářství' (On the Content of the Law of Planned Development of the National Economy), *Planovane hospodářstvi*, No. 12, 1961, p. 140.

under socialism'[3] Not only in theory but also in economic and political practice this meant that a completely harmonious development of socialist society, a development without internal contradictions, had been created. There existed only one interest, the interest of society as it had been formulated by the governing bodies, and all other interests were only an expression of bourgeois prejudices in people's minds. This dogmatic approach was an impediment to the real solution of the contradictions within socialist society; the principle of material incentives was only incorporated into economic management as a foreign body. The main emphasis was laid on the process of bringing the problems to light, on socialist emulation, on the Stakhanovite movement etc., that is to say on a solution of the contradictions between production relationships and the people's consciousness.

This necessarily led to an aggravation of the contradictions, instead of their solution. Against personal interests (and also group interests) which manifested themselves with objective compulsiveness, a strong barrier of administrative, political, penal and other measures had to be erected. In combination with the perversion of socialist democratism during the era of the personality cult, these facts weakened the unity within society and had many negative consequences which we can still feel.

Consequences of the dogmatic approach to the problem of identity of interests

Making absolute the identity of interests in socialist society in theory and in practice inexorably created a whole system of mistrust. That is to say, if only a unitarian, social interest is recognized in socialist production relationships the attempts at realizing any other interests, either personal or group interest, must necessarily be directed against social interests. This aspect, inevitably, led to the assumption that the interests of society had to be protected against personal interests which were foreign and dangerous to society. Thus it was not considered as essential whether these personal interests were directed against social interests. Many mistakes in the management by higher executives, resulting from ignoring contradictory interests, were interpreted as the subjective mistakes of people working in enterprises and caused by personal interests. It was generally stated that enterprise managers and leading executives were interested only in bonuses, that they always tried to achieve a reduction in the plans and to inflate the results attained, thus working against the social interests and for

3 Ota Šik, 'Počitat s dialektikou vývoje při řizeni socialistického hospodářství' (Consideration of the Dialectics of Development in the Management of the Socialist Economy), *Nová mysl*, No. 10, 1957, p. 889.

their own personal good. There is no question that such phenomena did exist. The problem is that their roots were not examined, i.e. the basic causes which often consisted in faults in the planning methods, indicators, etc., which created economic obstacles and put personal interests against social ones.

Thus there existed a general mistrust of economic incentives, and the governing bodies relied more on directives from above than on material incentives. And if some economic incentives were accepted, such thorough measures were taken for the protection of social interests against personal interests that these incentives lost their efficacy.[4] There was also mistrust in the independence of lower management and enterprises ultimately merely obeyed and executed directives received from above, since they were not permitted to decide independently.

The dogmatic, nondialectic approach to the problem of identity of interests – in spite of slogans and statements to the contrary – inevitably created an atmosphere of indifference to people and their justified personal and group interests. Behind the veil of the dogmatic interpretations of social interests the human being with his needs and wishes became lost. Not even basic directives for the development of the economy escaped this atmosphere. The quick development of heavy industry became an idol to which the development of the production of consumer goods was sacrificed. Key requirements of the national economy whose satisfaction was considered the main interest of society as a whole often absorbed so many resources that the satisfaction of other needs, especially the needs of the population – which is the aim of the development of the socialist economy – had to be relegated to the background.

It can scarcely be held that we have already completely overcome the heritage of the personality cult as far as distrust and indifference to people and their justified interests is concerned. Generally, we still take it for granted that in the realization of the interests of society as a whole or what we consider as such, personal interests have to go overboard and we do not seek ways to solve contradictions of interests. A social interest is a saving of socially necessary labor. This labor is saved, for example by a food shop foregoing one salesman, i.e. saving eight hours per day. But it is rarely taken into account that a queue of buyers will be created, that consumers will have to wait longer and that together they will lose tens and hundreds of hours per day. But this is not considered contrary to the interests of

---

4 A typical example was the imposition of a great number of indicators and conditions for bonuses of leading management workers in enterprises and for enterprise incentives. Naturally, this complicated the whole system of incentives, making it ineffective and completely tying the hands of executives. It should be emphasized that such attitudes still survive.

society, because it does not happen during working hours. One forgets here that socialist society wants to reduce working hours or working time gradually, to give people more leisure and thus enable them to lead a richer life, to devote more time to education, culture and sport.

Our planning, management, production and distribution enterprises, often show indifference to the needs of the people. They are satisfied, for example, with the aggregate balance between distribution funds and production funds but they do not make sure that the demand for specific products is satisfied. These are sometimes small things, attention to which would not create any difficulties within the national economy; it would require only a more attentive approach to the needs of the people. But even these little things can cause dissatisfaction among citizens and drive a wedge between personal and social interests.

Many more examples of indifference to the interests of the people could be given even today in the sphere of services, distribution, production, and also in central offices, national committees, etc. This, naturally, cannot be considered a general phenomenon, and the situation in this respect shows some improvement as the relics of the era of the personality cult are being overcome. But it is a phenomenon which in itself is foreign to socialism and has greatly damaging effects. For the very reason that socialist production relationships exclude the inevitability of a struggle between antagonistic interests, that they create a real possibility of a conscious solution for conflicting interests, it is necessary, basically, to alter this wrong practice which relegates the human being with his interests into the background and does not respect real life with its contradictions.

The attitude of indifference to personal interests in the era of the personality cult sometimes changed to actively hurting personal interests and infringing citizens' own rights. This had its theoretical roots in the dogmatic concept of an absolute identity of interests.

If interests in a socialist society are identical, harmonious and without contradictions, then society cannot hurt personal interests. Only the opposite can happen, namely that social interests are hurt by personal interests which arise as a consequence of bourgeois ideas in people's minds. This approach gave a free hand to damaging the interests of the working people; usually, this infringement takes the form of fighting for interests which were promulgated as social ones, at the cost of personal interests. In this respect, a kind of 'selfishness in reverse' was created, a ruthless realization of local, entrepreneurial, state and other interests as against those of the people.

Sufficient cases of this kind are known from practice. One typical example was the forced rise in the indicator of productivity of labor by an exaggerated intensification of labor. Rationalization measures and technical development were neglected but a rise in the productivity of labor was planned. To a certain extent, productivity of labor could be raised with the help of organizational measures or by mobilizing other reserves, but after these had been exhausted there was only one way left open: to increase the norms. But precisely in branches with a progressive organization of production, for example in the textile and shoe industries, it was necessary to use the whip of an exaggerated rise in the intensity of labor. Only a few years ago the conclusion was reached that this road was harmful and no longer practicable, and measures for a more rapid technical development were applied.

The period of the personality cult has left serious marks which are discernible even today and are attested to by cases of infringement of consumers' interests which occurred quite recently. The rounding off of prices of consumers' articles – which had its good reasons and with which working people agreed – was abused by some enterprises, especially in the services sector, by raising prices. Not only that the consumers are dissatisfied; the greatest mistake is that in these cases dissatisfaction is not directed against the real culprits but against the whole regime. But this, naturally, follows from an infringement of justified personal interests.

We could also mention an unnecessary infringement of the interests of working people by the general interdiction of a market for surplus agricultural produce, just at a time when there were difficulties in supplying the market with certain agricultural produce. The unfavorable consequences of this interdiction of satisfying the needs of working people on this market greatly outweighed its positive effect from the point of view of social interest. In the meantime, an attempt has been made to solve this problem in favor of the consumers.

From the indifference to personal interests and their infringement there was only a small step to the infringement of basic citizens' rights which was motivated 'by public interest'. If we criticize illegalities in the period of the personality cult, usually we have in mind excesses in penal law, the persecution of brave citizens and the meting out of heavy punishment to innocent people. After the XII Party Congress [1962] steps were taken to genuinely overcome the consequences of these illegal infringements. But we did not recognize sufficiently that these infringements of the law also had very serious consequences in other branches of law and led to outright arbitrariness in the decisions of various sections of the executive, especially the local and district ones. These executive bodies infringed citizens rights often in the false belief that this was necessary from the point of view of social interests. This was a juridical reflection of the distorted relationship between personal and social interests.

. . . There certainly can be no objection to the thesis that the main task of trade unions in a socialist society is the development of socialist emulation, the struggle for the growth of the productivity of labor and increased production, and the saving of socially necessary labor. But: 'Even under socialism, it remains the task of trade-union organizations to look after the material interests, social and cultural needs of the workers, to watch over the inviolability of workers' rights, to keep a strict eye on labor legislation, accident prevention, and protection of the health of the workers.'[5]

... However, it is not only the protection against direct law infringements which is important, but also protection of other interests of workers, even against their own State, their own enterprise. If a conflict of interests does exist within socialist society, then it is not only necessary to protect the social interests against infringements by individuals and groups of people but also individual and group interests must be safeguarded against infringements by the executive power. This is an important solution for these contradictions and will prevent nonantagonistic contradictions from intensifying, as a consequence of wrong directives, to an extent where in a certain situation they would change into antagonistic ones whose solution would then lie outside the executive power.

The above-mentioned distortions in the approach to an identity of interests in socialist society can lead directly to a split between abstractly conceived social interests and the interests of the people. In another work[6] we demonstrated the possibility of a split between the interests of an enterprise and those of its employees ... The interests of an enterprise in isolation and without connection with the personal interests of the working collective are only a legal fiction. They can acquire a real meaning only if their satisfaction affects, in one way or another, the interests of the members of the collective. The interests of an enterprise can, in practice, develop independently, according to their fictitious image, without connection with the personal interests of the enterprise staff and, as a consequence, they no longer affect the workers of that enterprise economically. This can have very serious consequences; the interests of the enterprise, if conceived as being independent, can set the management of a socialist enterprise against its working collective. It can even create a dangerous conflict between the personal interests of the collective and social interests. The social interests which to the workers are the interests of the enterprise, can then appear as foreign, external interests, which stand in contradiction to the interests of the working collective of the enterprise.

5 Ladislav Zajac, 'Leninské metódy vedenia más' (Leninistic methods of leading the masses), *Pravda*, May 15, 1963.
6 Andrej Lantay, 'Vzt'ah individuálnych, kolektívnych a spoločenských záujmov v sústave ekonomiských podnetov' (The relations of individual, collective and social interests under a system of material incentives), *Ekonomický časopis*, No. 5, 1962, p. 451.

An analogous situation can arise also in regard to social interest. It is not the interest of a fictitious person, separated from the people. As already mentioned, social interest is the basic, common, permanent interest of the members of society. It is impossible to identify it, as a matter of course, with the interest of the executive power of society or its representatives: the socialist State, or some of its executive organizations, etc., as society always functions through these institutions or organizations. Engels drew attention to the fact that the State at best (thus also under socialism) is an expedient, because the function of the State must be performed by executive personnel, by an apparatus of personnel, so that there is a contradiction between the leaders and the masses. This is also one of the important aspects of the contradiction within socialist society. The dogmatic conception of an absolute identity of interests, naturally, led to an identification of the interests of the State and its executives with the interests of society, and to the idea that the socialist State as an instrument of society cannot infringe personal interests. This approach inevitably enhanced the contradictions between the leaders and the masses and executives of society often found themselves isolated from the people as though they were an external foreign power, and not a State of workers and peasants. The blame for this separation can be put on bureaucracy whereby the narrowest interests of a branch, a national committee or an enterprise were always represented as social interests which had to be satisfied even against the justified interests of the working people.

The danger in separating the managing bodies from the masses became most conspicuous in the economy, in its management. 'Managing activity ... simultaneously means a certain influence by the manager on the working human being. Through this activity a certain will and certain interests always assert themselves and there is a certain relationship between these and the interests and will of the people'.[7]

When managers try to satisfy certain economic or entrepreneurial interests without combining them with the personal interests of the working people and these then do not combine those interests with their own interests, the activity of the managers becomes separated from the masses and the working people's participation in management is minimal or only formal. This applies particularly in cases when economic–political institutions, such as indicators that are wrongly chosen, inadequate methods of planning, and material incentives with negative effect, lead to a conflict between social and personal interests and in order to fulfill certain tasks the managers have to resort to administrative measures as against personal influence. But personal interests will break the barriers of these measures

7 Ota Šik, *Ekonomika, zajmy, politika* (Economy, Interests, Politics), Prague, 1962, p. 134.

with objective force, create negative results in the economy and thus aggravate the conflicts between social and personal interests and between managers and workers.

It is altogether natural that people cannot pinpoint accurately the sub-jective faults of the managers, the symptoms of bureaucracy that lead to an indifference to personal interests and to an infringement of the latter. People attribute these symptoms not to subjective faults but to society, the State, and the regime. In this way a poisoned atmosphere is created, an atmosphere of distrust and indifference. This phenomenon has greatly slowed down the growth of socialist consciousness . . .

. . . These negative phenomena could not be overcome by the great success achieved in the sphere of material production or by the quick rise in the standard of living. Working people knew that they were better off than under capitalism, that they received much from socialism, but many of them did not know how to combine this with the new relations within society or with the aims of society. The concept of the absolute identity of interests which they could only with difficulty connect with their own interests, did not convey to them that by attaining social aims the possibi-lity was created for greater satisfaction of their own needs. For many people socialism was advantageous for the purpose of getting as much as possible out of it for themselves; the whole atmosphere of the personality cult helped to create a disregard for the interests of society and the interests of their fellow citizens. We can mention a whole set of examples: neglig-ence in production, irresponsibility, lowering of the quality of products, waste of working time, disinterestedness in the cooperative production in agriculture, theft of national property, slipshod work, excessive rising of prices, etc. . . . Years of an atmosphere of distrust and growing contradic-tions can weaken even the greatest revolutionary enthusiasm, and bad experiences with preachings of the identity of interests will undermine even the most solid convictions. It would be unrealistic not to see that even today relations of comradely cooperation characteristic for socialist pro-duction relationships, have not yet become a matter of course in the national economy and attention to social interests is not always taken for granted. It would be extremely nocuous to deny the existence of negative aspects in people's attitude to work, socialist property, the interests of society and fellow citizens, or to consider certain phenomena only as the results of the surviving bourgeois ideas in the minds of the people. Such an approach would make it impossible truthfully to reveal the roots of these phenomena and to correct matters.

These problems, however, cannot be solved automatically but require well-thought-out measures.

The problems of the creation of unity within society

After the XIIth Congress of the Communist Party of Czechoslovakia, our society began to overcome on a broad front the consequences of the period of the personality cult. This is a very complicated task; it concerns all spheres of social life and entails the overcoming of ideas and customs which had been solidifying for years. Even though the measures taken in the spheres of politics, law, ideology, morals and administration are immensely important, we believe that these measures can be made effective only by creating a system of management of the economy and of the whole society that will guarantee the solution of the constantly self-reproducing contradictions between personal, group and social interests.

In this connection and in connection with the ideological tasks the XIIth Congress of the Communist Party of Czechoslovakia put in the forefront of attention:
- the teaching of a communist attitude to work;
- a resolute fight for a priority realization of the interests of society as a whole;
- the development of the most selfless comradely relationships between people.

These tasks aptly define the needs of our society at present. We believe, however, that our propaganda very often commits a serious mistake in wanting to carry out these tasks regardless of the direct material interests of the people or even directly against these interests. We could quote many examples from our daily press. In principle, this means the negation of the preferential realization of the interests of society as a whole, and implies that personal (and group) interests should be relegated in favor of the interests of society as a whole. From the above said it follows that this is an obvious consequence of the absolute theory of the identity of interests, according to the dogmatic ideas which do not solve the conflict of interests but negate it.

We mentioned that the social interest is the main aspect of the contradictions between the interests of society and personal and group interests. This social interest is not attained by a negation of the other side of this contradiction but by its conscious solution, i.e. by the managers creating preconditions for the regulation of personal interests by way of fulfillment of social tasks. In fulfilling this, personal interests (and also those of groups, such as entrepreneurial, local or branch interests, etc.) must inevitably be satisfied not against social interests but to their advantage, while justified personal and group interests must not be infringed by the executive power. In order to satisfy effectively the social interests it is necessary to create conditions that will allow personal and group interests to assert themselves as well, provided they are in harmony with the social interests. For example, if a worker wants to earn more by improving the quantity and quality of his work, he is fully justified in demanding that he be enabled to do so and that his justified earnings should not be threatened by a muddle in production or by subjective interventions.

Thus, the principle of preferential satisfaction of the social interest does not mean that the social interest must assert itself against justified personal or group interests; egoistic interests of society must give way. There is no reason to fight (by administrative measures, etc.) against the assertion of personal or group interests which do not directly help social interests but which also do not infringe them. The basic form of satisfying the interests of the whole society, in accordance with socialist production relationships, is a combination of interests – the exploitation of the principle of material incentives.

There are, of course, cases where personal interests cannot be harmonized with social ones. For example, it is necessary to transfer people from one enterprise to another, which creates disadvantages for them. Naturally, personal interests have to give way to social interests. But if social interests are given consideration administratively, by pressure, then the suppressed personal interest will nevertheless assert itself – in the above mentioned case by fluctuation, by abandoning work at the new place, etc. In such cases executives should try to eliminate at least the gross contradictions of interests, to compensate the workers affected, and, in particular, use moral incentives: persuasion of the inevitability of the proposed solution, of its correctness and equity, and the consensus of public opinion. In spite of all these guarantees, the satisfaction of the social interest at the expense of personal interests should be an exceptional case after exhausting all possibilities of another solution, or it will infringe the consciousness of the unity of basic interests . . .

O. ŠIK

Enterprise interests without erroneous ideological prejudices*

. . . What, really, is the core of the contradiction between [Oldřich] Truhlář's theoretical notion and objective socialist reality? The answer is that Truhlář and people like him created in their heads a scheme according to

---

* Excerpted from 'O podnikových zajmech bez chybných ideologických předsudků', *Politická ekonomie*, pp. 433–45, No. 4, 1964. [The article is directed against the positions taken by Oldřich Truhlář (in *Rudé právo* of Nov. 22, 1963) in response to Professor Šik's previous studies. (Ed.)]

which either commodity production can exist for the market with its market mechanism, whereby decisions on production are made in accordance with the selfish material interest of the commodity producer to attain the highest possible income from the sale of the commodities, production which is incompatible with the planned assertion of society's interests, or there may exist planned controlled development of the entire production according to the interests of the entire society, whereby production cannot take into account the development of the market and some development of incomes depending on the sale of commodities, in other words, which excludes the existence of commodity production and thus also 'enterprise interest'. This is again the metaphysical scheme of 'either-or' with no room for anything between the two extremes. Whatever appears in practice and does not correspond to this theoretical scheme is wrong, is somehow artificially and anti-socialistically created and must be eliminated. In reality, however, this imaginary absolute contradiction between capitalist and socialist economy does not exist. On the contrary, though objectively the necessity of such planned management of the entire socialist production asserts itself where the basic production and distribution processes are determined in advance by social management agencies in accordance with the envisaged objectively necessary development of social needs, here we can see the conscious assertion of social interests and a substantial difference as compared with capitalism where this does not exist. However, within these basic, long-range social decisions there must exist current concrete decision-making of certain socialist economic production units (enterprises) where certain specific interests of the entire staffs of the given units inevitably assert themselves, and they willy-nilly are an indirect reflection of certain interrelationships between these units (enterprises), though within certain socially planned and stipulated boundaries.

The point is that a metaphysician is unable to comprehend the unity and contradiction between the general and the specific, that for him the interests of socialist enterprises and of the entire society are either identical, and the contradictions between them are only an accidental expression of bad planned management, or there exist generally special interests of enterprises (or rather entrepreneurs) which assert themselves in their decision making; according to him, interests of the entire society then cannot exist and cannot assert themselves in a planned manner. In short, to the metaphysician the 'general' is something that is absolutely contained in every 'individual', permanently, constantly; it is absolute unity. If the interests of individual enterprise staffs are in accord with the interests of society, then according to him there cannot at the same time be contradictions between them . . .

. . . Under socialism there are conditions for the interests of the entire society to assert themselves as the decisive ones and for overcoming that character of contradictions and the way of their solution typical of capitalism. However, the dogmatic interpretation of this fact means mainly to absolutize it in the sense that there are no specific interests of individual economic production units, as if the interests of all the enterprise staffs were simply identical, i.e. absolutely social, and as if there existed only the direct relationship between interests of the entire society and individual interests, i.e. interests of individual workers . . .

. . . It is an objective necessity that the decisive interest of all people under socialism is still material interest, i.e. interest in ensuring the highest possible and constantly increasing material consumption on the basis of which and together with which the satisfaction of cultural needs can also grow rapidly. Material consumption will be the main interest of most people as long as there is not an abundance of consumer goods, i.e. as long as personal material needs grow in general more rapidly than they can be satisfied. Communism cannot be built under conditions of general shortages but only on the basis of abundance and overabundance of consumer goods. Since under the given technical and working conditions and with the given division of labor, which characterize an entire long stage of socialist development, work cannot be the first and chief necessity of life for most people (but remains an indispensable condition of the creation of all use values), consumption must also be linked to people's work for society. In other words, consumer goods must be distributed to people in dependence on their work contribution to society. On the basis of this the material interest of people under socialism is their main incentive to work. It thus follows merely from objective conditions that people will generally and chiefly carry out work in such an amount and insofar as it is linked to a certain material remuneration or the consumption mediated by it.

This is explained one way or another in every textbook of political economy, but some authors refuse to realize that in this we must seek also the basis of socialist commodity production. If 'labor' were a completely simple and unambiguous activity which will always and under any circumstances be automatically social labor, it would really suffice to remunerate every individual directly for carrying out a certain amount of work, and the matter would be settled. This would be direct material stimulation of social labor by according corresponding material remuneration. In reality this is not so, and not every expenditure of labor and creation of a product is social labor. In fact, the category 'labor' is an immensely complicated category expressing a very complicated social process, developing with internal contradictions, and not every labor asserts itself as social labor.

. . . The point is . . . to ensure such material remuneration (real content and relations between remunerations) and to link it to the development of labor in such a way that it in general stimulates the working people to the objectively necessary expenditure of labor, i.e. to its general assertion as social labor. Dogmatists usually agree to this statement without perceiving any problem in it. They believe that it suffices if from above downward, from the center to all enterprises and plants, a certain wage fund is stipulated and distributed, certain wage and bonus guidelines are issued, certain wage categories and tariffs stipulated, etc., and thereby remuneration according to quantity, quality and social importance of labor is ensured, as is usually preached. But how can one ensure that this remunerating system really promotes such expenditure of labor that production of really needed, constantly improved and new use values is ensured, that the use values are produced proportionately, that they are produced as economically as possible? The dogmatist will resolutely reply that this cannot be ensured by remuneration, this must be ensured by the plan!

Here we are at the core of the problem; here in the foreground is the connection between the material interests of people and certain objectively necessary economic production units and the existing system of planned management of production. If it were possible, as the dogmatists imagine, to determine from a social center, directly, constantly in a new way and in harmony with the objective laws of development, which use values to produce as to their quality, in what quantities to produce each kind and assortment, with what amount of labor (past and live) and with what division of labor (i.e. with what labor of each individual) to produce each item, then it would be possible to link a certain corresponding material remuneration of each individual to social labor thus specified. Then it would be possible to speak of the direct social stimulation of the work of individuals and there would really exist only the direct relationship between social interests asserting themselves in central production and remuneration instructions and individual interests asserting themselves in individual decisions on this or that expenditure of labor.

But such a notion is only an empty and lifeless abstraction. In reality such direct stipulation of the labor of each individual from a social center cannot exist. The stipulation of work by central agencies must be mediated by a large number of other, increasingly specialized managing agencies which stipulate the expenditure of an increasingly narrow and special field of labor. It is thus a hierarchical arrangement of an entire network of managing agencies whose task it is to stipulate the expenditure of labor increasingly concretely and directly, from the center to the workplace. But the dogmatist imagines the relation from the center toward the workplace to be one-sided, with the purely mechanical specification and concretization of directives in the direction of increasingly detailed production conditions. He takes this process to be only a process of increasingly concrete cognizance and decision making about individual aspects of production in which the general, social interest in the socially necessary development of production asserts itself seemingly uniformly all the time. Of course, this again is a one-sided and erroneous abstraction.

What is involved in reality is not only the one-sided relationship from the center toward the workplace, a one-sided process of concretization and the one-sided transfer of social interests to individual interests, but also a permanent relation from individual workplaces toward the center, a process of gradual generalization of certain facts concerning production and their connections, and a process of the assertion of the abundant individual interests vis-à-vis social interests with which they will never be completely identical. At the same time certain specific group interests of individuals joined together in enterprise collectives constantly crystallize. In relation to individual interests they are more general interests whereas vis-à-vis the interests of the entire society they are specific interests. Such group interests could be revealed and analyzed at various levels of grouping (cooperation) of working people, but there is only one specific level at which they are of extraordinary importance and have a substantial effect on economic development. These are groupings of working people in formations that are marked by a certain economic peculiarity and which are generally designated as enterprises, sometimes also more generally as independent profit and loss accounting formations, etc.

It is a special degree of cooperation of the working people in the production of certain specified kinds of products, marked necessarily not only by a certain relatively very independent decision making of the managing agency of the enterprise concerning the development of the production in question, but also by the origin of a strong specific material interest in all the members of this cooperation asserting itself very markedly in the decision making on production in question.

Although the socialist managing agency of an enterprise always decides of necessity within and on the basis of certain wider and more general central directives specifying the development of basic production and distribution processes, it has, on the one hand, an active influence on the creation of these central managing directives and, on the other hand, it has a relatively independent choice between a broad range of versions of actual production programs and procedures, which are always possible within the framework of general and even more or less one-sided central directives. In my article in the *Hospodářské noviny* of 14 February 1964 I tried to show how the central stipulation of the development of production is, of necessity, the stipulation of the quantitative aspect of production which in a very general way also affects its qualitative content (the production of certain use values on the basis of a certain production technique and technology), but that it cannot determine this content very concretely and prevent the existence of the most varied solutions. Enterprise cooperation will always have a substantial influence on the development of the qualitative content of production through its managing agency which is directly linked to the technical aspect of production.

It must be realized that at the same time the fund of remuneration (intended for remunerating individuals) is created in reality at enterprise level and depends on the development of the entire enterprise's cooperation stimulating some concrete expenditure of labor or other. Between certain economic production units (levels of cooperation) there must objectively always take place the exchange of the results of differing concrete activites. In these conditions, when the labor of all the members of these cooperations is expended within certain social limitations on achieving maximum material consumption, the rules of these exchanges (the way of obtaining material means needed, but produced outside the given cooperation) will have a substantial influence on production decisions, i.e. on the concrete expenditure of labor within these cooperations. This is precisely where the specific material interests of members of these cooperations will manifest themselves, aiming at the creation of the largest possible fund of remuneration (indirectly of consumer goods from other enterprises) for the entire cooperation with the aid of joint specific expenditure of labor.

Such a cooperation, which appears not only as a specific production unit but at the same time also as a unit exchanging with other units and obtaining material means from other units in dependence on its own work, may be called an enterprise (even though the name here is not decisive, and we use it only as probably the most suitable designation for the characterized degree of cooperation). On this general level (of political economy) of explanation such a stipulation suffices, even though a more concrete economic explanation requires a more detailed specifying of the characteristic of various degrees of cooperation. However, this does not change anything in the objective existence of such a basic production, exchange and materially interested link in social production. All that may happen is that in certain cases, say, two levels of materially interested cooperations will exist (e.g. enterprise and association of enterprises). Within the narrower cooperation a narrower, more specific material interest will originate, as compared with the broader and more general material interest of the broader cooperation. However, this more general interest will again be a certain specific interest in relation to the interest of the entire society, in dependence on the special task of this cooperation in the social production and exchange process and in the obtaining of material means of all their members by specific economic activity.

And precisely the existence of the specific material interest of such an enterprise unit, which has considerable relative independence in deciding on its production or the concrete expenditure of its labor, must always find expression in such an expenditure of this labor that it achieves the greatest possible material remuneration. Yet expenditure of labor may be such that it corresponds exactly to the general central directives and regulations (is within their limits) and in spite of that does not correspond to the needs of the consumers or the objectively necessary development of social labor altogether. Of course, this may be so because the central planning directives themselves are wrong or one-sided and do not determine the development of production in the enterprise in accordance with the objectively necessary development of social labor. The adversaries of commodity relationships between state enterprises admit this. But they refuse to recognize that within the general central directives (no matter at which level) such concrete decision making by the enterprises as producers will always be promoted; that a certain one-sided, specific interest of these producers will assert itself unless it is constantly corrected by the opposite interest of the consumers.

This is not unsocialistic. It is simply objectively necessary under those conditions of labor and consumption about which we spoke above and on which there is general agreement among all theoreticians. However, as soon as the discussion concerns enterprise decisions on labor, these objective work stimuli are, for some theoreticians, wiped out as if by a magic wand. Truhlář believes that it suffices if the central agencies nominate the managers of enterprises, and that henceforth in these enterprises social interests will prevail constantly, directly over individual interests. Truhlář not only, in fact, equates the social interests with the central planning and managing directives, but he is unable to understand that 'social interests' are an enormous abstraction which disregards the actual existence of a mass of one-sided, specific, mutually contradictory interests whose unity asserts itself only by the constant overcoming of contradictions.

How should we assess a manager who nowadays endeavors, for instance, to achieve the highest possible gross output (from which also productivity of labor is calculated) in order to ensure for his enterprise the highest possible wages per employee; moreover, he does so in accordance with the central plan, wage regulations, etc.? Yet he does not, for instance, introduce new products, although it would be technically possible, only because it would prevent him from achieving the planned gross output. Production in such an enterprise, in fact, comes into conflict with the interests of society and the objectively necessary development of social production although it develops fully in accordance with central directives. The dogmatist reacts immediately by saying that this is an expression, on the one hand, of shortcomings in the central management, on the other hand, of the unsocialist morals of the manager in question who, they maintain, should act in accordance with the interest of society in the developmental and the qualitative aspect of production. But firstly, he is unable to say how to abolish the necessarily general character of central directives and also how to plan the development of the qualitative content of production of enterprises from the center without duplication of the managing activity of enterprises (which is practically impossible anyway). Secondly, he suddenly and against Marxist principles accords more importance to the moral factor than to the material incentive (because he wants enterprises to produce in accordance with social needs, e.g. even at the price of nonfulfillment of the planned increase of gross output and the development of wages linked to it); moreover, he is unable to understand that any moral tendency, any moral exhortations to introduce new products, etc., are necessarily general.

The point is precisely that the general interest in the introduction of new products or in other aspects of production also has in each enterprise, necessarily, its more concrete specific expression. In each enterprise the improving of products or introduction of new products into production always develops in a certain quantitative relation to the development of production costs, production proportions, growth of output, etc. These interrelationships are not only different in every enterprise and at every period even if they develop optimally, but they may, moreover, develop absolutely differently when internal contradictions of various levels between these mutually related aspects of production grow. It is precisely these specific traits in the internally complicated development of production within each enterprise that every dogmatist ignores, relying on the omnipotence of general moral exhortations. Without functioning commodity relationships and with the decisive weight of one-sided administrative plans from above, the enterprise manager cannot know at all whether a certain concrete decision gives rise to an internally contradictory development of production or not, whether it ensures optimum harmony of all production aspects or not. Moreover, it is quite understandable that while fulfilling planned indicators given from above, achieving the highest possible material remuneration per employee is for him the decisive criterion in determining the concrete development of a certain production aspect. His decision is not prevented by the fact that under the present system of planned management he achieves maximum remuneration in contradiction with the interests of the consumers (because he fulfills what superior agencies demand), and besides, in most cases he is not even aware of it. He cannot know at what rate he should, e.g. introduce new products even at the price of a somewhat slower growth in productivity of labor, etc., if the decisive criterion to him is not the development of demand but the fulfillment of output indicators imposed from above.

Enterprise interests mean the joining of individual interests of members of enterprise collectives into a certain common mainstream which has its specific features in each enterprise. They manifest themselves by the endeavor to attain the highest possible shares in social consumption by the specific determination of the development of individual aspects of production (and their effective interrelationship), i.e. also by specific expenditure of labor in its relationship to objectively necessary social labor. Existing economic relations and the economic position of enterprises in them manifest themselves precisely in the specific development of enterprise interests, and economic relationships between enterprises can assert themselves only through these enterprise interests.

If by the administrative system of management we prevent the consistent assertion of socialist commodity relationships between enterprises, we thereby in reality prevent the consistent assertion of socialist economic relationships altogether. Even under such a system enterprise interests do not disappear but they are deformed, they develop absolutely one-sidedly and at variance with social interests. They cause a one-sided development of production and a growing contradiction between production and consumption, in consequence of which the interdependent growth rates of production and consumption slow down increasingly.

When socialist commodity relationships are consistently applied within the limits specified by socially planned and determined broad production and distribution processes, the entirely one-sided interests and decision making of enterprises do not disappear completely – but the clashes of these interests are solved constantly and are flexibly corrected. The essence of these commodity relations is such a clash and mutual adjustment of material interests of producers and consumers where on an average the direct interest of producers is created not only to expend a certain amount of labor as productively as possible as a prerequisite of obtaining back the same amount of most productively expended labor in another form (law of time economy and, simultaneously, law of equivalence), but where also the interest is created in the full satisfaction of the needs of consumers in all kinds of products and in the creation and stimulation of their constantly new needs by the production of new and better use values (law of proportionality and law of development of use values).

A condition of this, of course, is the commodity and monetary exchange between enterprises, whereby such a price movement asserts itself which reflects the mutual relationship between demand and supply and in which the prices will really solve the contradiction between use value and value. It is a contradiction that reflects certain clashes of interest of people, stemming again from the analyzed objective working conditions and consumption of people and inevitably causing contradictions between socialist enterprises . . .

. . . As regards means of production, an overwhelming majority of them is produced according to plan and ahead of the moment of their sale, although it would be desirable that again the majority were contractually ensured at the moment when enterprises decide on their concrete production (except for products with a very long production cycle where the consumer possibly does not even exist yet, e.g. a new enterprise, etc.). Only a small part of the means of production is produced for inventory and sold according to the concrete development of demand. Of course, also in the case of means of production produced according to plan in advance, in accordance with future (mostly contractually ensured) consumption, price movement, as we discussed before, is of immense economic importance. It ensures that enterprises, when deciding on their actual production program, really have an interest in producing needed and constantly improved new means of production; that they are led to the most productive production of socially necessary goods not by administrative order but chiefly by their own interest. If such an economic price movement is not ensured one way or another, the contradictions between the interests of enterprises as producers and consumers must grow, one-sided, socially undesirable decision making on production matters must occur, and no administrative planning, no matter how centralized, can remedy that (on the contrary, it only compounds it).

In the case of consumer goods, on the other hand, production is chiefly in advance, and on inventories and the movement of inventories (in dependence on actual sales of goods on the market) production decision making should be oriented as flexibly as possible in the direction of the actual development of demand. Therefore, price movement here must constantly direct the interests of producers in the direction of the development of demand on the part of the inhabitants. Rigid prices that do not reflect the changes in the development of relations between supply and demand cause growing contradictions between production decision making by enterprises and the development of demand from the inhabitants or home trade. But it would be demagogy to state that the market regulation of actual production programs in case of such price movement, or flexible reaction of trade and production agencies to changes on the market from their own interest and initiative would be more deleterious to the socialist society than the present immensely belated and cumbersome reaction (sometimes altogether absent) by the entire hierarchy of planning and managing agencies to current changes in demand by the inhabitants. It is not at all necessary that prices constantly fluctuate; it is enough if there is the possibility of such fluctuation and sufficient production reserves and modern computing and communication means between trade and production for actual production proportions to adapt quickly and flexibly to details in the changes of demand. It is, for instance, known that even under contemporary capitalism there are no excessively lively fluctuations in prices of consumer goods produced by large monopolies. Before prices are lowered or raised in consequence of lower or higher demand by the population for some goods, production reacts flexibly to the changing stocks (with the aid of the most up-to-date automatic information from retail trade all the way to production) by reducing or increasing output. However, a potential change in price is a condition without which production could certainly not react so readily to changes in demand.

If the dogmatists object to this linking of socialist production with the market and claim that the market cannot solve our structural problems, determine basic proportions, etc., they simply ascribe to the defenders of commodity production other views than the latter really hold, and then it is easy for them to disprove such views. However, here again they wrongly reject any influence of commodity relations on the origin of even basic production proportions. Of course, it is much more indirect than it seems to them.

Indeed, the immediate development of the market cannot decide the basic structure and proportions of production. This is not even the case under contemporary capitalism, and it can be even less so under socialism. It is precisely the enormous advantage of socialism that under it there exist conditions for the long-term planned ensuring of necessary changes in the basic production proportions within the entire social production, regardless of the limited possibilities of accumulation by individual branches of production or enterprises. This socially planned determination of the most effective changes in the basic structure and branch proportions in the entire national economy, in accordance with long-term trends of development of needs, makes it possible to ensure in time and with sufficient reserves of time changes in basic production conditions (changes in the extent of branch capacities, distribution of labor, etc.) for future changes in production proportions. If we do not create in time, with the aid of long-term plans, changes in production capacities of individual branches of production, we are later unable at a certain moment, no matter how hard we press and mobilize enterprises, to ensure the necessary increase in output in a certain branch.

However, it is important that the necessity of producing for the market, the necessity of realizing commodities really effectively asserted itself already as a substantial factor in the creation of these long-term plans. It is important that enterprises should not be more or less passively waiting for production plans from their superior agencies; they themselves should have the greatest interest in their creation, knowing that their future production will have to be most consistently harmonized with the future market since the future development of their incomes will depend on it. There is a great deal of difference whether the main driving force for enterprises is the fulfillment of plans given from above, in which quantitative indicators are of necessity decisive, or whether the main incentive is the attainment of the highest and most profitable sale of goods. Whereas under the former conditions the enterprise endeavors, e.g., to attain the absolutely highest possible investments to facilitate as much as possible the planned increase in output (to which it also adapts all the information for superior agencies, thus inevitably creating subjectively distorted conditions for drawing up central plans), under conditions of real commodity relations the effectiveness of investments would be calculated very thoroughly and deliberately, even by the enterprises, and they would really seek the optimum versions in individual branches and in the entire economy. It is thus an advantage of the planned economy that the concrete utilization of certain existing production capacities, concrete production programs, must occur in harmony with demand and if possible on the basis of previous contracts between buyers and suppliers. Furthermore, the creation of the production capacities themselves must be ensured beforehand according to interbranch relationships (of course, only in rough aggregated values) and according to trends in the general structure of demand (again in accordance with the foreseen development of productivity of labor, incomes, the basic distribution processes, etc.). If we accept the basic prerequisite that the higher the incomes of enterprises, the more consistent will be the long-term harmony between the development of production capacities and the structure of demand and the more effective will be the utilization of these production capacities, then more effective prerequisites (information, calculations, etc., from enterprises) and criteria for really optimum planning will be created.

Whoever would want to deny this connection between socialist commodity relations and long-term planning is obviously more concerned with his personal prestige than with discovering objective economic connections. A really profound examination of all the basic contradictions and connections within the socialist economy shows the first-rate importance of the consistent utilization of the socialist commodity relations for the solution of all the other economic problems. Without the application of these commodity relations the endeavors of economists to solve some economic problem or other is usually only a partial and, unfortunately, often also an ineffective attempt. Truhlář's attempt to positively solve the internal contradictions of our production with the aid of a better system of final inspection of the quality of products, by a different method of awarding bonuses and determining production norms, is not directed towards the main problems and cannot solve the existing basic contradictions.

As long as the old centralistic and administrative method of current planning remains in force and the interest of enterprises is linked to the fulfillment of directively stipulated detailed planned indicators dictated from above, all atempts at eliminating the one-sided and ineffective development of production with the aid of even the broadest or most complicated external controls are bound to fail. The point is not that control and inspection are not necessary. No management system can waive them altogether because this is an essential feedback in managing. But the point is that the system of management should not constantly cause certain contradictions which subsequent control cannot resolve or prevent. If we find that control constantly ascertains the same contradictions *post festum,* we must examine the management system which constantly causes them. If the given method of production planning and of stimulating enterprises provides too little scope and causes insufficient interest (or even complete lack of interest) in real improvement of the products, the introduction of new products into production, technical development and improved production technology, etc., subsequent control is bound always to be proven weaker. Moreover, as internal inspection of the enterprise it is subject to the same enterprise interest, and as external random control it is altogether ineffective and cannot change the basic prerequisites. To introduce such control did not need Truhlář's proposals, but the real overcoming of the existing contradictions in production requires completely different proposals.

The same applies to the awarding of bonuses, the remuneration of the working people and the norming of their work. As long as financial means of enterprises earmarked for wages will not be amassed in dependence on the value of the produced and sold goods but will be stipulated centrally from above in dependence on the fulfillment of some one-sided production indicator, it will be impossible to overcome the rigid wage and bonus regulations which do not correspond to the changing conditions and only fetter the enterprises. As long as the increase in productivity of labor will be administratively planned from above and will not be the result of real technical and technological changes in production and of the initiative and interests of enterprises, it will be impossible to overcome the administrative stiffening of norms and the undermining of the real material interest of the workers. Moreover, it must be realized that any wage and bonus system under the existing one-sidedness of enterprise interest must evoke a one-sided development of production. It is and remains most important whether the main aim of the enterprise as a whole is the fulfillment of planned quantitative indicators or the real and effective satisfaction of social needs. If the incomes of enterprises were dependent on the real sales of goods, the necessary order in remunerating employees would be quickly introduced, and the interest of the enterprises would concentrate on the effective and socially necessary development of production.

If we take note of the real gravity of insufficient technical development of our production, its disproportionate and uneconomical development, all of which nowadays cause immense economic difficulties and losses, and if we find more or less beyond doubt, that all this was caused by the already completely unsatisfactory system of planned management, we really must have the courage to penetrate to the root of the matter and put an end to the very deep-rooted ideological notions which have nothing to do any more with creative Marxist theory. If we cannot solve the existing contradictions in production without commodity relations – and all past attempts at reorganizing management within the old model of limiting commodity relations prove it – we must have the courage to begin using socialist commodity relations deliberately as a condition of making socialist planned management more comprehensive and more scientific. It is a decisive step on the path toward the real development of the initiative of our enterprises and of all working people, without which we will not overcome our material difficulties. And in applying this endeavor we must be able to conquer also all erroneous ideological prejudices.

B. KOMENDA AND C. KOŽUŠNÍK

Some fundamental problems of improving the system of management of the socialist economy*

... The improvement and introduction of scientific methods into the system of planned management of the economy must ... be understood not simply as a partial adaptation of the present system by improving individual indicators and the like, with the aim of remedying only the most glaring shortcomings, but rather as a fundamental reappraisal of the basic principles and main methods and instruments of planning. This is the only way to abolish the chronic disharmony between the development of social

* Excerpted from 'Některé základní otázky zdokonalení soustavy řízení socialistického národního hospodářství', *Politická ekonomie*, XII, No. 3, 1964.

needs and social production, the constant tension between social needs and the resources for their satisfaction, and constantly to increase the effectiveness of social labor expended.

The core of the entire problem is found in questions of commodity production or, to put it more concretely, in the function of value categories – especially the market and its mechanism in the society economy – and in the questions of material interest of the staffs of socialist enterprises. The hitherto existing management systems proceeded from the idea that the material interest of enterprises and the system of monetary and commodity relations among enterprises are irreconcilable with planning, an alien element in the socialist economy, a remnant of capitalism and a source of spontaneity. All the measures of planned management therefore aimed at suppressing these necessary evils as much as possible and at containing them within the rigid framework of the state plan. Reality proves that such methods of struggling against objective economic conditions and their influence on the actions of the masses of working people are ineffective, that plans thus conceived cannot be fully realized and that harmonious and efficient development of the national economy cannot be ensured with their aid.

Scientific planned management must not set itself unrealistic aims; it cannot suddenly change the given material conditions under which society lives and try to abolish the economic forms of connection among enterprises unless it provides a substitute which is at least as effective. It must therefore rely on a certain mechanism which is based on commodity and monetary relations. Only if market relations are utilized is it possible to create a system of planned management of the social process of reproduction in which it would not be necessary to prescribe from the center every step for every link of social cooperation, but in which it would instead be possible to make use of the fact that in each of these links there are thinking people at work who are able to find their bearings unaided and to make rational decisions. It would then be sufficient for national managing agencies to create objective conditions for the activity of individual enterprises such that enterprise interests coincide with social interests. There would then be no need for a system of directive instructions or for detailed indicators.

Social agencies of course must have a concrete idea of the planned development. In individual cases the detailed knowledge of interrelationships of the planned processes will probably have to be the same or even better than under the present system of management. But the purpose of this knowledge will be not the elaboration of directive production targets for individual enterprises but rather such intervention in external conditions as will influence the actions of producers, bringing enterprise interests more into line with social interests. The most important aspect of the work of managing agencies must be activity resulting in the constant orientation of enterprise staffs toward the satisfaction of social needs in a way which corresponds to the basic political and economic aims contained in the long-term plan. There is no substitute for this function of the managing agencies.

As mentioned above, a condition for this concept of planning is the utilization of commodity and monetary relations and of the material interests of enterprises. Both these issues have to be looked at and solved concomitantly. For the first, the core of the problem is the price policy; for the second, it is chiefly the system guiding the creation of the incomes of employees of socialist enterprises. Experience so far (especially that of the changes in management carried out in 1959), indicates that interference with the system of material interest cannot yield results if it is not correctly combined with measures in the sphere of price policy. Conversely, changes in the price system alone do not lead to a fundamental improvement of the whole system of management. This also finds its expression in the fact that price adjustments, carried out from time to time, are seen not as measures concerning the system of management but more or less as technical changes within the framework of the existing system.

Although we emphasize the utilization of commodity and monetary relations and the material interests of enterprises, it does not mean that we want to deprive social agencies of all possibilities of interfering directly with the reproduction process and of using administrative forms of management. The aim is not to juxtapose different forms of management and then to exclude one of them. A scientific system of management must use all suitable forms. We emphasize commodity and monetary relations and material interest not only because so far they have been neglected and have been likely to be classified as negative phenomena, but especially because the administrative forms of management themselves can be really effective and yield positive results only if they do not clash with the material interest but instead act in harmony with this interest. Since it is not inevitable under socialism that antagonistic contradictions arise between social interest on the one hand and personal and collective interests on the other, it is always possible to find solutions to the inevitable contradictions between these interests, where the directive-administrative form of management will be an exception used under special circumstances or for special purposes. Even in these exceptional cases, however, it is necessary that the whole matter is not disposed of merely by an administrative order.

The system of planned management of the economy, which would abolish the contradictions of the former methods of management, does not in principle presuppose directive stipulation of output, of the structure of production, or of the limits to the use of specific factors. The satisfaction of the needs of society with minimum expenditure on production can be ensured, as mentioned before, by creating suitable economic conditions and by guiding the material interests of enterprises. If the enterprise does not receive directive tasks as to output and structure of production, it can learn about the development of social needs only through the prices at which it sells its output. But this requires both that prices really express the relation between social production and social needs, and that the enterprises be suitably interested in actual prices. Since the core of this management system is the solution of these problems, it is necessary to investigate further the material interest of enterprises and the planned guidance of price creation under this system.

The system of material interest of enterprises

The principle of material interest used to designate the general motivation or orientation of the economic activity of people is based on the fact that every economically active individual endeavors to achieve some maximization of results (effect) obtained from his activity in relation to the effort, i.e. chiefly the work effort. This endeavor is the more pronounced, the greater the expended effort has to be and the smaller the effect may be. Since these circumstances are completely dependent on the economic conditions under which people produce, this endeavor is also a special expression of these conditions.

If this fact is to be consistently utilized in the planned management of the socialist economy, the results of production must be oriented correctly, and, on the basis of this, the share of each individual in the social product can then be stipulated. The basic problem here is that the results of the labor effort of each individual cannot, under present conditions, be directly determined. The difficulty is not, however, that practically all products are the result of combined labor. The entire production process can be broken down into individual production operations, and for these it can be ascertained who carried them out, how long it took him and what the result was. The known methods of setting norms for work and of technical inspection make it possible to determine fairly accurately all these circumstances connected with the worker's participation in production. The development of socialist production is undoubtedly largely dependent on a system of piece rates, norms, bonuses for using raw materials, fuel and power economically, for using and maintaining production equipment, and for the quality of production, and on the other forms of material incentives used nowadays, all of which are bound up with demonstrable and technically measurable merits of individuals (possibly of certain groups). All these methods and procedures can be maintained and further improved. The proposed system of management does not require any radical changes in this sphere. However, these means are not the whole answer to the problem of combining the individual's interest with the interests of the entire society.

The shortcoming of all these procedures is that they concern only the technical aspect and do not touch upon the economic content of production. It does not follow simply from the fact that all the workers engaged in producing a certain product obeyed all the known technical principles, used up not one superfluous gram of material, and did not exceed the necessary time by one minute that the labor expended was actually socially necessary labor. That depends not only on the technical conditions of production but chiefly on the relation of production to social needs.

If material interest is to be used to make employees of socialist production enterprises consciously link their personal interests with the interests of society as a whole, it is not enough to link their personal income or the possibilities of improving their workplaces only to the results of work measured by technical means; their material remuneration must be linked to those economic indicators of the work of their enterprise which express the relation of the entire production to social needs. Under present conditions, the labor of an individual receives social recognition only as part of the labor of the entire productive staff engaged in the production of the given use value, because each individual worker is only a part of the collective labor. Therefore, the income of each individual due to his work must be determined not only by the features of his work as individual labor, but chiefly by its characterization as social labor, i.e. as value-producing under present conditions. In this sense, the material interest of individuals must be understood as collective interest.

As long as commodities are being produced, no plan can absolve individual commodities from the necessity of carrying out the fateful somersault, i.e. of passing through exchange. It is only the exchange of a commodity that proves in effect that the labor expended on its production was social labor. Commodity exchange at the same time solves two important aspects of the problem of the social merit of an enterprise. If exchange is effected, it proves that the commodity contained social labor, that the labor expended satisfies some social need. At the same time, the price at which the commodity is sold relative to the costs defrayed by the producer shows to what extent the quality and quantity of the products correspond to social need and to what extent production was effective. Thus, if the material situation of employees of individual enterprises depends on the results of exchange of their products, there will be an economic incentive for their active participation in social production, and there will also be an incentive for the labor expended in production to be expended on the production of articles that are socially useful. This linkage also serves as a safeguard for society against the damage that might be caused by having individual collectives expending ineffective or inexpedient labor.

If the material interest of enterprises is to be really effective, the monetary incomes of enterprises and the incomes and all other rewards of the workers must be strictly linked to the actual sales of the commodities. It follows from this that all the links mediating the circulation of commodities and the connection of producers with consumers must be organized on commercial lines so that they can bear the risk in case the goods ordered by them do not sell at the originally expected prices.

Another prerequisite for the effectiveness of the entire system is that the actual assortment of production be predominantly a matter to be settled by the enterprise in direct negotiations with its customers. The central plan may serve the enterprise for orientation but it must not absolve the enterprise from responsibility if its products do not find social application. It is, of course, assumed that prices express the actual relation between social production and social need.

However, the price does not in itself characterize the result of the productive activity of the enterprise. The contribution by the enterprise to society is not determined by the entire value of production but only by the new value created by the labor of the staff of the enterprise. This labor is what the enterprise really contributes to society, since the value transferred from consumed and used-up means of production must return to the sphere of production to enable the enterprise to continue to produce. Therefore, the monetary incomes of employees and, possibly, the other financial funds of the enterprise should in principle be determined as a function of the magnitude of the newly created value.

When the price is fixed independently of the enterprise, the monetary expression of the newly created value and the gross income of the enterprise will be the greater, the smaller the consumption of material and power, the larger the quantity produced and the larger the proportion of the goods produced that are really sold. On the other hand, if material expenditure is given, the magnitude of the gross income will fluctuate according to the fluctuations of the price. If the price movements correspond to changes in the relation of social production and needs (i.e. to changes in the relation between supply and demand), the fluctuations in gross income can serve as information helping the enterprise to concentrate on the production of socially needed use values.

If the enterprise is to be interested in selling all the goods produced and in maintaining a minimum of inventories, it is necessary to include in the prime costs of the sold goods the expenses on the increment in inventories. In that case, a change in the proportion of goods sold to the entire amount of goods produced and a change in the amount of inventories will immediately find expression in a change of material expenditure on the goods sold. The larger the share of goods sold, the relatively lower the cost of the goods sold, with the price given, and the larger therefore the gross income of the enterprise.

The linking of the material position of the employees to the magnitude of the gross income they produce will therefore cause the employees to have an interest in saving material expenditure and in producing goods which are socially useful and of high quality and which can therefore be profitably sold. In certain cases, the enterprise may desire a price reduction for its products in order to sell all the goods produced.

The enterprise may actually influence the price (even if it does not decide on it) by the quality of its production, on the one hand, and by the quantity, on the other. By restricting supply, it may in fact raise the price of its products and attain higher gross income, which would be advantageous for the enterprise. However, at the same time the utilization of production funds and of labor is reduced, which is disadvantageous from the point of view of society. If the interest of the enterprise and the interests of society are to be brought close together, conditions must be created, by action from the center, so that a price reduction (which is only the reflection of increased output, with the extent of social needs given) is more advantageous for the enterprise than is less effective utilization of labor and production funds.

A certain interest in increased output could be generated if the magnitude of depreciation were not dependent on the method of utilizing fixed assets but were instead a fixed item in the annual prime costs of production. The influence of suitable distribution of the net product could be utilized in the same way. In any case, social control and planned guidance of pricing will be necessary in the future, too, in order to prevent enterprises from abusing their monopolistic position vis-à-vis their customers.

The system of material interest described above requires that one of the basic tasks of the national plan be the stipulation of the gross income to be created in individual enterprises or in entire branches of the economy, along with stipulation of the way it is to be distributed. In general, we may say that gross income per employee should somehow be differentiated among the individual branches, depending on the qualification structure of the employees of the branch (it is assumed that simple unskilled labor in any branch in principle creates equal gross income within the same time period). The planned pricing of products in individual branches should also be taken into consideration in the planned stipulation of gross income, or, to put it conversely, the basic task of planned pricing of the products of each branch must be the economically justified stipulation of the overall gross income of the branch of the economy. We shall return to these questions below.

There can be a number of methods of distributing gross income. When a certain version is chosen, it is necessary to take into consideration the principles of financing the reproduction process of enterprises – in the first place, the financing of the needs of expanded reproduction. This is a complex of problems all by itself and one with which we cannot deal in detail in this article. We shall assume that enterprises finance simple reproduction, i.e. current maintenance and major overhauls of production equipment, from their own resources, that they use short-term credit for operating capital, and long-term credit for financing extensive reconstruction and new construction.

Under these assumptions, the distribution of gross income could be roughly arranged according to the following principles. If the enterprise created, in the course of a year, that gross income per employee envisaged, then it would pay a previously stipulated part of this income to the treasury. The remainder of the gross income would represent the net income of the enterprise. From this net income, the enterprise would first cover its commitments to the State Bank, i.e. it would pay interest on credits and repay the appropriate part of long-term credits. The remainder of the net income would form the fund for the personal incomes of the enterprise employees. During the year, the enterprise would pay the basic wages of its employees from this fund. The share of wages in the fund of personal incomes should in principle be a function of the magnitude of possible inaccuracy in the plan of creation of gross income, but it should never exceed about 90 per cent of the fund. The remaining part of the fund – the fund of supplementary incomes, which would remain in the enterprise at the end of the year – would be paid to all employees of the enterprise according to special rules, but in principle according to the size of the basic wage . . .

. . . The interest in saving social labor expended in production is equal (provided the enterprise must adapt to the needs of the customers and is interested in selling all its output, even at a lower price) to an interest of the enterprise in lowering the value of the products. It follows from this that enterprises would be interested in increasing the productivity of labor (since this is only another expression for lowering the value), in using new equipment, technology, and progressive organization of work, and in increasing output, for these are factors which increase the effectiveness of the means and labor expended, and which therefore, with prices given, also increase gross income. We may safely say that under such conditions increased output, productivity of labor and technological improvement of production would not be treated as formalities or as an end in themselves, but would be economically justified.

It is thus clear that all of the substantial aspects affected by the level of socially useful productive activity of enterprises could be captured in the single indicator of gross income. There is therefore no need to seek a system of various indicators and to invent conversions by means of which we could then bring those various indicators to a single common basis which would show unambiguously how the enterprise should be evaluated on the whole.

On the other hand, the indicator according to which the enterprise is evaluated must not be confused with the various indicators that must be used in every economic analysis in order to elucidate individual aspects of the activity of enterprises and reveal the influence of the various factors affecting the development of these aspects. There may be a large number of such analytical indicators, and it is impossible to determine generally which of them should be selected.

The system of material interest will have a more intensive effect, the more long-term are the interests of the employees. It is therefore necessary to work out a set of measures that could stabilize employment, especially of economic and technical executives. If such employees had to change their place of employment, it would be necessary to ensure that they could not evade possible negative consequences of their activity in the former enterprise.

The system of material interest cannot by itself solve the problem of technical development of products nor prevent the rise of prices. These problems are closely interconnected. Their solution must be sought, on the one hand, in a complex of measures that will ensure equilibrium in the market and a certain stability of the price level and of money in circulation, and on the other hand, in the national guidance of technical development.

A special problem is the interest of enterprises in economical and economically effective investment construction. As mentioned before, the proposed system assumes that this interest could be aroused if investment construction within the framework of functioning enterprises were financed by long-term investment credits. Credit would be granted on the basis of a thorough evaluation of the economic effectiveness of the project. The investor would thus be put under pressure by the size of the credit, the time of recoupment and the interest rate, all of which would be a burden in his future activity. Drawing on the credit would have to be subject to stringent conditions concerning the course of construction and the extent to which the planned technico-economic indicators were met. In the case of unfavorable deviations, sanctions could be imposed in the form of an increased in.erest rate for additional credits.

Problems of planned price formation

The gross income of an enterprise expresses the contribution of the enterprise to society only if the actual market prices do not lose their relationship to the economic conditions under which they function, i.e. only if they constantly express conditions of production and the relationship between social production and social need (the relationship between supply and demand). They must therefore constantly be equilibrium prices. This means that exchange relations between enterprises must not be governed by any means other than the price level (e.g. by a system of allocations or preferential supplies).

Only under this condition will the price inform the producer of changes in the relationship between production and social need, and thus be able to replace the direct central stipulation of the assortment to be produced and so remedy the hitherto existing isolation of production from social needs. With the system of material interest of enterprises described above, the profitability of every product to its producer will depend on the ratio of the gross income contained in its price to the basic wages that have been paid towards its production. Therefore, as a result of changes in the relation between supply and demand, enterprises will modify their production program in such a way that their market prices will approach prices with the average ratio of gross income to basic wages. In addition, equilibrium prices would automatically adapt the extent of actual social need to the given production potential and would exclude any erroneous information on the growth of needs.

Under such conditions, the function of central planned price formation – and especially the instruments and methods of price policy – would change. Under the present system of management, price policy and price formation in principle fall within the domain of central managing agencies. This is the only way of ensuring that the interests of the entire society are heeded and of preventing enterprises from achieving advantages by raising prices at the expense of society. However, the practical results achieved by applying this view have serious shortcomings. It is obvious that central price formation for the majority of products cannot be carried out except by freezing prices for a relatively long period, in the course of which the prices are necessarily being isolated from the developing economic conditions. Besides, the greater the number of prices that are centrally stipulated, the more the interests of individual enterprises may assert themselves in proposing prices, since it is impossible to check all price recommendations by enterprises. If some strict general principle of price formation is applied against the interests of the enterprises, the price relations of individual products cannot be economically justified even at the very beginning of their use, for without detailed knowledge of the economic conditions under which individual products are produced, a general principle can be applied only mechanically.

The isolation of prices from economic conditions is intensified by the fact that the preparation of every single price modification takes several years, and during that time economic conditions may diverge considerably from the original estimate, since even the production plans of enterprises are usually not definite.

The essence of the central direction of price formation in the proposed system of planning and management cannot be the stipulation of individual prices but rather the creation and maintenance of conditions which prevent enterprises from manipulating their prices in accordance with their own narrow interests against the interests of society. Conditions must be such that the price will serve enterprises as an objectively given social criterion of their activity, which they can change only in a way that is of benefit to society. In all cases where enterprises would be under pressure, by the development of supply and demand, to lower prices while maintaining the high quality of their products, central management could be confined to general supervision and evaluation of the overall trend of proportions of social production, and the enterprises could be given wide powers in stipulating prices.

In connection with the new task of central management in the sphere of price formation, it is necessary to abandon the present ideas of the importance of price stability. It follows from the concept of price as an economic category whose inalienable feature is its functional dependence on the relation between supply and demand, that price stability cannot be considered a generally mandatory principle of price policy. Although it is now a principle which facilitates the management by central agencies of enterprises and of economic processes, it will certainly disorganize relationships within the national economy if it is applied as the basic principle of price policy . . .

. . . Using stability of prices as a general principle inevitably leads to rigidity in the structure of social production and social consumption and in the final analysis to wasteful and ineffective satisfaction of social needs. Thus, if the essence of planned management of social production is the goal of achieving constantly improving and more effective satisfaction of social needs, the principle of price stability must be considered as a subordinate principle which does not fully express the basic task of price policy. Stability of prices can be only a transitional and basically short-term phenomenon, dependent on the relative constancy of production conditions. The period during which the prices of individual products are stable must be shorter, the faster is technical progress in the sphere of their production and the greater is the influence of technical upheavals on the value of products . . .

KAREL KOUBA

Plan and market in the socialist economy*

Origin of the problem and a contemporary formulation

. . . The renewed discussion on the functioning of the socialist economy first started under quite specific conditions in Yugoslavia in the early 1950s and later, due to a favorable social atmosphere, continued in many other European socialist countries. This discussion has enriched the traditional debate on socialism which had begun as a polemic between the critics and supporters of the socialist system shortly after the revolution in Russia.

Ludwig von Mises stated in the 1920s – and further elaborated in the 1930s – the view that the economy cannot operate effectively under socialist conditions. According to him, the socialized ownership of the means of production precludes a market for these goods and, therefore, prices for the means of production cannot exist, i.e. the conditions of a socialist economy do not provide the knowledge of the relative prices which are the basis ('under a given system of preferences and available resources') for rational choice among alternatives.

In contrast to him, other supporters of the same view, especially L. Robbins and F. A. Hayek, did not exclude the theoretical possibility of effective allocation of resources in a socialist economy; what they did exclude was the possibility of finding rational prices for the means of production through mathematical calculations and determination by a central organ.

Fifty years of experience with the development of socialism, its influence on the world's development and in the thinking of our century makes it possible to continue this 'debate on socialism' which has already proved its historical vitality. At the same time critical analyses, due to the recent favorable conditions in the socialist movement, result in a more critical attitude toward unresolved problems and enable us to look for answers in all kinds of directions.

* 'Plán a trh v socialistické ekonomice', *Politická ekonomie*, xv, Nov. 9, 1967, pp. 773–83.

In his remarkable and original work 'On the Economic Theory of Socialism' Lange suggested that the problem of effective allocation of resources could be solved without having a real market for the means of production.[1]

Lange's solution for a rational price structure points to a socialist system in which a real market for consumer goods exists and a free choice of profession and working place is maintained; equilibrium in the market for consumer goods and in the market for labor are achieved as in the competitive market in the West. Since, however, a real market for producers' goods does not exist and thus real market prices do not exist for them, the problem is solved by positing that the Central Planning Board replaces the competitive market with centralized decisions, *and* compels the production managers to conform to the centrally determined prices (which are of parametric character, i.e. every production manager considers them as given and adjusts to them). Such prices would provide data on effective allocation of the production factors.

Simply put, Lange's solution could be defined as follows . . . The Central Planning Board determines prices and insures that the enterprise and branch managers carry out their calculations on the basis of these prices only – no other way of calculation may be allowed. If prices are viewed as stable parameters, the price structure will be in equilibrium. Every price differing from the equilibrium price would result in either surplus or deficit of certain goods, and it would show up as such at the end of the period of accounts. Thus, every failure of the Central Planning Board in determining prices would assert itself objectively, by a deficit or surplus of certain goods or productive factors which would have to be eliminated in order to achieve a smooth flow of production. As Lange puts it:

> Our study of the determination of equilibrium prices in a socialist economy has shown that the process of price determination is quite analogous to that in a competitive market. The Central Planning Board performs the functions of the market. It establishes the rules of combining factors of production and choosing the scale of output of a plant, for determining the output of an industry, for the allocation of resources, and for the parametric use of prices in accounting. Finally, it fixes the prices so as to balance the quantity supplied and demanded of each commodity . . . Thus the accounting prices in a socialist economy can be determined by the same process of trial and error by which prices on a competitive market are determined.[2]

1 He proceeded from older works of V. Pareto and E. Barone, and from the problem suggested by F. M. Taylor, who in 1936 was one of the participants in the debate. Abba Lerner's view was similar: therefore, this approach is known in economic literature as the Lange–Lerner solution. See O. Lange. 'On the Economic Theory of Socialism', *The Review of Economic Studies*, Vol. 4, 1936–37.

2 *Ibid.*, pp. 63–4 and 66 of the English text.

Even today, Lange's theories appear remarkable and original not only in the way they resolve tasks but especially in the way they pose the issues. Today also, an objective price structure is viewed as axiomatic for effective economic decisions under socialism. From the beginning of the investigation, free choice of goods on the consumption market is considered as an essential feature of the economic model of a functioning socialist economy. In this sense Lange's theoretical model of a socialist economy is topical and modern. An objective price structure, and thus the mechanism which maintains the effective price structure as the source of more or less accurate objective economic criteria, is considered as the indispensable prerequisite for economic calculation and successful planning.

As far as Lange's solution of the central economic problem of the socialist economy is concerned, I doubt that its practical realization and utilization would be possible, even though Lange proved theoretically that the central planning organ does not have to deal with millions of equations and could achieve the same results as the competitive market with the method of approximation. However, from the point of view of our present experience, we can state that his was only a theoretical proof. If, as mentioned above, we continue the old discussion [on the economics of socialism] it is only fair to concede that some of F. A. Hayek's arguments were reasonable. The central planning organ cannot replace the firms' initiative and cannot bear responsibility for the firms' current decisions. Even the most developed contemporary techniques could not collect such detailed data as required for the replacement of the producers' goods market with central decisions.

Reality has forced us to revive discussion on these problems . . . It is true that in a socialist economy the central planning organ possesses a much deeper knowledge of the economic system than any entrepreneur could have, and thus correct equilibrium prices could possibly be reached in a shorter period of experimentation than in the competitive market. However, the mutual exchange and transfer of data between the central planning organ and the enterprises presupposes accordance of enterprise and social interests.

The socialist revolutionary process which eliminated private ownership of the means of production and thus destroyed the bourgeois structure of society, also eliminated the main impediments hampering harmony of economic progress and pure economic aims with social progress and social aims. However, this does not mean that in the system of a centrally managed socialist society no critical issues remain – and this certainly can be said of every system of management of a given level of division of social labor. Initial data collection is influenced by the enterprises' interest. And this is a controversial interest because it concerns earnings, social funds, and accumulation. Data processing in the center is likewise not a purely technical matter. The relative autonomy of the executive organ and the previous system of representative organs in the social structure give evidence of the fact that the determination of the development aims of the society and the scale of preferences are problems which cannot and must not be considered as satisfactorily resolved.

Research on the structure of interests with regard to the division of social labor in a socialist society brings us to the conclusion that controversy on short- and long-term interests between enterprises and the center and between production collectives and production managers, and controversial social standpoints (especially those of a noneconomic character), make it impossible to rely on exchange of information as a source of credible data which could replace the market. We are concerned here not only with the credibility of data provided by bearers with different interests, but with the source of enterprise motivation, the center's decisions and consumer influence on production.

Lange 'defended' socialism against those critics who stated that central decisions cannot determine the effective price structure when a real market for means of production does not exist. Experience and also the theory of socialism show, however, that the essence of our 'debate on [the economics of] socialism' does not lie in this sphere.

Specific functions of the price system cannot be replaced successfully by central decisions or by the plan. The price system operates as a signal device and as the source of incentives. In certain circumstances the price system is the most flexible and at the same time the cheapest mechanism for providing the production managers with information as to what, how, and for whom to produce.

Lange accepted the thesis of the critics of socialism that national ownership of the means of production eliminates the existence of markets for producers' goods. I suppose that this thesis is the basic weak point in von Mises' and Hayek's concept and cannot be accepted. The contemporary 'debate on socialism' is conducted under different theoretical and practical conditions than those which are to be found in the works of von Mises and Hayek, and on the other hand, in the Lange–Lerner theory.

A specific kind of market can also be created as far as producers' goods are concerned. Socialist enterprises, the economic subjects of the market, can introduce real exchange of these goods at real prices, especially if the socialist economy is not isolated from the international market . . . A real market of producers' goods among socialist enterprises is also compatible with regulation of individual and enterprise income which ensures the socialist character of the distribution of national income.

The precondition for the effective functioning of a realistic price mechanism on the market for producers' goods lies in maintaining the parametric character of prices; here Lange's assumption is fully justified. The reality of today, however, entitles us to have serious doubts about Lange's solution of the issues of parametric prices. It is difficult to imagine that the real solution lies only in the system of commands. Rather, I see the solution in the effective structuring of the socialist market, in the possibility of free entry, in maximum support of competition. If an economically motivated monopoly exists, the country's frontiers must be opened in order to utilize the regulating influence of world prices on the internal economy. The accelerated process of innovation is accompanied by great changes in assortment. Practical experience in setting prices of new products shows that even firmly set centralized prices cannot be maintained when the preconditions mentioned above are not taken into consideration. The parametric character of prices causes very difficult theoretical and, especially, practical problems.

For some economic decisions, particularly in investment allocation, utilization of accounting prices would be adequate and reasonable. The simulation of the market, made possible by contemporary mathematical–economic methods, is a useful instrument for decreasing risk and improving effective decisions. However, we are also concerned here with accounting prices which result from an analysis of the real market and which take account of projected market tendencies. Corrections of the chosen alternative will be a matter for the real market.

Planning calls for an effective price structure not only as far as accounting prices are concerned, but also as far as the actual price mechanism is concerned.

An objective price system in the absolute sense of the word cannot exist. However, we are concerned here with conditions under which the price level and price relations develop together with balanced relations of supply and demand and follow tendencies analogous to those of world prices.

The socialist society is exposed to the great risk of having an ineffective economy if its planning is not based on an objective price structure. I dare say that optimal planning without a rational price structure is impossible. If the solution cannot be found in the simulation of real prices on the market of producers' goods, the problem, as recent experience shows, must be tackled on the basis of the actual linking of the plan and of the market through a regulated market mechanism. Mutual correlation of effective decisions on the basis of the market and effective decision by means of the plan can be considered as the central theoretical and practical problem for an effective functioning of the socialist economy.

Concept of economic planning

The basic idea of the economic reform centered on the linkage of the plan with the regulated market mechanism, is the gradual creation of a rational price structure, as a precondition for economic planning. This is not always fully understood. The traditional concept of the plan remains essentially untouched; changes are effected only in the structure of plan indices and in their methodical regrouping into guiding indices rather than into compulsory indices. The plan reformed in this manner is complete with a price mechanism; this price mechanism, together with the complex of other economic factors is the instrument for carrying out the plan. This kind of reform operates within the framework of the administratively managed economy. Frequently, the function of the plan is confused with the techniques of planning. Actually, identical planning techniques can be used in different kinds of planning and in different concepts of the plan's function in the economic system. Moreover, planning techniques are to a certain extent neutral, no matter whether they are concerned with a socialist or capitalist economy.

Only a reform which completely eliminates the traditional administrative system and replaces it with [real] economic planning can achieve long-lasting results. A price mechanism based on a realistically functioning internal market, simultaneously influenced by the world market, will be one of the most important instruments for creating the central plan . . . Economic planning in the full sense of the word has hitherto not been realized in any socialist country, and thus, theory could not have been supported by general practical experience.[3]

The hitherto well-known ways of planning enable us to determine the task of planning.

Analysis of the function of the directive plan enables us to aim at a detailed investigation of the problems concerning the linkage of the plan with the market mechanism. Gradual resolving of the problems will enable us to create a system of socialist planning in which both the theoretical and the practical methods of planning will participate. The experience and the theoretical concepts of planning in capitalist countries could also provide help. Besides the kind of planning used in the majority of socialist countries, capitalist countries in the postwar period also developed theories and

---

3 This also applies to the decentralized system of Yugoslavia's economy. In the theses on the 'System of social planning in Yugoslavia' one may read that 'The development of the self-management system and the level of development of production forces achieved, have discredited the old way of planning; however, a new system of planning with a more adequate mechanism of managment and coordination which would correspond to the commodity character of production and to self-management, has not yet been built up', *Ekonomist*, No. 3, 1965.

practices of planning under market conditions. First of all, for more than twenty years prosperity planning has been applied. As a matter of fact, it is short-term forecasting of development for one year which helps to choose economic policy ensuring full employment, a stable currency and equilibrium in the balance of payments. This theory and practice of short-term prosperity planning is well-known, especially in Holland, where recently longer periods have also been introduced. The improved kind of planning under conditions of a capitalist market mechanism is structural planning for a period of approximately five years. Partial structural planning has been applied since 1947 in France, and later also in other West European countries (Italy, Belgium, Holland). In West Germany specific features of regional planning have been used. They concern partial planning in specific production branches, especially with regard to regional projects. Later, in France and partly also in Norway, general structural planning was developed; it determines specific priorities and supports structural changes in the national economy within the framework of the capitalist social structure. Since the 1960s, medium-term planning in France has changed gradually. The selective character of the plan and subventions have been decreased, and tax policy vis-à-vis branches has lost its selective character. The plan has been provided less and less with selective instruments and operates only as the complement of the market, as the instrument for improving the market and competition.

. . . Planning under market conditions enables us to extend the period of economic policy and to plan the strategy of economic growth. The planning organ, proceeding from the fact that the market is effective, can improve and complement its effectiveness.

The plan is sometimes considered as the model of the future market. I think that from the standpoint of interrelations between plan and market an important aspect comes to the forefront, and I do not see any reason why this concept should be rejected. Long-term planning, especially under the conditions of socialism, calls for an accurate definition of this concept of planning.

The indispensable starting point of planning under market conditions is the analysis of the economy and the forecast of the future market. Speaking of forecasting – in contrast to the plan – we have in mind forecasting variants of economic development on the basis of exogenous factors.[4]

---

4 L. Rychetník and O. Kýn distinguish between plan and forecast as follows: 'When speaking of forecasting, we have in mind forecasting possible variants of the development of the economy on the basis of the development of economic factors which, from the standpoint of central decisions, are exogenous and cannot be directly influenced by them.

When speaking of planning, we have in mind a concrete variant selected among the possible variants of development. The optimal plan is the variant which corresponds best to the given criterion', *Czechoslovak Economic Papers*, No. 10, 1968.

Some specific kinds of forecasting take into consideration factors of an endogenous character also. One of the valuable sources for initial data when setting the plan is a forecast of possible variants of economic development which proceed from the model of the future market, and which take shape under the given exogenous factors either in a fixed or variable economic policy. The choice of economic policy depends on the decisions of central organs and determines, together with the endogenous factors, the trend of the endeavor. Thus, forecasting does not only have a passive task, since it serves as the source of data for confronting alternative variants of development with anticipated goals. However, that does not mean that forecasting of the future market is the plan; it only represents an initial phase of planning.

The plan represents the model of the future market only under specific preconditions. The competitive market, together with the plan, can be the instrument for achieving the economic optimum. If the economic optimum is selected in accordance with the enterprises' decisions and balanced growth is ensured, conditions can be created that will result in the mutual complementing of market and plan, which together represent the instrument of effective economic development.

The plan can be considered as the adequate and even necessary instrument for improving the market. The market operates under uncertainty with entrepreneurial risk, and is unstable. Balanced growth, and especially structural changes of a more important character are realized very slowly and with fluctuations. The imperfectness of competition linked with the oligopolistic structure of the market multiplies its negative features. Thus, the plan can be considered as the instrument for improving the market, as the 'catalyst' of the market. This applies to the kind of plan which aims at an economy with a developed market and competition. The idea that the plan 'decreases uncertainty', that it is the 'catalyst of market', and of the necessity of 'excessive research on the market' do not have their origin in the socialist countries. Some medium-term plans of the French economy starting with the third plan (1958–61) embody this idea. The approach has been strengthened in the fourth plan (1962–65) and later, in the fifth plan (1966–70). Former plans (1947–57) used selective instruments to a great extent and managed the development of the market.

The concept of planning as a model of the future market is also compatible with the socialist economy.

. . . The plan does not represent the essence of socialism, and the market is not the alternative to a socialist economy. The difference between socialism and capitalism does not lie in the fact that one society is managed by the plan and the other by the market. Since the sixties, many countries of both systems, have aimed at linking the plan and the market. The difference between the systems, caused by their diverse economic and social structures, is expressed in the goals of the given economic decisions which are independent of pure market forces. Autonomous decisions are likewise not the essence of socialism. The contents and arrangements of goals are specific of socialism. They are conditioned by the given structure of society.

Socialist planning and the utilization of the market mechanism surpass the task of modeling the future market. The specific structure of socialist society enables the plan to become the instrument of coordination in the activity of economic subjects, to achieve concordance of interests, and to determine the grade of preferences expressed by the hierarchy in the structure of goals.

Integration of goals in the activity of socialist enterprises determined by the plan results in establishing a hierarchy in the structure of targets. At the top of this structure is the main target which can be called the target of the first order. Instruments serving to carry out this target directly are targets of a second order. Instruments serving directly to carry out these targets are targets of a third order, etc. The goals of different enterprise activities have various degrees in this hierarchy of targets. Thus, while hierarchy in the structure of targets is the expression of planning in the socialist economy, the integration of the goals of individual socialist enterprises is at the same time the expression of the manner of effective socialist production. This effectiveness, expressed by the hierarchy in the structure of targets, does not appear at the onset of socialist production relations. It is created gradually, with difficulty, and concomitantly, with the development of socialist production.[5]

The plan exceeds the limits of the market's function, especially when it concerns the conditions under which resources and incomes should be divided. The play of market forces results in a polarization of incomes which, from the standpoint of socialist humanism and social equality, is undesirable. Planning and the instruments of a socialist economy can have a great many features similar to those used today in the capitalist economy. The essential difference, however, is in the social–economic conditions under which incomes and goals are divided; the criterion of the enterprises' effective decisions is in accordance with the goals of social development. The fact that the model of income distribution in socialist society has not yet been resolved – the difficulty in harmonizing the goals of socialist humanism with the mechanism of the effective functioning of

5 Oskar Lange, *Politická ekonomie. Obecne otazky* (Political Economy. General Problems), pp. 167–8, Academia, Prague, 1966.

the economy – does not negate this characteristic of socialist development.[6]

Planning exceeds the limitations of the effectiveness of the market in other fields also. Socialist planning ensures a great possibilities of surpassing the principles of rational decisions and of applying them in those economic and social spheres where the functioning of the market is not reliable. The sphere of social needs depends on the development of the productive and social infrastructure (resolving the problems of transport, communication, health-service, education, housing, social security, etc.). The smooth and effective flow of these solutions exceeds the possibilities of the market mechanism, as does the resolving of production and social problems. Development of the infrastructure is a typical feature of our present civilization and creates favorable conditions for the development of human capital and of the standard of living in a progressive industrial society. A paradoxical phenomenon is that in the administrative system the plan often fails to resolve these important and long-term tasks of development; in this kind of planning, problems of production and techniques have priority. However, this is not the failure of socialism. The function of the plan in those spheres where we cannot rely on the market mechanism belong to the main task of socialist planning; a humanistic conception and accordance of economic effectiveness with noneconomic criteria for social development should become the tasks of central management.

Under conditions of socialism the concept of the plan as the model of the market (in the sense of anticipated market tendencies) is not sufficient.

Sound development of the socialist economy calls for market impulses; however, it is not a market economy in the full sense of the word. The market mechanism is a system in which profit is not only the motive but also the goal of economic activity. The socialist economy needs the market mechanism as a signalling and motivating device which ensures the smooth working of the economy. Profit is the goal of the economic subjects' activity in this sense. Socialist economy as a whole, however, exceeds the framework of the market mechanism; socialist society aims at establishing an economy and society with high ethical norms. Socialist development aims at achieving such goals of social development and conditions of economic life by which income division proceeds from the ethical norms of socialism ... The market mechanism has in this development an important but limited function. The objective price struc-

6 In the socialist literature Lange tried to find a possible solution to the problem. He suggested that 'only a socialist economy can distribute incomes so as to attain the maximum social welfare'. See O. Lange, 'On the Economic Theory of Socialism'.

ture is the indispensable source of criteria in economic calculation, which is the instrument of effective decisions. The regulated market mechanism is at the same time the irreplaceable part of the motivating system. In this sense, the market mechanism under socialism can contribute to the increase of material wealth and the increase of consumption. An adequately applied market mechanism can contribute to the economic progress of socialism.

. . . The linkage of plan and regulated market mechanism, however, forces us to face a complex of caveats and unresolved problems. How can socialist society avoid – when applying the positive effects of market incentives – the market's negative effects, which are in contrast to the socialist concept of equality and with the development of the human personality? The socialist concept of planning, utilizing the market mechanism, calls for an exacting attitude to problems linked with the creation of a social and political system which would ensure democratic determination of the goals of social development on a scientific level and the application of modern progressive techniques of planning. These problems of the socialist concept of planning are part of the program of the economic reform. Though our present knowledge of the problems enables us to formulate them, we are still looking for an efficient methodical and practical solution which can be used in planning procedures.

The shift in the economic system involves a much more difficult task than only complementing the traditional plan with a regulated market mechanism. The essential feature of the shift to a higher system of management is gradually achieving a rational price structure which will become one of the criteria for setting and carrying out the plan as an instrument of economic development, an instrument for the coordination of the economic subjects' activity and of determining the goals of development. The shift to the new concept of planning linked with a regulated market mechanism is part of the change in the functioning of the socialist economy; it is characterized by a certain structure of institutions with adequate tasks, activities, attitudes, and methods. The economic reform implies changes in the whole system of socialist institutions; it is concerned not only with their influence on the effective development of the economy, but also especially with their influence on a profound democratic and human development of socialism. Linkage of plan and regulated market mechanism is the initial phase of this development.

The forms and intensity in the linkage of plan and market mechanism will not hold for ever; they will undergo changes depending on the degree of economic development, the influence of external conditions, and experience.

The most challenging theoretical and practical tasks are tied to the process of replacing the administrative system with a system built on the plan and the regulated market mechanism.

The economic reform represents not only a process of purely economic changes. It is part of the general effort to achieve an improved economic, social, and political socialist system. Seriously impeding the realization of the reform are bureaucratic links in the managing apparatus and the pursuit of selfish interests, which hamper the successful carrying out of the reform. Whether the principles of the economic reform as part of the general program of democratization and intensified socialist humanism will be carried out and developed will depend to a great extent on social and political circumstances.

Index